ALPINE ELITE

ALPINE ELITE

German Mountain Troops
of World War II

JAMES LUCAS

JANE'S
LONDON · NEW YORK · SYDNEY

DEDICATION

This book is dedicated with love and gratitude to my dear wife, Edeltraude, for the help and encouragement she has always given, and for the great happiness with which she has enriched my life.

CONTENTS

Dedication   v
Acknowledgements   ix
Introduction   xi
The Genesis of Gebirgsjäger Organisation   xv

THE GEBIRGSJÄGER AT WAR

The Years 1935–1939   3
Poland 1939   7
The Year 1940   13
Norway   14
The Year 1941   21
The Balkan Campaign   22
Crete   32
Russia 1941   82
Uman 1941   86
The Year 1942   127
The Caucasus 1942   128
The Years 1943–1944   145
Finland 1944   147
The Year 1945   153
Austria 1945   155

Epilogue   201

ORGANISATION

The Order of Battle of the Gebirgsjäger Formations   205
    Divisions, Corps, Armies and the
    Hochgebirgsjäger battalions of the German
    Army   205
    Divisions, Corps and the Tartar Brigade of the
    Waffen SS   214
The organisation, tactics and equipment of Gebirgs units   221

Mountain artillery 229
Uniform and specialist equipment 235
The senior commanders of Gebirgs formations of the German
    Army 241
Bibliography 251
Index 253

ACKNOWLEDGEMENTS

To all those who assisted me in the writing of this book I am deeply indebted. To Barbara Shaw, my daughter who typed most of the manuscript, and to all my German and Austrian ex-Service friends, the records of whose experiences are recounted here. Also to the various institutions and libraries in the United Kingdom, Germany and Austria, the staff of which gave the fullest assistance, mentioning particularly Susan Bardgitt of the Department of Education and Publications at the Imperial War Museum, the officers of the Department of Documents and of the Department of Printed Books of that museum. And to Dr Manfried Rauchensteiner of the Austrian Heeresgeschichtliches Museum go my especial thanks.

INTRODUCTION

The first Gebirgsjäger I ever saw was kneeling, stone dead, by a shallow slit trench just below the crest of Monte Gemmano, a mountain in north Italy.

He had been killed in one of the battles of the Gothic Line offensive fought during the autumn of 1944. The task of the Queen's Brigade of 56th Division, to which I belonged, was to capture Monte Gemmano from the German force which was holding it. We were not aware, I think, that the mountain was being defended by 100th Gebirgsjäger, one of the crack mountain regiments of the German Army, but none of us had any doubt, when we were relieved a day or two later, that our foes had been first class soldiers; the best we had encountered in Italy.

Crossing the start line of our attack at 14.00hrs in the afternoon of 8 September our company files had struggled through the dense scrub of the steep and forested slopes of the eastern end of the massif. We lost men at every bound to snipers who had concealed themselves at our approach and who emerged after we had passed over them to pick off the unwary. Machine gun fire swept the open stretches across which we toiled; fire from the front, from the flanks, and even occasionally from the rear, pinned us down. Mortar bombardments and artillery barrages tried to break the pace of our attack but we pushed on until, just below the crest, we halted to regroup. The platoons of my company were then to storm across the peak and to capture the stone-walled village which crowned the summit of Monte Gemmano.

Sweating in the afternoon heat and panting with the exertion of the climb a few of us stood, backs bowed under the weight of equipment. Arriving with the frightening sibilance to which no familiarity could ever accustom us, shells from 88mm guns crashed on every side. We went to ground. Near the crest I flung myself down almost beneath a burnt out Bren gun carrier, victim of an earlier and unsuccessful assault by 44th Reconnaissance Battalion, and found myself staring into the single, vivid blue eye of a dead German who was crouching on the grass holding a rifle in his left hand.

The body of another man lay flat on his back on the floor of the shallow trench, his machine gun, silent now, upside down and sprinkled with earth. The kneeling man had been killed, and that recently, by a shell fragment which had cut away most of the right hand side of his face. The blood on his shirt had not had time to dry.

His long, blond hair had fallen so that it hung partially obscuring the wound that had killed him. His left eye, blue and clear, gazed in death across the ground over which he had advanced. The machine gun post was one of those groups which had held us pinned down and it had a field of fire which dominated a wide arc of our brigade's attack. Around the trench lay shining in the bright afternoon sun hundreds and hundreds of empty cartridge cases, proof of the part that these two had played in contesting our attack.

I concentrated upon details around the slit trench in an effort to distract my mind from the exploding shells and with such success that those particulars are still clear and distinct, although more than three and a half decades have passed. On the parados of the trench lay a blood-soaked cap and shining on its side a metal badge formed into the shape of a flower. The shoulder straps on the dead man's shirt were edged in green; he was a Jäger and if I had correctly identified the flower in his cap then he was a Gebirgsjäger. His ankle boots were square-shaped and heavily nailed, his brown socks had been rolled down to the ankle leaving the calf bare. He looked about sixteen years old.

When the German barrage of shells ended, our platoons went over the top of Gemmano's crest, fought their way into the village and had soon captured half of it. Counter-attacks then flung our platoons back until they held only a pair of houses which were under attack all night. An attempt at a fresh advance on the following day brought the Queen's depleted platoons no farther forward. The Gebirgsjäger held their every attempt and drove back each incursion.

All day the battle was fought for the ruins which now constituted much of the village and late that evening our battalion was relieved from the line. Not until more than a week later when a whole Indian division was put in against them did the 100th Regiment finally leave the feature. The village itself fell to an attack by 2nd Battalion The Queen's Own Cameron Highlanders but the Gebirgsjäger on Gemmano had not been fought off the mountain; they withdrew for fear of being outflanked.

The mountain had been held by a crack unit which had withstood the furious and repeated assaults of the best units of 8th Army for over two weeks. The Gebirgsjäger left at least nine hundred unburied dead in the village and around the peaks. They had held Gemmano but, more than this defence, they had also played a vital role in halting 8th Army's advance northwards and with it the hope of ending the war in Italy before Christmas.

A year later with the war over I was climbing in the Hochschwab mountains in Styria and saw how effortlessly the former Gebirgsjäger in our party tackled the ascent; moving with practised ease. Several months later I saw a one-legged, former Gebirgsjäger ski-ing down the steep slopes of the same range with as much confidence and daring as any man with both legs. That unconquerable spirit was the trait that was most common in mountain men. For them difficulties existed to be overcome and these slow-talking men, who moved with deliberation as if calculating each step, seemed able to surmount any problem, natural or artificial, material or psychological. They had fought from Poland in 1939 to capitulation in 1945, often in bitter hand to hand battles. Some had spent months in the dark and frightening isolation of the gloomy pine forests of Finland, others had conquered the highest peak of the Caucasus mountains and, by penetrating farther into the Soviet Union than any other unit of the German Army, had taken the war from Europe and nearly into Asia. They had also served in Africa and in the Balkans where they played a vital part in the battle for Crete.

Those were Gebirgsjäger; men against whom I had fought in Italy and some of whom, since those far-off days, have become close personal friends. It is with a special feeling that I write of them and of the campaigns in which they fought.

I must add that the Third Reich was an avowedly anti-Christian political system which tried hard to substitute for the Christian Messiah, born in the Middle East of Semitic parents, the pagan deities of Thor, Wotan, Freya and the other Scandinavian gods of myth and legend. It is therefore strange to think that the men of the Gebirgsjäger, who came mainly from the most conservative and deeply religious provinces of Germany and Austria, should have fought so long and so well for a Nazi regime which, if it had won the war, would have destroyed without qualm the Catholic Church and the Christian values in which they so fervently believed.

The first part of this book traces the history of the raising of mountain troops. Then follow accounts of operations carried out by Gebirgsjäger during World War II. Inevitably there is, as in the case with all elite units, an embarrassing choice of battles in which they played a prominent or decisive part. From these I have selected eight, five of which are short outlines of the part played by Gebirgs divisions in those campaigns. The remaining three are treated more exhaustively. The second half of the book gives details of their organisation and equipment.

The stories begin in Poland in 1939 and Narvik in 1940. Before the long section which deals with the actions of 5th Division in Crete during 1941, there is another short outline of the fighting in Yugoslavia and Greece where 5th Division smashed the Metaxas Line. In the war against the Soviet Union Gebirgsjäger fought with all three army groups and I have chosen two of the many battles which were fought there. The first of these is the encirclement battle around Uman in the autumn of 1941 and the second the advance to the Caucasus during the summer of 1942. The seventh account is that of 7th Gebirgs Division's retreat from Finland in 1944. I conclude the first part of the book with a description of the battle fought by 99th Gebirgsjäger Regiment in the Austrian province of Steiermark during the final weeks of the war.

These then are accounts of battles fought by Gebirgsjäger during World War II, men for whom I had, and still have, the most profound admiration.

The Genesis of Gebirgsjäger Organisation

The final decades of the 19th century took the armies of Europe out of an age of soldiers fighting stylised, day-long battles inside short campaigns limited by the need for suitable weather, and into the area of modern warfare. Of year-long struggles of nations against nations; peoples against peoples.

The railway system made it possible to move armies of men and thus to effect a rapid concentration of force in order to strike the enemy host with lightning blows of massive power. There had also been an increase in the range and destructive power of weapons and explosives. Thus the General Staffs of Europe's major armies faced new and heavy burdens of defence and security which caused the military to believe that their forces were generally too few to maintain and uphold national sovereignty. An expansion of armies to a point where it was considered they were sufficiently large to secure the national frontiers and to guarantee the safety of the State became a common feature of those final decades. There were certain nations in Central Europe for whom this new mobility, brought about by the railway, posed strategic problems not shared by the other Powers. By accident of geography their frontiers ran through Alpine areas, for the defence of which there were insufficient well-trained men.

High mountain areas had previously been considered by the military as sectors in which, because of the difficulties of terrain, reinforcement and supply, there could be no major clash of forces. An attacker had always sought to pass through the mountain barrier at speed so as to debouch on to the plains beyond. The strategy of the defending army was to meet the attacker before or behind the mountain, either in approach march or as he came out, piecemeal, from the mountains. He could then be engaged in battle before he had had time to concentrate his forces. The military forces raised for the defence of the high country had, therefore, been left to locally raised levies of riflemen whose task it had always been to slow down the enemy's progress. Railways and roads now ran through Alpine passes and in the light of this new mobility the locally raised militia could no longer guarantee to retard the advance of an enemy host. Small and scattered detachments could no longer withstand the swift blows of a mass invading army. To overcome the attacking mass required a massive defence; large forces of specially trained and equipped soldiers were required. That was the held opinion of the 1880s. The new force of mountaineers must be sufficient in number to manoeuvre and fight and also be able to survive in an Alpine area devoid of vegetation, cover or natural food resources. These needs were the genesis of those battalions and regiments of Gebirgsjäger, Schützen, Alpini and Chasseurs Alpins which were raised before World War I in the armies of Austria-Hungary, Italy and France and which were intended to fight en bloc along a mountain frontier line, using their local knowledge of the ground and their tactical skills so as to be able to withstand any mass assault.

It was the introduction of the machine gun which passed the superiority decisively into the hands of the defender, for it was shown that the advance of an enemy through the mountain barrier could be seriously delayed by small groups of men armed with machine guns, and far more effectively than by regiments of men standing on the heights. The nations with Alpine troops on their establishments then adopted the idea of locally recruited, specially selected men, trained to fight in small groups. They would have a threefold task. As defenders obstructing an enemy thrust, as Alpine assault troops whose function it would be to spearhead attacks upon enemy positions or, thirdly, and more importantly, to act as guides to lead the main bodies of their own army's forces in safety through the high peaks.

A study of military history shows that the need existed, for well recorded is the fate of those forces whose commanders had failed to prepare for the unusual problems of moving mass armies through the high peaks. The forces of Alexander the Great lost 50 per cent of their effective strength crossing the Taurus. Hannibal in the Alps, Napoleon on the Saint Bernard pass and Suvorov on the Saint Gotthard, all had suffered heavy casualties through lack of preparation and of guides. In more recent times the Russian forces, during the Balkan Wars of 1877, had spent only between two and six days in crossing the mountains but their numbers had been decimated in that short time.

Three major armies of Western Europe, of France, of Italy and of Austria, had a need for soldiers trained in mountain warfare and it was in those lands that its principles were laid down and subsequently enlarged upon. Each of these countries, facing the same problems, had arrived at the same conclusions and each, broadly speaking, followed indentical patterns of training and equipment. In those days, at the turn of the century, Germany did not have its own Gebirgsjäger establishment, for in event of war it had been planned that the defence of the mountainous front would be the responsibility of the soldiers of Austria-Hungary. Germany was able, however, to increase the amount of Alpine knowledge through the various mountaineering organisations which had been formed. There were, in those early years, too few military men with sufficient Alpinist capability and, in the cases of both Austria and Germany, recourse was made to civilian mountaineering clubs whose members instructed army classes in rock-climbing, traversing glaciers and in the techniques of survival in sub-zero conditions. Civilians ran the courses, wrote the regulations and laid down the training programmes upon which military mountain units were trained.

That there were sufficient civilians available to help develop military Alpine techniques was due, in part, to the social advances which had taken place in Western Europe. Increased leisure gave to the city dwellers who were using the new railway system, the opportunity to explore the mountains where they learned the delights as well as the dangers of those formerly remote, isolated regions. In the less advanced lands of southern and south-eastern Europe there had been no similar social advances and there was, therefore, no core of civilian enthusiasts able to instruct the soldiers. This lack was to be bitterly felt during the first winter of the Great War. The soldiers of the Turkish commander, Enver Pasha, trying to invade Russia through the Caucasus mountains lost 78,000 from a total of 90,000 men, and the Tsarist winter offensive, aimed at forcing the Carpathian mountains, collapsed and failed with losses whose immensity has never been accurately calculated.

All the books which were written on warfare in mountainous terrain, all the lectures and pamphlets laid great stress on the moral fibre of the individual soldier, his strength of character, the need for speedy reflexes and fast reactions. To achieve these goals the training of the mountaineer-soldier was exceptionally thorough. The ideal which Alpinist-minded officers had was of an elite force composed of hand-picked men in well equipped and highly trained units. Mountain soldiers would not be treated as heavy infantry but as rifle detachments; that is to say as formations whose men were capable of acting either in small numbers or even upon their own initiative. They would all be first class shots and capable of using to their own advantage the terrain in which they had to fight. Recruiting for the Alpine detachments was restricted to local areas and from men who lived among and were, therefore, at home in the mountains.

When war did come, as it did in August 1914, there was initially little call for the skills of mountain trained troops. The main battle areas were in Flanders, Northern France and in Russian Poland, all of these being either flat or set about with low hills. When Italy declared war upon Austria in 1915, the course of military operations changed dramatically for the Austrians for soon much, then most of, and finally the greatest part of her armies were needed to man the mountain frontier. It was found during this time that many theories of troop employment, formerly held valid, had in fact been false. It was found not to be essential, for example, for all the troops holding the line to have been trained in Alpinist techniques. The chief requirements were that those standard units were aware of the dangers and difficulties of fighting in the high country and that their ranks had a "stiffening" of expert mountaineers.

It was around that "stiffening" in its own forces that the German Army built up its Gebirgsjäger organisation out of the few battalions of Jäger, trained and equipped to fight in hilly country. In the Kingdoms and Principalities of Germany there were large numbers of men who lived in the mountains but there had been no need of their skills and it was not until 1915, when the move began of large numbers of German troops to the battle area of Italy, that the first true Alpine units were formed. An initial impetus had come much earlier as a result of the fighting in the Vosges mountains when the German troops fighting in that region found themselves outclassed by the Chasseurs Alpins. There was then a need to match the forces of their enemies France and Italy, as well as of their ally, Austria, by forming

Gebirgsjäger detachments. The human material was to hand in the armies of the Kingdoms of Bavaria and Württemberg.

The first snowshoe (ski) battalion was raised in November 1914 and was followed by a mountaineer company. This elite troop was formed of soldiers from Alpine areas who had also seen front line service in France and Flanders. By March 1915 the units had been taken out of State control and passed into that of the German Empire. The War Establishment of these *German* as opposed to *States* units included a Bavarian Alpine ski battalion, a Württemberg company and Jäger battalions from the States organisations of Bavaria, Hanover and Mecklenburg. All these units were then grouped regimentally, and to their strength was added the Bavarian Leib (Household Troops) regiment. The whole was then re-organised into two brigades, further expanded, and eventually given the title of the German Alpine Corps.

The composition of No. 1 Brigade was the Bavarian Leib Regiment and the Bavarian Jäger battalions. The 2nd Brigade contained all the other Jäger and also the ski battalion. Artillery units were also raised so that eventually there were seven on establishment, as well as pioneers, trench mortar and signals detachments; all of them skilled mountaineers.

The regiments of the German Alpine Corps served in the Tyrol and in Macedonia. Their fighting ability led to them being used as straightforward assault troops and it was in that role that they were put into the fighting around Verdun in 1916. They were then switched to Romania, returned again to France and to the Vosges in May 1917, before moving down into Italy for the German offensive at Caporetto. The corps was switched from one threatened front to another: Mount Kemmel during the 1918 German spring offensive; the Chemin des Dames, back to Serbia and then to the Eastern Front where it served until the war's end.

The traditions of the small but potent Alpine Corps were retained by three Bavarian units of the Army of the Weimar Republic and these were then taken back when the German Army expanded, as it did under Hitler in 1935. The Gebirgsjäger establishment was enlarged to the strength of a brigade and subsequently to that of a division. With the annexation of Austria in March 1938, other Gebirgs divisions from the forces of the former Austrian Republic were added.

When the German Army mobilised for war in the late summer of

1939, there were on its active establishment seven regiments of Gebirgsjäger formed into three Gebirgs divisions. The 1st Division had 98th, 99th, and 100th Regiments. The 2nd Division had 136th and 137th Regiments while the 3rd had 138th and 139th Regiments. The gap in the numerical sequence between the 1st and 2nd Gebirgs Divisions is attributable to the fact that all the Jäger were considered to be on the infantry establishment and that standard regiments of the infantry line had been raised between the formation of the two Gebirgs formations.

During the summer of 1940 there was an expansion of establishment when 142nd and 143rd Regiments were formed, but the intention to create a 4th Gebirgs Division was not proceeded with at that time. Not until much later, in 1940, when "Operation Barbarossa", the invasion of the Soviet Union, had been decided upon and planning for the new war was in active preparation was the raising of the new Alpine formation undertaken. At that time certain standard infantry divisions were being converted into panzer grenadier and panzer divisions and with this conversion a number of their infantry regiments became surplus to establishment. Six of these supernumerary regiments were then formed into three new Gebirgs divisions. In 1941 a seventh division was added when 99th Light Division was converted to a mountain role and an eighth was formed in the final months of the war. In the last weeks of the war two 9th Gebirgs Divisions were formed, one first given the description "Nord" and the other "Ost", but neither seems to have been marked as such on the operations maps of the time.

From individual divisions fighting within the framework of standard infantry corps there evolved Gebirgs corps and then an entire army, most of whose units were Alpine formations. It must be admitted that, with very few exceptions, the fighting which was carried out by the great mass of those units was not mountain warfare, the task for which they had been formed, but winter warfare with whose techniques they were also familiar as a result of their high Alpine training.

In addition to the Army's Gebirgsjäger establishment there were SS corps and divisions formed along the same lines as those of the Army. Other foreign Armies which had previously not included mountain divisions on their establishments raised such units during World War II. The British had one which served in the campaign in north-west Europe, the Russians raised some to fight in the Caucasus and the Americans also brought mountain units into their Army. The Soviet and the United States units, like those fielded by the Scandinavian countries, seem rather to have been winter warfare specialists than experts in Alpine techniques. This book is the story of the men and units of the German Army who, in addition to their basic abilities as infantry soldiers, were able to rock climb, to ski, to maintain direction in Alpine fog or total darkness and to survive where nothing grew that sustained life.

The Gebirgsjäger at War

The Years 1935–1939

As a result of the reintroduction of conscription by Hitler in 1935, the Gebirgs battalions of the German Army amalgamated to become a brigade and this was then expanded by such an influx of young men that it rose to the strength of a division. Through the accession of Austrian Gebirgsjäger divisions this establishment rose to become a force three divisions strong.

Conscription ensured a regular flow of replacements to the Jäger regiments both in peace and war but the recruits who came in did not enter unprepared into military life. All of them had served in the *Reichsarbeitsdienst* (RAD) the German Labour Service in which they had learned to live a community life, had become fit through physical labour in the open air and had learned the value of discipline. Thus when they joined the Army to become, as they believed, one of the elite, a weapon bearer in the National Socialist State, the recruits had completed much if not most of the training necessary to turn them into skilled soldiers; service life was to them no bewildering separation from the family circle, but an extension of those years of allegiance which lay behind them. There were, of course, differences between life in a para-military unit like the RAD and that in an elite Regular Army unit, but these differences were slight.

Service in the German Army was compulsory and every able-bodied male citizen was required to present himself when called. At certain times during the year a registration was made and those obviously ineligible, the blind, the crippled and the deformed, would be rejected. The selected ones returned home to await the call-up papers and the placards which would announce the days on which they would be required to report. A summary of the experiences of a group of Austrian Gebirgsjäger serves to illustrate the path from work on a farm to service as a rifleman in a Jäger unit.

Throughout Styria, in every town and village, the placards had been displayed detailing the days on which recruits had to report and for many of the new soldiers to reach the reporting centre they had had to leave homes and farms before sunrise and to tramp through fields and silent woods, meeting en route other individuals dressed in their best suits walking to Feldbach or some other centre in Austria's eastern province. Outside the school building which had been commandeered for the day the small knots of men gathered, their civilian hats and jacket lapels decorated with flowers, the signs of a recruit, who saw with peasant indifference the arrival of a bus in which travelled the officers and permanent staff of the military commission.

When all was ready the main doors were opened and the recruits streamed in to stand in place in the queues. In pre-war days the commission members were nearly always Germans whose questions and instructions issued in clipped, Prussian accents were almost incomprehensible to the Styrian peasants and wood cutters, most of whom had never left their county. The initial registration was soon completed and then there were lectures on how to allocate money for family allowances, on the reporting dates and procedures and on completing the final details. The recruits were then marched to the medical officers and once they had passed this stage were issued with their military identity card. They were in the Army now. They were fit, they had their documents to show that they were future soldiers, future Gebirgsjäger; now only the call-up day had to arrive and then they would be off.

It was usually the Gendarmerie officers of the villages and small towns who brought the call-up order and then for the Austrian Jäger the trains left for Graz, Salzburg or Innsbruck and recruit training began. It is not necessary to describe the duration or nature of the period during which the young men were moulded, but usually about the end of the second week, when they had become truly absorbed, the oath of allegiance would be taken. This was the climax of recruit training and marked the formal entry into the Army, the transition of a soldier from recruit status to the higher, privileged caste of warrior. Such an act of passing was, therefore, one set about with elaborate ceremonial.

Long before the appointed day the recruits who were to be passed were drilled in the marching and movement required for the parade and instructed in both wording of the oath and its significance. On the day itself a short parade, a sort of dress rehearsal, was held. For the actual ceremony the men of the battalion or depot with which the recruits were serving were paraded in hollow square with the Reich's war flag and other military symbols decorating a podium which had been set up along the inner wall of one side of the square. Directly opposite the podium stood the recruits whose clothing had, until this time, been the white denim jacket and trousers of fatigue dress, now dressed for the first time in correct uniform: often walking out dress, but more usually Service dress and steel helmet. No firearms were carried although in some units side arms were worn. Forming the left and right walls of the square stood the remainder of the battalion, the "old sweats", who on this occasion also renewed their own oath of allegiance.

At regimental or even at divisional level the ceremony was more elaborate and both the standard and band would parade. The colour would be marched on, borne not as in the British Service by an officer and escorted by sergeants, but carried by an NCO and guarded by officers. The main guard turned out to greet the arrival of the commanding officer with bugle call and with presented arms and then began an inspection of the uniformed ranks. The files of Jäger stood stiffly at attention with their immobility broken only by the movement of the head and eyes which, following European drill practice, were to look at and to follow the commander for three paces before the head was brought back to the "eyes front" position. The commander then made a short speech and a group of Jäger, representing all the recruits, were marched forward and at a command placed their left hand on the regimental colour. The officers drew swords. The men on parade, rigid with concentration, raised their right hand and intoned the words which made them all comrades in the army of Greater Germany. Although it was customary for the infantry to swear on the colour, gunners on the barrel of the gun and machine gun detachments on their tripod-mounted weapons, some detachments swore the oath on a sword blade; but in whatever fashion the oath was administered now at last they were no longer recruits but soldiers with the warrior's responsibilities and obligations to fight and, if need be, to lay down his life.

But before the excitement of active service with a regiment lay training: intensive but interesting or repetitious and boring, but always thorough and designed to turn them in a few months from half-trained young men into combat soldiers. Courses in rock climbing, compass marches, cross country ski-ing and always the happy hours spent on the ranges with the smell of cordite drifting in fresh mountain air and the feel of the rifle's kick against the shoulder. And always the route marches. Some of these were long, lasting all day, with the companies singing in chorus as they began the trek through the red dawn, singing perhaps that marching song that told of other dawns, red dawns that would light them to an early death. Other marches lasted all night through villages lying quiet under the Alpine stars, or across frosty fields, kilometre after kilometre, through the silent and watchful mountains of their homeland. Manoeuvres, exercises, marching and still more marching dominated their lives. Their monastic life was often enlivened by unit dances or Open Days, when civilians and especially girls came to gape at the splendid weapons and to listen to the young men telling with pride of the hardships of Army life.

The Munich crisis of 1938 came and went with a partial mobilisation. The rump of Czechoslovakia was swallowed in the spring of 1939 and the crises of that last golden summer of peace renewed the rumours of war and brought about the recall of reservists and a flurry of intensive training. During August the 1st Division began its move eastwards towards the Polish frontier and took up position with the rest of 18th Corps in Army Group South. On the first day of September 1939, Adolf Hitler announced that fire from the Poles was being answered with fire and bombs by bombs. War had come and with its declaration, and in obedience to the orders of their Supreme Commander, the men of the German Army's Gebirgs units crossed the border and entered Poland. The Gebirgsjäger were at war.

Ahead of them lay years of battles and suffering, of death in any one of a dozen terrible ways. Singly or in groups they would fall. Some would be buried in the sandy soil of Poland or in the frozen tundra of the northern countries of Scandinavia. The sour soil of Finland would cover those who had fought and died in the extensive and neurosis-inducing deep and silent woods. Some Jäger were to battle against the British troops in the barren Tunisian hills or in Italy; or in Russia, in the flat steppes of the Ukraine, the swamps of Kuban or the high mountains of the Caucasus. In the last years of that terrible war some were to be killed in western Germany or in lands like Romania or Hungary, which had once been under the rule of German princes or of the Emperors of Austria. The very last to fall were those who sacrificed themselves to hold the eastern provinces of Austria against the drive of Marshal Tolbukhin's forces. On every front upon which the German Army fought during World War II, Gebirgsjäger were present and it is with them in the campaign against Poland in September 1939, that this half of the book, dealing with the Gebirgsjäger at war, begins.

Poland 1939

Although all three of the Gebirgs divisions on the German Army's 1939 establishment fought in the Polish campaign it is not an account of their operations with which these next paragraphs will deal, but with the disappointment of a victory snatched from the grasp of 1st Division.

On 25 August the 1st and 2nd Gebirgs Divisions were in garrison in southern Germany when they received orders to journey eastward and to take up positions in the north Slovakian province of Moravia across whose border with Poland they were to advance shortly after the declaration of war. Their journey from Bavaria was not an easy one. The German railway system was at that time handling a tremendous amount of traffic and other trains containing the men who would make up the assault wave, and whose priority was therefore higher, rolled east towards the concentration areas along the Polish frontier. The war had begun and had already run two days of its course before the main of the two Gebirgs divisions had reached and grouped in their designated area. The other division in 18th Gebirgs Corps, Dietl's 3rd, had been stationed along the border before hostilities began on 1 September, and had begun its move into Poland on that day.

A glance at a map will show how the Polish frontier with Germany projected as a salient in the west and that, therefore, the armies defending western Poland were deeply and seriously outflanked both to the north and to the south by the territory of Germany or of nations friendly to her. The frontier area in the south of Poland where it bordered with Moravia was characterised by a range of mountains, the High Tatras, which unless they were quickly crossed and their defenders neutralised would pose a threat to the advance of the German Army's right wing. The location of the Gebirgs divisions in the extreme southern part of the German line was deliberate. It was the task of 18th Gebirgs Corps to penetrate the mountain barrier and to gain the low country beyond. From that point the divisions, echeloned from left to right (that is from west to east), Dietl's 3rd, Feuerstein's 2nd and Kübler's 1st, were to wheel and in line abreast were to advance towards their first major objectives, the towns of Tarnov, Jaslo and Sanok respectively. Their ultimate objective was the city of Lemberg or Lvov, the capital of Galicia.

For the war against Poland the German Army's High Command formed a northern and a southern army group. That of the north was made up of 3rd and 4th Armies under Küchler and Kluge, respectively. The 8th Army under Blaskowitz, the 10th commanded by Reichenau and List's 14th Army together formed Army Group South. The battle plan of OKW (*Oberkommando der Wehrmacht*), the Supreme Command, for the war against Poland was to envelop the enemy in a double pincer operation, and thereafter to destroy him. The 18th Gebirgs Corps formed the southern pincer of the outer jaw and, together with the rest of 14th Army, was to wheel northwards from Lemberg to meet the descending pincer of 3rd Army. To reach Lemberg the Jäger would have to carry out long and exhausting foot marches but once that town was reached then, as the outer flank unit on the great wheel northwards, their march rate would have to be very fast and the distances covered each day would need to be prodigious. They would have to march farther and faster than the units on the inner flank of the wheel.

The war had run for five days before the 1st and 2nd Gebirgs Divisions crossed the frontier and joined the advance of 3rd Division. Matthew Cooper, in his excellent book *The German Army 1933–1945,** claims that the outcome of the campaign was decided during the first four days of fighting. This assessment may have been known to the leaders at Supreme Command Headquarters but the mountain men were unaware of it. Indeed, the Jäger might have pondered on the truth of that statement given the heroic resist-

* Macdonald and Jane's Ltd, London, 1978.

ance offered by the Poles, the stubbornness of their defence, the determination of their rearguards and the élan that the Polish infantry displayed in the attacks which they mounted and executed with fiery fanaticism from the first until the last day.

The first Polish Army units that the men of 1st and 2nd Gebirgs Divisions met were the mountain soldiers of 1st and 2nd Alpine Brigades supported by the Rzezov Motorised Brigade. Those units formed part of the three divisional Przemysl group which held the left wing of the Polish battle line and who, under the German assault from both east and south, were forced to fight on two fronts, under which pressure they began to give ground. The Gebirgsjäger, fighting in their natural element, had soon passed through the High Tatra mountains and had descended on to the plains ready to undertake the first of the long and exhausting foot marches that they were to carry out throughout most of the eighteen-day campaign.

The roads in southern Poland were ankle deep in dust and their state was unbelievable to soldiers accustomed to the neatness and firm surfaces of the highways of home. The thick dust slowed the pace of the advance and to lead the 1st Division's advance and to bring it quickly forward, the divisional commander formed an advanced guard around a battle group. This advanced guard or point unit was a convoy of soft skin vehicles led by armoured cars and accompanied by artillery. The lorries were filled with Jäger armed and ready to undertake immediate infantry action. The confidence of the German units in this sort of situation allowed them to take risks which sober judgement would have rejected. As the hours passed and the motorised group drove deeper eastwards its advance left miles behind it the bulk of the Jäger regiments force-marching in a vain attempt to keep touch. The point group was isolated from the main and each might have been intercepted, held and destroyed by a sudden Polish attack. But this risk was accepted, and the two detachments made their individual way forward. The fast lorry-borne assault broke through the thin lines of Polish resistance and soon the German vehicles and men were in the rear areas of the Przemysl group. As the lorries roared towards their objective they passed columns of enemy troops moving away from the front and others marching forward to take their places in the battle line. Whenever a marching group was encountered, whether on the road up or else moving down the line, each was sprayed with fire or blown apart by shell fire. The Poles could make few attempts to set up blocks or to form rearguards to hold the storming Jäger, for these were moving too fast for Polish counter-measures to be taken. Indeed, many Polish units had long since been out of touch with their general headquarters and were acting either on their own initiative or upon the orders of their immediate superiors.

Here and there some Polish detachments, quick to react to the danger that the point group represented, formed a front and opened fire fights. The employment of the advance guard artillery pieces was sometimes sufficient to clear the way, but on many more occasions the Jäger riflemen had to launch set piece attacks to fight down the resistance before the drive could be continued. The Poles who had been scattered by the advance guard's rapid thrust reformed after this had passed through them, and met with fire and determination the Jäger regiments trudging through the dust. The ferocity of the Polish resistance and the number of their infantry attacks slowed down the foot-marching elements and separated them even farther from the point unit. The speed of that advance guard had been so great that on one occasion it formed a salient penetrating deep into the Polish line and stood more than 120kms in front of the main German line.

The days and nights of battle were filled with violence and fury. The Luftwaffe ensured that many obstructions on the road forward were destroyed by Stuka bombardment but even these did not always quench the fire of the survivors. After even the heaviest air assaults the Jäger advance would often be contested by machine gunners, concealed in the rubble of destroyed and ruined houses which needed the action of a time-consuming infantry attack before they could be overcome. But nothing halted the flowing advance of 1st Gebirgs Division for long and by 13 September its leading elements had reached the outskirts of Lemberg and had driven into its streets intending to capture the town by coup de main. The few Jäger detachments which undertook this penetration were soon met by desperate charges mounted by Polish infantry, were held and then thrust out of the parts of the city into which their storming advance had brought them. Driven from Lemberg the shattered German detachments regrouped and dug in, holding their positions against the force of Polish infantry attacks until the foot-marching regiments began to arrive. Battalions of these stormed and captured the hills which lie to the north of and dominate the city while the remainder began to prepare for the grand assault which would seize their principal objective. Reinforced, rested and determined to win, the Jäger in front of the city returned to the offensive and flung themselves into patrols and battle groups establishing jump-off points in preparation for the fight which lay ahead. This was certain to be hard and bitter and would have to be carried out with the battles involving civilians as the combatants fought from street to street and from house to house.

To succeed in street fighting operations the attacker must always outnumber the defender by a ratio of at least 2 to 1. For the assault upon Lemberg the number of German soldiers deployed was vastly inferior to the host of those employed by the Poles and, despite the fact that the division built up its strength in men and weapons for the trial which lay ahead, it was a reversal of ratios and it was the attackers who were outnumbered. During the pre-battle preparations there came a sudden crisis and it seemed as if the corps assault plan would be thwarted when there appeared on 1st Division's left flank a whole Polish corps retreating from Przemysl. The impetus of the Polish corps' drive seemed likely to take the mountain division in flank and to overroll it but the arrival of a German panzer and an infantry division deflected the Poles and relieved the Jäger from the spectre of having to fight a two-front battle against overwhelming odds. The men of 1st Gebirgs Division then returned to concentrate upon the final battle and soon all was ready. Then the introduction of a new factor destroyed the division's elaborate preparations.

The Red Army had intervened and had crossed the frontier to strike the Poles in the back. In accordance with the political settlement drawn up between the German and the Soviet governments the city of Lemberg would be within the Soviet zone of occupied Poland and there was, thus, no longer a need for the Gebirgsjäger to assault the town. Robbed of the triumphs of victory in the last minute it seemed to the mountain men that all for which they had marched, fought, suffered and bled during the weeks of campaigning had been for nothing and they prepared to march back again across the new demarcation line. But before they began that march their spirits were raised. The commander of the Polish forces in Lemberg, conscious of the worth of his opponents, sent out a plenipotentiary under a white flag and offered the surrender of the city and its garrison to the representatives of 1st Gebirgs, one of the elite divisions of the German Army. It was a knightly gesture and one deeply appreciated by all ranks. Two years later the 1st Gebirgs Division was to move once again upon Lemberg, this time during the opening offensives of "Operation Barbarossa", the German attack upon Russia. But that war lies in the future and with the campaign in Poland completed we now turn to the battles of 1940.

The Year 1940

It was during 1940 that certain events occurred which shaped the course and outcome of the war in Europe. The first of these were the victorious campaigns entered into by the German Army, against Norway and Denmark in April and against the Western Powers in May.

During the time that Dietl's force (a regiment from 3rd Gebirgs Division) was fighting a defensive battle around Narvik the 1st Gebirgs Division was involved in the fighting for bridgeheads across the river Seine and along the Chemin des Dames, the scene of so much sacrifice during the Great War.

The campaign in the West was a short one. Within days both Holland and Belgium had been defeated and the battle for France ended with an armistice on 22 June. The British Expeditionary Force evacuated France through Dunkirk and the ports of Brittany leaving behind most of its guns and heavy weapons. Isolated and without allies Great Britain seemed to be defenceless against the triumphant Germans. Hitler and the OKW planned for a cross-Channel attack and invasion of the United Kingdom, "Operation Sealion", for which 1st Gebirgs Division, together with other elite units, underwent weeks of training.

It was planned that the Jäger of 1st Division would form part of the assault wave and that they would cross the Straits of Dover in assault craft and barges. They would debark in Dover, scale the cliffs and establish a bridgehead before moving inland towards Ashford, the first main objective. The pre-conditions for "Sealion" were never attained. The RAF established its superiority in the air over the Luftwaffe and as Britain slowly grew in strength the Führer, less reluctantly than might have been thought, first postponed and then cancelled the order for invasion. His failure to subdue the United Kingdom was a second event which shaped the course and outcome of the war. A third was his intention, first stated in concrete terms during July 1940, of embarking upon a war against the Soviet Union. There were other plans of less importance formulated during 1940 of which one, "Operation Felix", is noteworthy because 1st Gebirgs Division was selected to take part in it. The division was removed from invasion exercises in the Channel ports and taken to Besançon where it began training for an attack upon the Rock of Gibraltar. Like "Sealion" before it "Operation Felix" was cancelled and 1st Division marched back into Germany.

During 1940 the establishment of Gebirgs divisions in the German Army was increased to six by the raising of three fresh divisions.

A fateful year ended during which all the countries of Europe, excepting only a handful of neutral nations, had been conquered by Germany or had become her allies. Hitler was on the pinnacle of success; he was master of Europe. The victories which he had achieved in Scandinavia and in the West had been gained through short campaigns and, therefore, without the high blood count that had marked the battles of World War I. He could view the battles of the coming year with a calm and resolute mind.

Norway

The year 1939 had not run its full course when Hitler decided to follow up the military success which he had gained against Poland with two new campaigns aimed at the Western Powers and against Norway. Britain and France were his major enemies but these could be dealt with after a more pressing need had been filled. Hitler had listened to the arguments of Admiral Raeder who maintained that military force would need to be exerted to secure control of Norway, an area strategically important and economically vital to Germany.

Since the outbreak of war the Royal Navy had blockaded Germany but Norway outflanked the British Isles and from harbours on the west coast of an occupied Norway German ships, blockade runners or armed raiders, could sail out and return, slipping past the British naval patrols. There was also the importance of Norwegian

iron ore to Germany's economy. A war industry required vast quanti-
ties of iron ore to produce the weapons and munitions required by
the fighting forces and the output of German mines was insufficient
to meet those needs. Eleven million tons of ore were imported from
Norway and Sweden and one third of that tonnage came through a
single port—Narvik—and was brought by ship to the north German
ports. At any time the government of Norway could halt the export
of iron ore and thus cripple the German war effort. Even if supplies
were maintained the Royal Navy might take action to sink the ore
ships. Raeder's argument that it was necessary to occupy Norway,
both to provide ports from which to strike at Britain's command of
the sea, as well as to protect the coastal sea routes along which the
iron ore ships sailed, was accepted by Hitler and plans were laid.

Great Britain, too, had been aware of the strategic and economic
importance of Norway and on 8 April 1940 ships of the Royal Navy
mined the lanes used by German shipping. By a strange coincidence
both Great Britain and Germany had chosen the same date on which
to move against Norway. The British action was mining; the German
was the invasion of Denmark and Norway. The plan put forward by
OKW, the German Supreme Command, proposed a strike at six of
Norway's principal ports at which places German forces would land,
take possession, and then move out into the hinterland and thus,
eventually, take over the whole country. One of the objectives was
Narvik and the unit whose battles we are to follow in this short
campaign is 139th Gebirgsjäger Regiment of 3rd Gebirgs Division,
whose objective was Narvik and whose mission was to occupy the
town and the important iron-ore railway line which ran from Sweden, a scant 70kms from Narvik.

The war diary for the Norwegian campaign was opened by 3rd
Division on 5 April at 21.00hrs and described the embarkation. A
Jäger battalion was embarked on each of three destroyers forming
part of the German naval task force and the diary recorded the departure from Wesermünde on to the high seas and the journey to
Narvik. The foul weather, heavy seas and the cramped conditions did
not make for an easy or pleasant voyage but during the morning of
9 April, with the seas abating, a flotilla of German destroyers entered
Narvik fjord and from three of these the sea-sick Jäger began to disembark. The 1st and 3rd battalions landed at Bjervik; the 2nd Bat-

talion disembarked in the harbour of Narvik and occupied the town. All three battalions landed without casualty.

Narvik lies at the tip of a peninsula bounded on its northern and southern sides by two fjords: Rombaken to the north and Bjetsford to the south. Along the southern shore of the peninsula ran the iron-ore railway into Sweden. North and north-east of Rombaken fjord were high mountains which dominated the peninsula on which Narvik and the railway stood. It is the story of the Jäger landing and their exploitation of the situation; the Allied counter-attacks which drove them out of the town and almost into Sweden and their desperate struggle to hold on and to win that make up the story of those weeks of struggle around this small but vital area.

The German battalions had barely taken up their first positions when the first effect of British naval supremacy was felt. Royal Navy destroyers penetrated the fjord, destroyed the German ships and established a blockade outside Narvik fjord. The Jäger, some 1750 men in all, were now isolated from their homeland and from their Army. No help would be able to reach them and soon the Allied troops would be moving against them. Aware of his numerical inferiority, the energetic Dietl added to the strength of his ground forces by forming a naval battalion from the men of the ships destroyed by the British in their several penetrations of the fjord. This naval battalion the Gebirgsjäger commander placed on the northern shore of the peninsula to guard the railway while his Jäger battalions began to probe northwards and north-eastwards into the mountains which rise sheer from the edge of the fjords.

As he was without adequate artillery, the Gebirgs commander organised salvage detachments which dismantled the guns, the anti-aircraft artillery and the wireless sets and removed these from the sunken German destroyers. Ammunition was also brought up out of the wrecks so that a modest degree of artillery support would be available to the Jäger in the attacks which they were now making against the enemy. A welcome reinforcement came when a flight of Ju 52 aircraft air landed a battery of 7.5cm mountain guns. Dietl surveyed the potential of his small command. He was without transport and heavy weapons or equipment. Air drops were likely to be few and far between, and there was no other way of obtaining those supplies of food and clothing which would be essential for men fighting in the mountainous region of Norway in the bitter climate of

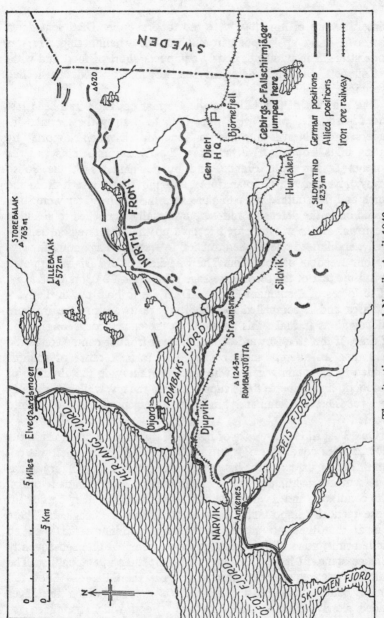

The situation around Narvik. April 1940

Map labels:
SWEDEN
STOREBALAK △ 763 m
LILLEBALAK △ 572 m
Elvegaardsmoen
HERJANGS FJORD
OFOT FJORD
NARVIK
Ankenes
SKJOMEN FJORD
BEIS FJORD
Djupvik
Bjord
ROMBAKS FJORD
Straumsnes
Sildvik
△ 1245 m ROMBAKSTÖTTA
△ 620
Björnefjell
Gen Dietl HQ
NORTH FRONT
Hundalen
SILDVIKTIND △ 1235 m
Gebirgs & Fallschirmjäger jumped here

5 Miles
5 Km
N

German positions
Allied positions
Iron ore railway

winter. Aware of how low were the food supplies Dietl sent down divers to bring up supplies from a sunken whaling ship. He was understrength in numbers, poorly equipped, short of food and without support. But his orders had been to hold on and this he had every intention of doing.

The reaction of the Allies to the German invasion had been fast and co-ordinated plans were drawn up to destroy the German invaders. In the Narvik area the 6th Norwegian Division supported by strong units from the British Army, the Chasseurs Alpins and the Foreign Legion from France, and by detachments of the Polish Army, invested the German force and moved against it from the north and the south. Under this pressure the Gebirgsjäger were soon forced on to the defensive and were eventually compelled to abandon the town. Hitler was prepared to give up the whole region, temporarily, and indeed telegraphed to Dietl in April and again in May giving him freedom of operation. The war diary of 3rd Division quoted in full the text of the second message sent out at 20.03hrs on 8 May. "The forces of Lieutenant General Dietl are to hold out in the Narvik area and if compelled to withdraw are to destroy the iron-ore railway so as to make this unusable to the enemy for a long period of time. If the area forward of the Swedish frontier can no longer be held then an attempt must be made to form a cadre of soldiers trained in mountain warfare who are to withdraw in the direction of Bötobodö and who are to be supplied from the air, while the remainder [of Dietl's Command] may in emergency cross over into Sweden".

On 13 April began weeks of battle, of fighting for positions in the mountains in conditions of intense cold and deep snow. Dietl was determined to gain space for his group and to retain the military initiative, sent out fighting patrols to seize and to hold dominant peaks. The conditions under which the companies fought as they battled for those tactically important heights can scarcely be imagined. There was at that time no proper camouflage clothing; there were no quilted suits, none of the winter warfare equipment that subsequently became standard issue. The late winter weather was appalling. The visibility was frequently reduced to yards by the thick fogs. Snow fell almost continuously causing deep drifts through which the Jäger waded slowly towards their objectives. Food which had been rationed since the opening of the fighting was reduced and the small

portions were then further reduced. During the whole of the period
from mid-April to the end of May the men of the Jäger battalions
had only three hot meals. Their normal daily ration consisted of five
slices of bread washed down with melted snow water. They lived in
small tents, covered by a single blanket and were without fires or
heating of any sort, for there was little combustible material in the
bare mountains or on the open, stony heights. The number of men
lost through sickness mounted more quickly than those who were
wounded in action and battalions were so reduced by those continual
drains upon their strength that soon they had little more than company establishments. Positions which should have been held by platoons were occupied by little groups of men, hungry, cold, tired and
outnumbered. Conditions for the Allied soldiers were little better but
they had at least regular supplies of food, and, because of their
greater numbers, could have occasional relief from the strain of constant battle against the human enemy and the terrible weather.

Step by step Ringel's men were forced back along the railway line.
Fighting was for the tunnels, dark and echoing caverns in which patrols met and clashed, or outside on the mountains where Dietl's
men, invisible in the blinding snowstorms, held the rearguard positions while behind them their comrades sought to build a perimeter
which could be held. For eight weeks they fought and held and then
the stories of their endurance which had filled the headlines of German papers vanished completely. On Friday, 10 May, German forces
had struck across the borders of Holland, Belgium and France. The
campaign in the West had begun and soon it became clear that the
Allied armies in France and Flanders were in difficulties. The Jäger
in the Narvik area must have hoped that some of their enemies might
be called back to the defence of their own countries so that the battle
might be fought on more even terms. But this was not to be. Rather
more did the Allied forces try to bring about a decision in northern
Norway by repeated and heavy assaults. By this time nearly 15,000
Allied troops had been put into the battle against the Jäger and the
sailors. There was, however, some help en route. The successes of
the German armies in the West permitted the despatch of reinforcements to the northern Norwegian front and during late May a
group of about one hundred Gebirgsjäger, hastily trained in para-
chuting techniques, were dropped into the small perimeter near the
Swedish frontier. Within an hour they were in action. A fresh Allied

offensive was capturing one mountain top after the other from the exhausted mountain men. The air drop of Jäger reinforcements was soon followed by that of a complete parachute battalion which came in during the last days of May, but even this scale of reinforcements did not cover the losses which the Narvik area garrison had suffered in the weeks of its endurance.

On the first day of June Allied attacks reduced the perimeter and the pressure was maintained throughout the first week. On 5 June Jäger patrols reported a build up of Allied strength which forecast the resumption of an all-out offensive. The motley garrison of mountain men, sailors and paratroops prepared themselves for what many thought would be their last battle. Two days passed and when, by the end of 7 June, the expected attack had still not come in patrols were sent out. They returned with the astonishing news that the British, French and Poles had evacuated the Narvik region and that only the Norwegian Army was still offering battle. The subsequent fighting was brief and three days later the enemy commander came in to surrender. It was all over. A regiment of Jäger and a sprinkling of troops from other arms of service had held the north. The town of Narvik was retaken and thus those economic prizes, possession of which had been one of the principal reasons for the expedition, were regained. The 3rd Division war diary recorded the Orders of the Day which both the commanding general and the Narvik Area Commander issued to their tired but happy troops, but there was to be a more tangible reward to commemorate their action: the Narvik arm shield.

This, the first of such decorations to be authorised, was instituted on 19 August 1940 and bestowed by Dietl upon those who had been present between 9 April and 9 June. The metal shield, in gilt for the Navy and in silver grey for both the Army and the Air Force, was worn on the upper left arm. On its surface was a propeller, an anchor and an edelweiss surmounted by the single word "Narvik".

The Year 1941

This year marked both the high tide of German confidence in victory and the first rebuffs which demonstrated that its Army was not invincible.

In the spring the Balkans were overrun and in May Crete fell to a combined paratroop and Gebirgsjäger assault. Political pacts bound the countries of central and south-eastern Europe to Germany and those nations supplied troops for the war against the Soviet Union which opened on 22 June 1941. The opening months of the new war seemed to confirm the belief that the German Army was all-powerful, invincible and that it was only a matter of months before Russia lay defeated. The months passed without that dire prophecy being realised. The mud of autumn held fast the under-powered German vehicles and then the snows came. In the period of the severest winter for thirty years came the Red Army's offensive which all but broke the divisions of Army Groups North and Centre and foreshadowed the awful fear in the minds of the General Staff that the war against Russia would be no walk over but a titanic struggle which would bleed Germany white.

With the exception of 2nd Division, which was in Norway, all the other Gebirgs divisions, of which there were now six, served on the Eastern Front at some time during the year 1941. The 1st and 4th were with Army Group South; the 5th with Army Group North and 3rd and 6th Divisions in Finland fighting on the Murmansk front. A seventh Gebirgs division was formed during November 1941, but did not go into action until 1942.

The Balkan Campaign

Less than a month after France had signed an armistice Hitler had decided upon a war which would decide, once and for all, whether it was Teuton or Slav which was to be the dominant race in Europe. He decided to attack the Soviet Union, a country to which Germany was at that time allied and which was supplying him with the wheat and oil to prosecute his war against Britain, the only nation which was still in the field. But before turning East he had to ensure that England's power was reduced so that she should present no threat to "Operation Barbarossa", the invasion of Russia.

To destroy Great Britain's influence and to seize her overseas possessions on the borders of continental Europe, Hitler was prepared to attack both Gibraltar and Suez and even to intervene, with a token force, in North Africa where the Italian and British Empires were embattled. A British attack there in December 1940, coupled with a diplomatic rebuff by General Franco, cancelled "Operation Felix", the attack upon Gibraltar, for which Gebirgsjäger of 1st Division were to have been used and for which they had trained.

The British were not, however, to be kept out of Europe and when, on 28 October 1940, Mussolini launched his invasion of Greece, the British in retaliation occupied the islands of Crete and Lemnos. These actions brought the Balkans sharply to the attention of Adolf Hitler for the occupation of Lemnos gave to the British a stepping stone from which they could re-enter the mainland of Europe or an advanced air base from which the oil fields of Ploesti, vital to the German war effort, could be bombed. The Führer conference of 4 November ordered that the Romanian oil fields be protected and ordered the drawing up of plans for an invasion of Greece (Operation Marita) to be launched out of Romania and Bulgaria. A second reason for an attack upon Greece was to help the Axis partner, Italy, whose armies had been flung back everywhere in rout by the Greek Army. The Balkan campaign which began with plans, grudgingly made by OKH to aid Germany's ally, ended with Yugoslavia, Greece and Crete overrun and occupied by the Germans and the British driven from Euorpe's south-eastern region.

Under the terms of the Führer Directives issued after the conference of 4 November, teams of German technical experts from the
Army and the Luftwaffe began to arrive, in civilian clothes, in both
Romania and Bulgaria, the forerunners of the forces which would
soon come in strength. An iron ring was being drawn around Greece.

Shortly after the signing of a pact between Germany and Bulgaria
the 12th German Army crossed the Danube on 1 March 1941 and
took up positions along the Greek/Bulgarian frontier. The increase of
German pressure had tended to isolate the Kingdom of Yugoslavia
and on 25 March, the Regent, Prince Paul acting on behalf of the
young King Peter, signed a pact with Hitler. The way was now open
for an invasion of Greece which was now isolated and faced on her
north-eastern and north-western borders German armies flushed with
military victories, equipped from the finest arsenals of Europe and
who would strike in support of the Italians whose offensive of
12 March had failed miserably.

Politically the initiative certainly seemed to lie with Germany but
there then came about a popular uprising in Yugoslavia which destroyed Hitler's plans. King Peter, at the instigation of his Army
commanders, repudiated the pact which his uncle had signed. This
action, coming so soon before the German Army's D-Day for the
campaign against Greece, was seen by Hitler as the blackest of treach-
eries and in a fury he decided, on 27 March in Directive No. 25,
that he would annihilate the Yugoslav nation. On 27 March he
gave orders for an operational plan for an extension of "Operation
Marita" to be prepared, and ten days later this was in his hands.

The forces to attack both Greece and Yugoslavia were 2nd Army
under Weichs and 12th Army under List. Gebirgs divisions were to
serve with both of these armies, fighting in the mountains and as a
corps for the first time in the history of the Gebirgsjäger arm of service. In the Graz region of southern Austria was 1st Gebirgs Division,
forming the main of 49th Gebirgs Corps. The southern group of 12th
Army had 5th and 6th Gebirgs Divisions as part of 18th Corps, while
with Kleist's 1st Panzer Group was 4th Gebirgs Division.

For the 4th, 5th, and 6th Divisions the Balkan campaign was to be
their baptism of fire and for the 5th it was another first; the first time
that any force had attempted to attack such strong fortifications as
the Greeks had built in the wilderness of mountains along her north-
eastern border. It is with only a short outline of the operations car-

ried out by 4th and 5th Divisions that this chapter deals, but before these accounts it is perhaps interesting to know of how some Jäger reacted to the new war.

My family had formerly farmed way down in what was, under the old Emperor, German-Austria. Under the Treaty of Saint Germain this had become part of Yugoslavia and my father, together with all his family had come up into Obersteier [Upper Styria] where they had a smallholding on which I was born in 1920. According to my mother I had been conceived among strangers but had been born among my own people. Lots of the Austrian-German families stayed on in what my father, an old soldier using old Army words called "that land far away from the Sava river and from soap". When we knew that we were going into the Krain area of Yugoslavia, which was once Austria, we felt ourselves to be all Germans; we this side of the frontier and they on the other side. When we first entered the towns we were greeted as liberators with flowers and wine and for the first days it was just like a manoeuvre; a battle of flowers.

A second Jäger, stationed north of Graz, recounted the excitements and disappointments of his first military operation.

It was a lovely spring evening and we were off duty when the alarm came bringing us back to barracks. The stand-by platoons were ordered back by bugle and trumpet calls which were blown in cinemas and restaurants. Everywhere one saw soldiers running back to barracks. Within the hour we were ready to march, and ball ammunition had been issued. We were at 15 minutes readiness to move but then came hours of waiting during which most of us lay down on the ground fully dressed and tried to sleep. At about four in the morning, as no marching orders had been received at regiment, we were dismissed. The movement order did not in fact come until late the following afternoon and we embussed in troops carriers.

Our convoy went straight through Gleisdorf and headed towards Mureck. We halted for the night outside Radkersburg and for the first time in my military life I was on sentry duty on active service with live ammunition in the breech of my rifle. We stood to at dawn and then in foot marches moved along the frontier, keeping well out of sight of the enemy watchers. We halted that night near a castle and took up positions with men from a Frontier Defence company. My company had a six-kilometre stretch of ground to cover and my own platoon was a standing patrol on a commanding height. We were to safeguard the passage of the main of the army through our sector. Thus we were not in the assault wave when war did come on 6 April, although we could hear the sounds of battle quite clearly. On the following day my company together with one from the Frontier Defence attacked and stormed the Radl Pass. It was a well executed attack but we lost four men; two killed and two wounded. We consolidated on our objective and waited for a counter-attack but none came. Next morning our OC sent out a patrol down to the Drava river and this was fired upon by the Yugoslavs but without loss.

We then had one night of excitement. The area which we were holding was densely wooded and rolling country. One night parties of Yugoslav soldiers, led by local Serbian settlers and acting as guides, attacked us out of a wood. The trees of this wood came to within a couple of hundred metres of the village. Our company was out of the line and was billeted in some of the village houses. Our sentry was completely taken by surprise and thought that the figures which he had seen moving through the trees had been one of our patrols. The Serbs opened fire with rifles but their firing was premature and gave us time to turn out. The enemy soon penetrated into the village, firing into houses which they had been told were occupied by us. There were wild shots and hand grenades all over the place. Windows shattering, doors being blown in and, of course, as we had been off duty most of us had undressed and were sleeping rolled up in our blankets on the floor. In the dark we had to find our rifles, helmets and boots. Some of the Jäger, including my own No. 1 and 2 on the LMG [light machine gun] rushed out to engage the enemy, even though they were dressed only in their underclothes, boots and helmets. Once in the open our counter-attack went in like clockwork; we had practised it often enough. One enemy MG was firing from across a small stream with his back to the trees and we made a left flank assault upon him, holding the gunners' attention by aiming at the muzzle flashes of their weapons. The outflanking group was now in posi-

tion, opened fire and forced the Serbs to withdraw. A reserve platoon of our company moved even deeper on to their flank and
began to spray the retreating Serbs with bullets. Then a battle
group from the Frontier Defence company, alerted by the firing,
came down and between our fire from the front, that of the reserve
platoon from the front, and that of the battle patrol from the rear,
the Yugoslav attack broke up and the men vanished into the trees,
leaving behind their dead and wounded as well as some equipment.

Like the 5th and 6th Divisions the 4th Gebirgs Division experienced its baptism of fire in the Balkan campaign. From garrison in
Germany it went by train to Romania and entered Bulgaria on
2 April to begin its approach march to battle. One of its Jäger battalions, in the course of that march, covered 160kms in two days.

The sudden change in the situation in Yugoslavia, as a result of
King Peter's actions, then required another Gebirgs division to
strengthen the attack by Kleist's panzer group upon the Yugoslav
capital, Belgrade, therefore the 4th was taken off the establishment
of one part of 12th Army and taken on the strength of another. The
task given to 4th Gebirgs Division was to strike westwards across the
Bulgo-Yugoslav frontier and to capture the high ground on both
sides of the Sofia–Belgrade road. The Jäger regiments set out,
climbed the almost trackless mountains, battling their way forward
against gale-force winds and blizzards to keep pace with the advance
of the panzer group. Opposition from Yugoslav military groups
varied between light to quite severe, but resistance, however determined, could not hold the drive of the mountain men. With the fall
of Belgrade on 12 April, Yugoslav resistance began to fail and while
the main of Weich's 2nd Army drove the defeated Royal armies
southwards, the 4th Gebirgs Division stayed in the Belgrade area on
occupation duties. These were pleasant months of light patrols, company and battalion exercises in the hills around the city and a peace-
ful existence untroubled by partisans for, in those early days, neither
Mihailovic nor Tito had organised themselves sufficiently to take part
in guerrilla operations.

Before long the call to action came again and this time to take part
in the new war which had begun upon the Soviet Union. The division's task was to participate in a drive upon Lemberg where, only

23 months before, other Gebirgsjäger had fought in the first campaign of World War II.

The actions of 5th Gebirgs Division in the Greek campaign came at the end of a 450km march through Romania and Bulgaria during which the division crossed snow-blocked passes above the 2000 metre level. The Jäger regiments were then dispersed along the Greek/Bulgarian frontier. The mountain range on which the 18th Gebirgs Corps (5th and 6th Gebirgs Divisions) was positioned are those which march eastwards out of Yugoslavia, fall abruptly into the valley of the Struma river and then ascend steeply again, running ever eastwards along the northern frontier of Greece. The valley of the Struma river is, therefore, the natural pass into Macedonia and thus the gateway to the western seaboard of Greece and the city of Athens as it is to the eastern and Salonika.

In the war to take out Greece the valley of the Struma and the mountains rising out of it were to be of vital importance to the plans of both sides. The 18th Gebirgs Corps was ordered by 12th Army to break the Metaxas Line, a Greek system of fortifications. The corps commander placed Ringel's 5th Gebirgs Division directly in front of the line and gave to it the task of carrying out a frontal attack against an alert foe positioned in strong fortifications. The 5th was to smash the Metaxas Line and to seize the Rupel pass through which the remainder of 12th Army would then follow. The Greek defensive line was based upon the design used by Maginot in France. The main line consisted of concrete and steel bunkers connected by underground tunnels. Each of these bunkers gave cross fire to defend the others, each had been sited in tactically good ground and, to add to the strong defences of some, a smooth, open glacis gave to the soldiers in the pill-boxes clear fields of fire. Undergrowth, trees and bushes had been cleared in front of the works so that no lurking enemy infantry group could rush out with explosive charges. Nor was it easy to bring heavy guns into positions from which they could engage the cupolas in the Metaxas Line. The roads on the Bulgarian side of the border had never been designed to take the weight and size of the artillery pieces which the Germans intended to use.

The heavy German guns had to wait down in the dripping valleys until corners had been widened, the road width enlarged from its narrow three metres and the degenerating surfaces made good. Only when that essential work had been completed could the next task begin, the slow haul of the guns, metre by metre up the inclines, inching them into carefully selected sites from which they could bring fire to bear. Next came the task of portering forward the ammunition which would be used in the barrages needed to clear a path of fire through which the Jäger could advance on to their objectives. The lighter guns, the artillery pieces specially designed for use in the mountains, could be broken down into horse loads but then there came the point past which even the sure-footed mules could not go. Then it was the gunners who carried the heavy pieces—barrels, carriages and wheels—stumbling along goat tracks to bring forward sufficient fire power to help their comrades in the forthcoming assault.

The last preparations had been made. The German armies in the Balkans waited upon the word of their Supreme Commander and when this came and "Operation Marita" began the German host moved down upon both Greece and Yugoslavia.

By midnight on 5 April 1941 the assault groups of 5th Gebirgs Division were in position and at 05.20hrs, in the first light of dawn on 6 April, the Jäger moved forward to begin a bitter four-day-long battle. To begin they would have to drive in the Greek outpost line occupying field fortifications on the rocky heights. In the bloody fighting that was certain to come the German mountain men would be facing other mountain men who would be battling to defend their homeland not only against the Germans but more particularly against the Bulgarians, traditional enemies of Hellas.

It is no easy thing to imagine oneself in the situation of Ringel's Jäger on that first dawn. Scattered among the stunted bushes they had lain in full equipment for hours. No fires; no smoking and the only talk was military orders given in whispers. The April night was bitterly cold and the last hot drink had been given out long before the assault groups had crawled on their bellies into the empty area which lay between the two frontiers. Shivering and trembling in the cold most were wondering how they would react to being in action for the first time and whether they would stand the ultimate test of manhood: combat in war.

Just before dawn and while yet it was dark, far away there was the sound of aeroplane engines and this grew louder as the light became stronger until ten minutes after sun-up the chains of Stuka aircraft were overhead, shining in the light of the blood-red dawn. The flying artillery had arrived and then the machines began to dive upon their targets, their fitted sirens howling and screaming. Then, as the Ju 87s climbed away again, below them the bombs they had released burst and sent fountains of earth and rock rising into the sky. Before the air attack had run half its course the Jäger of the assault detachments were on their feet ready to rush forward before the shattered defenders could recover from the shock of the bombardment. The screaming aircraft had had as little effect upon the nerves of the Greeks as the HE bombs had had upon the fabric of the defences and the Jäger, moving forward across the cratered ground, were met by a well co-ordinated cross fire which pinned them down. Under cover of artificial smoke they pulled back and called for the Stukas to go in again. This time the storming units began their advance before the air attack had ended, accepting the possibility of casualties and weighing the losses against the advantage of surprise.

Dust still hung in the air, the roar of aircraft engines was still loud when the assault pioneers, the point of the Jäger spearhead, rushed in. To the smoke and dust clouds was added a newer cloud, that produced by burning oil. With a sibilant hiss and then a roar as teams of flame throwers directed the flaming nozzles of their weapons towards the pill-boxes. Sheets of flame poured through the embrasures or smothered the outside of the bunkers in burning oil and phosphorus. Behind the "flamers" came other engineers with satchel charges which they pushed through machine gun slits and whose thundering detonations shook the steel and concrete forts.

It was not just a simple matter of flame and bomb. The projector and satchel charge attacks had to be made under constant fire from machine guns, mortars and snipers. Then the Greek artillery opened up its own destructive barrage trying to crush by bombardment the few groups of Jäger jinking about in the torn up ground. The Greek guns fired for a good ten hours and then as the sun's rays passed below the mountain crests and darkness began to fall, their infantry reserves, encouraged by the Germans' lack of success, charged in with the bayonet to drive the invaders from the soil of Greece. Their bravery was undoubted, their determination and will to win unbounded, but their weapons and tactics were obsolescent and in the rapid fire of Schmeissers and MG 34s they were cut to pieces.

The bright sunshine of the first day of the new war was replaced on the second by a steady downpour of freezing rain which cut

visibility to metres and made the task of the Forward Observation
Officers of the artillery more than usually difficult. Down in the mist-
shrouded valleys there was a continuous roll of thunder as the German guns opened fire and then the sharp crack as their shells burst
along the mountain crests. Under this barrage the engineers and the
Jäger went in again and by 08.00hrs on 7 April, the first bunker was
captured. Great waves of flame had roared around it and gobbets of
fire hissed in the steady downpour. The Jäger moved in towards the
bunker. There was no burst of machine gun bullets, no hand grenades. A senior soldier kicked open the blackened, paint blistered
door. Still no enemy fire, nothing except the sound of moaning. There
were wounded in this black hole and the sour smell of burnt human
flesh and hair. A sergeant jumped through the door and then from a
passageway the first shots came. More shots and then a whole fusillade as Greek soldiers came thundering down the dark corridor to recapture their lost position. A flame thrower team and an LMG detachment slid quickly into the pill-box. This was a terrible risk that
they were taking in using the projector inside a confined space. If
the flame did not go true into the corridor but hit a wall it would
rebound and possibly incinerate the German soldiers. "Flame" came
the order and the hissing fire projected across the pill-box cascading
in a golden rain when the fire touched the low ceiling and then
unrolling into the corridor, a sea of flame poured through the passageway. The screams of the Greeks caught in the fire were cut off by
the noisy reverberation of the machine gun firing in a bare and hollow space.

By flame and explosive charge; machine gun fire and hand to hand
combat; by desperate assaults across bare mountain tops and savage
fighting to hold off frenzied counter-attacks: by all of these and more
Ringel's men fought and fought until by 11.15hrs the first signs of
disintegration in the Greek defences became apparent. The key position of Istiby fell to a storming Jäger charge and then the first line of
bunkers was taken. Within twenty-four hours the Greeks seemed to
be in disarray although the garrisons of individual forts battled on
until death trying to hold back the Gebirgsjäger drive. Patrols from
5th Gebirgs Division slipped through the Greek lines and penetrated
into the Jiammutsitsa valley to reach the bridge at Lutra which spans
the Struma river. On the main battlefront fighting flared again and
each bunker had to be fought for, captured and then held as the iso-

lated Greek units battled to hold their own individual positions. Those Greek soldiers knew as Leonidas and his Spartans had known at Thermopylae that they were holding one of the gateways to Greece. Their heroic defence was to last only a little longer. The advances in other parts of Greece had left the defenders of the Metaxas Line outflanked and holding a militarily senseless position. The general commanding the Greek Macedonian Army offered the unconditional surrender of his forces and this was accepted. Some Greek garrisons in the bunkers of the Metaxas Line preserved their honour by fighting on after the local armistice, even though they knew this could lead to them being considered as franc-tireurs. When the last of these small groups came out, unwashed and hungry but dignified with honour preserved, the Jäger officers and men saluted their opponents, respecting the bravery which the Greeks had shown and the staunchness of their defence. The 5th Gebirgs Division had suffered a loss of 7 officers and 153 other ranks killed in the four days during which Ringel's men had forced the Metaxas Line, but the campaign was not yet over. Leading the advance of 12th Army through the Rupel pass 18th Gebirgs Corps then met the British for the first time and in violent actions drove off their rearguards from Mount Olympus. The mountain was climbed in a dense blizzard and the Reich's war flag was flown at its peak. By 19 April the 5th Division had broken the British defence and had captured Larissa. Then followed a pursuit battle across the Plain of Thessaly with hot little actions against determined British rearguards as the German armies pushed farther and farther southwards. On 23 April, the 6th Gebirgs Division forced the pass at Thermopylae compelling the British to withdraw to Athens.

The sudden and total collapse of Yugoslavia had allowed the whole might of the German war machine to be turned upon Greece and any hopes that the Royal Army might have had of fighting a successful defensive battle were destroyed. The end was inevitable and, when the armies of the Centre surrendered to the Germans on 21 April, this could not be long delayed. From ports in the south and in the Gulf of Corinth Royal Navy warships and light craft began to evacuate Greek, British, New Zealand and Australian soldiers and to take most of them to Crete.

Ringel's Gebirgsjäger had fought and won but ahead lay not a pleasant life as soldiers in the Army of Occupation in the tavernas of Athens, but even harder fighting in the arid, comfortless mountains of Crete.

Crete

The attack upon Crete and its capture in May 1941 was a German victory, but a Pyrrhic one. The sacrifice of so many first class fighting men, particularly paratroops and glider troops as well as transport aircraft immediately before the opening of "Operation Barbarossa", the war against the Soviet Union, weakened the opening offensive of that undertaking. Nor was Crete's strategic potential ever able to be fully exploited by the Germans and that, after all, had been one of the main reasons for the launching of "Operation Mercury". The scale of the losses was so high that thereafter only local and tactical assaults were made; no further major German airborne operations were undertaken for the remainder of World War II. It is not, however, with the paratroops whose initial landings formed a bridgehead that this account deals, but with the exploitation of the first successes and the final conquest of the island by the men of Ringel's 5th Gebirgs Division. The mountain men proved their mastership of such terrain. And the flexibility of their Command structure and the amount of responsibility given to quite junior officers were remarkable. The outflanking thrust through the Cretan mountains by 85th Gebirgsjäger Regiment, which is one of the several engagements described here, is a very considerable achievement in the history of mountain warfare.

During the spring of 1941, the German armies had overrun Yugoslavia and had conquered Greece, expelling from that country a British expeditionary force which had been hastily assembled and shipped there. When the Balkan campaign ended there was no place on the mainland of Europe, except Gibraltar, where there was a British garrison and the Germans could boast with truth that they "had swept the Tommies from the Continent". In North Africa the remnants of the Army of the Nile, the strength of which had been severely reduced by the despatch of much of its force to fight in

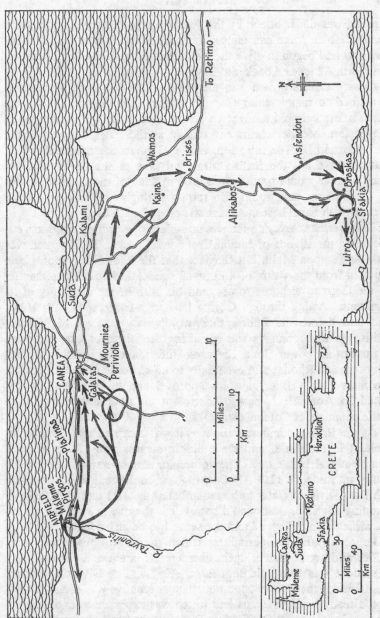

Gebirgsjäger movements; Crete 1941

Greece, was under attack by the Afrika Korps. This recently arrived small German force had almost immediately gone over to the offensive and had begun to drive the weak British detachments out of Italian North Africa and back into Egypt.

Great Britain's presence in the Middle East was under threat and it seemed to many senior German officers that the time had come when a strategic blow might be struck against British sea routes in the eastern Mediterranean and chiefly at the bases between Malta and Alexandria. The intention, as the German commanders saw it, was to drive out the British from that area of the Mediterranean. Such a move would protect the southern flank of the German armies in the Balkans and would also seize a springboard from which the great British naval base at Alexandria could be attacked.

The German Army's planners considered several possible targets, including the islands of Malta, Crete and Rhodes. Their option was an assault upon Malta but the fact that the choice fell upon Crete resulted from the vision of a Luftwaffe general, Student, commander of the German airborne forces, and his faith in the capability of its regiments. Acting through Göring he had a conference with Hitler and laid before the Führer the revolutionary concept of ignoring British naval supremacy and of seizing the island of Crete through the use of air power alone. Crete, as Student saw it, would be a stepping stone to Rhodes and eventually to an airborne operation against the Suez canal. Hitler gave his approval and in Directive No. 28, dated 25 April 1941, passed control of the operation to the Luftwaffe commander Colonel General Löhr.

As the British dominated the seas it was accepted that the assault, at least in the initial and the build-up stages, would have to be a completely airborne one. The forces for the operation were to be found in Student's 11th Air Corps which contained the battle-tested 7th Para Division (later to be renumbered the 1st) and the 22nd Air Landing Division. Both would be needed: the one to seize the principal airfields on the island and the second to be airlanded in Ju 52s, in order to expand the perimeters which the paratroops would have gained and from which bridgeheads set out to conquer the island.

Student was then told that 22nd Air Landing Division was not available for the Cretan operation. The alternative was to find a division already in the Balkans and which was experienced and reliable. The choice fell upon 5th Gebirgs Division; the ideal choice in view of the mountainous terrain over which the campaign would be fought, even though the Jäger were without experience in the techniques of air landings.

To form the airbridge there would be a fleet of some 550 transport planes whose task it would be to tow the gliders, to ferry the paratroops, then to air land the Gebirgsjäger component and, finally, to bring over the heavy stores from the mainland of Greece to the island. The 4th Air Fleet under General Löhr was to set up and to carry out "Operation Mercury", for which a time-table of ten days was allowed, to cover from the first drops to the final battle. Air superiority was a pre-requisite of the operation and the Germans were able to gain this because they had airfields in Greece and on the offshore islands from which they could fly off their aircraft. The nearest British bases were in North Africa. The Stukas, the Heinkels, the Messerschmitts and the Focke-Wulf aircraft were usually the only machines to be seen in the skies during the battle and the German attack opened with a combined assault by bombers and low-level strafing. Reduced to a simple proposition it may be argued that British command of the sea was beaten by German control of the air and therein lies the whole story of the battle for Crete.

The following account must, in its opening pages, dwell more upon the airborne aspect of the campaign than upon that of the mountain men. Had the paratroops drops all failed to seize the first allotted objectives, then there would have been no need for the Gebirgsjäger to enter the battle. But success at just one place could be exploited to bring victory. Initially then, the emphasis is upon the dispositions and battles fought by Student's 7th Para Division and this is then followed by the account of 5th Gebirgs Division.

The role of the mountain division is secondary to that of the paratroops only in that they were follow-up troops. The actions which the Jäger fought, the terrible country which they traversed, and the outstanding results which they achieved, would have given pride of place in any other battle but this, for the campaign in Crete is remembered chiefly because it was the first mass use of airborne soldiers in war.

Ringel's 5th Gebirgs Division went to battle in two types of carrier: ships and aircraft. It is the tragedy surrounding the ships of the light flotillas which opens the Gebirgsjäger section of this account. Also contained within the main body of the story are translations of contemporary, unedited and unexpanded reports written by two jun-

ior commanders of Gebirgs units on the roles played by the formations under their control. The one, Advance Guard Group Wittmann,
led the division in its pursuit battle, while Krakau Group carried out
the encirclement action at Stylos which was instrumental in forcing
the British to withdraw from their prepared defence lines covering
Canea, the island's capital.

The part played by all the troops on Crete was soon overshad-
owed by the greater drama of the German attack upon the Soviet
Union, but before we move, as we shall do in the next chapter, into
Russia to follow the fortunes of Gebirgsjäger units in the great encirclement battles which took place on the desolate steppes around
Uman, let us consider the action of 5th Gebirgs Division in the Cretan mountains in the late spring of 1941.

Crete lies about 100kms distant from the southernmost point of
the Greek mainland and is a mountainous island approximately
260kms long and between 20 and 50kms wide. There are four principal mountain ranges which divide Crete of which two are of especial
interest to this narrative. These are the White Mountains in the western end of the island which rise to a height of nearly 2700 metres
and which, extending eastwards, give way to a central feature, the
Ida range. The mountains on Crete are eroded, barren and steep and
in certain areas are considered to be impassable. The southern side
of the island is characterised by the abrupt descent of the mountains
into the sea and the absence of any large harbours. There are on the
hostile southern shore only a few fishing ports. Although the northern side of Crete is also rocky and has cliffs, there are small areas of
beach behind which lies a fertile strip of intensively cultivated land.

There were, in 1941, three small airstrips located at Maleme,
Canea and Heraklion, all on the northern side of the island as was
the large natural harbour of Suda bay. A single major road ran
east–west and connected the towns on the northern side of the island, but even this main road was reduced to a single carriageway in
its passage through the mountains. North–south communication depended upon a few minor roads which threaded their way through
the ranges. Considering these factors it can be appreciated that the
British were in a poorer placed position than the Germans in the
matters of supply and reinforcement. The Germans could more easily
build up their forces attacking the principal objectives, the airstrips,

which were all on the side nearer to Greece and which had easier terrain. Any British attempt to reinforce the island's garrison had to rely upon the few fishing ports on the southern side of Crete from which their units would have to traverse the width of the island using a few minor roads.

In 1941 the British garrison on Crete consisted of three infantry battalions as well as two heavy and three light anti-aircraft batteries. This force had been sent to Crete in October 1940, shortly after the attack upon Greece by the Italians, and since the island had been envisaged as a supply depot for the British expeditionary force which was then sent to Greece, little had been done to put it into a proper state of defence. The garrison was then reinforced, if that is the proper word, by the remnants of the expeditionary force which had been driven out of Greece and which had been evacuated to Crete. This force of some 25,000 men, chiefly New Zealanders and Australians, had lost all their heavy equipment in the fighting on the mainland and were, therefore, only lightly armed. Indeed, there was a grave shortage of all equipment. There were, for example, insufficient anti-aircraft guns to defend all the probable targets on the island and it was decided to locate the greatest concentration of guns around Suda bay. Defence of the airstrips was left chiefly to infantry units who were backed by the armoured strength of a handful of old and slow tanks. The few British field artillery pieces had been dug in, consequently reducing their effectiveness by rendering them immobile.

Intelligence had warned of the likelihood of a German airborne attack upon Crete and General Freyberg VC, the British commander, had deployed his troops covering the most probable targets. The remnants of 2nd New Zealand Infantry Division's 5th Brigade was kept in the west of the island to protect the Maleme airfield. The town of Retimo and its area was defended by an Australian brigade. British troops defended the aerodrome and town of Heraklion. Added to these forces were a few Greek battalions of poorly armed, low-calibre troops. German sources also mention, with some bitterness, the bands of Cretan civilians who fought on the British side and whose actions as partisans were responsible for the reprisals which were carried out against the civil population.

From the time of the issue of the order to launch "Operation Mercury", to its D-Day, was only a short period and General Student had been given only a few weeks to plan and to organise the operation. The equipment which his para division required was scattered in stores throughout Germany and needed to be brought to central points for sorting and for distribution. There were insufficient transport machines to carry out the whole operation of bringing in the paratroops in a single wave. Thus a shuttle service would have to be organised and operated. Heavy losses in the transport aircraft would then place an additional burden upon the surviving machines and this, in turn, would reduce the amount of supplies which could be ferried in.

The interpretation of aerial reconnaissance photographs by Luftwaffe specialists was so poor that many British gun and tank positions were not identified, nor were the interpreters able to advise the paratroop commanders on the terrain difficulties which would be met. Those commanders were, thus, ignorant of many of the problems facing them, but of one they were in no doubt whatsoever. They were aware that the airstrip runways were very short. The one at Maleme was only 170 metres long by 80 metres wide and the others were fractionally larger than this. The paratroop commanders were also aware that to capture and to hold those strips was the key to victory. The airfields were as vital to the success of the opening stages of the campaign as possession of the few main roads was to be in the final part of the operation. It was essential to the German build up that the airstrips be captured quickly, for upon them would land the transport aircraft from which would debouch the reinforcements who would take over from the lightly armed paratroops and then go on to capture the island.

The risks against the operation producing a victory were incredible and the difficulties were enormous. To quote one minor example of the difficulties, because of the short runway at Maleme and the dusty soil on which it was laid, only one Ju 52 could land at any one time. As soon as the machine touched down it would have to be braked sharply to halt it quickly. Its load of men would be debarked and then the pilot would have to take off again, threading a way through the wrecks of those aircraft on both the incoming and outgoing journeys that would fail to make a safe touch down. And all the while the next Ju 52 waited until the clouds of dust thrown up by the landing and the take off had cleared sufficiently for it to make its own run in.

To capture the landing strips it was planned that parachute descents and glider landings would be made at four main points on the island. Because of the shortage of aircraft these landings could not take place simultaneously and thus smother the British defences. Instead of a single drop there would be two. One at dawn on 20 April would attack targets in the western part of the island, Maleme, Canea and Suda bay, while targets in the central sector, Retimo and Heraklion, would be assaulted in the afternoon of the same day.

Preceding the paratroop and glider landings there would be severe and long bombardments by Stuka and heavy bomber squadrons to soften-up the defence. In the event this bombing offensive was so successful that the last remaining RAF machines on the island, three Hurricanes and three Gloster Gladiators, left Crete on 19 May. The Germans now had mastery of the air over Crete and the airborne landings could now take place. The units and their objectives follow.

Battle Group Maleme had five objectives; of which the principal one was to seize and to hold the airstrip. An important part of the Maleme assault was the capture of Point 107, a tactically important hill to the south of the airstrip which, therefore, not only dominated this but also the country surrounding it. With Point 107 firmly in German hands reconnaissance could be undertaken and a link up made with the troops who had been dropped at Canea where it was proposed the main effort was to take place.

The importance placed upon the success of the Maleme assault can be seen in the composition of the force chosen to accomplish it. The 1st Battalion of the Para Assault Regiment, minus Nos 1 and 2 Companies, was to attack the anti-aircraft batteries on either side of the Tavronitis river. No. 3 Company was to assault the British guns, while nine gliders, under the command of Major Braun, were to capture the river bridge and to cut the road from Maleme to Spilia. These landings would all take place on the western side of the airstrip. No. 4 Company had as its objective the capture of Point 107, upon which depended the success of the landings at Maleme. The airfield itself was to be attacked by 3rd Battalion of the Para Assault Regiment which would be dropped to the east of the field.

The second of the assault groups was Battle Group Canea, which it had been proposed was to be the main task force for the whole assault. Two platoons of the Para Assault Regiment were to take out the anti-aircraft guns south of Canea, while No. 2 Company of the assault regiment was to go on to attack other gun positions of the Akrotiri peninsula. The whole of 3rd Para Regiment was to jump over the area Galatas–Daratos–Alikianu–Canea. The 1st Battalion was to descend over an area extending from the Canea road to Suda, while 2nd Battalion was to jump in the Canea area. These assaults would be preceded by the drop of 3rd Battalion in the Galatas–Daratos area where it would guard the southern flank of the regiment's assault. The Para Engineer Battalion was to be dropped around Alikianu. The battle group's task was for it to attack Canea and to carry the fight forward to Suda bay.

The third grouping was 1st Para Regiment which had orders to capture and to hold the airstrip at Heraklion, so that air-landings could take place. The town of Heraklion was to be occupied and contact established with the Retimo battle group. The subsequent advance upon Canea would be made in conjunction with that battle group.

The 2nd Para Regiment was to drop over the town of Retimo, the fourth objective, to secure the town and its exits preceding an advance to capture the airstrip. This group, too, was to link up with and to support the Canea battle group.

The air invasion began in the morning of 20 May with successful attacks against the anti-aircraft positions at Tavronitis. The drop to capture Point 107 did not succeed and this failure affected the course of the fighting during the first few critical days. At other points the paratroops had been fired at while still in the air, while defenceless upon the ground or had been dropped over British troop concentrations. The drop at Suda bay was a débâcle. The 3rd Battalion of the Para Assault Regiment, for example, was scattered over such a wide area that it did not fight as a cohesive unit for several days. In an even worse state was the 3rd Para Regiment's 3rd Battalion. This formation was dropped over British positions and was shot to pieces upon landing. The few survivors who escaped death or wounding while still in the air were pinned down and unable to launch a concerted attack. They formed small islands of hard-pressed men battling against overwhelming odds, but most held out until the Gebirgsjäger relieved them days later.

In this context it is interesting to note that stories of heavy losses inflicted upon the paratroops as they floated down were discounted by the Germans. Experiments carried out by trained troops firing at dummies showed that at a distance of only 150 metres one shot out of 185 hit the target and at 350 metres this, already high, figure had risen to 1708 rounds fired to score a hit.

As if to reinforce this point the regimental medical officer of the Para Assault Regiment reported in a paper to the Luftwaffe study group that relatively few of the German dead were found in their parachute harness, which would have indicated that they had been killed while descending.

So disjointed was the pattern of the first engagements and so sparse the information coming into 11th Air Corps headquarters on that first morning that no true picture of the ground fighting could be gained. Only seven transport aircraft had been lost in the first drops and this light loss, together with the optimistic but inaccurate reports by pilots and crews, led General Student to assume that the operation was progressing smoothly. He was unaware that the airstrip at Maleme was still not securely held by German forces, that Süssmann, General Officer Commanding 7th Para Division, had been killed in a glider crash and that the commanding officer of the Para Assault Regiment, Meindl, had been seriously wounded. The loss of these two men meant that neither the Maleme nor the Canea groups had a commander and lacking this central direction each sub-unit fought its own battle in isolation. It was fortunate for the Germans that the officers had all been well briefed before the operation.

Problems with refuelling delayed the afternoon take-off. The schedule could not be kept and it was not possible to cancel in time the bombing attacks which were to open the way for the paratroop landings. The result of that bombardment was to alert the British to the arrival of the transport aircraft bearing the paratroops and so the defenders were prepared to receive the airborne attacks. When these assaults did come the paratroops came under heavy and accurate fire as soon as they had landed and were killed or wounded before they could reach their weapons containers. Their losses were enormous and the drops may, generally, be considered to have been unsuccessful. Soon small groups of men were holding all-round defence positions and waiting either to be overrun by British counter-attacks or to be relieved by a back-up force. They themselves were too weak in numbers and armament to carry out any major offensive operation. To hold out until relieved would be, in itself, a victory.

Not until the evening of 20 May was 11th Air Corps in a position to assess the results of the day's operations, building up their picture from the mass of wireless signals which had come in from the men fighting on the ground. These messages showed that only in the western part of the island, at Maleme, did the Germans have any sort of hold and even this ground was dominated by the still uncaptured Point 107. An attack by the paratroop survivors had gone in at 15.00hrs but had faltered and stopped in the face of a counter-thrust by two British tanks supported by heavy and accurate machine gun fire. Still, tenuous or not, the perimeter at Maleme was a foothold which could be exploited. Student thereupon decided to switch the main attack from Canea and instead to build up the effort at Maleme. Made aware of a reserve of some 550 combat-ready paratroops on the mainland he ordered Colonel Ramcke to lead this group into action. These reinforcements were dropped during the morning of 21 April and made a landing west of Maleme, almost upon the tactical headquarters of the Para Assault Regiment.

The situation Ramcke found was not encouraging, even though the capture of the airstrip had in the meantime been consolidated and men of 2nd Battalion of the Assault Regiment had conquered the crest of Point 107. The hold was firm even though the airstrip was still under the fire of British guns which bombarded the transport machines as they came in to land. The whole runway was littered with destroyed or burning aircraft and these wrecks had to be cleared to allow other Ju 52s to make their attempt. The paratroops were hard-pressed men but some had to be spared from the firing line to clear the runway of the crashed aeroplanes. Using the power of a British tank captured and pressed into German service, the fuselages were dragged to one side, craters were filled in and the surface of the runway levelled ready to receive the next machines. By late morning the first platoons of 3rd Battalion of 100th Gebirgsjäger Regiment had emplaned at Tanagra and were en route, flying over the ships of the light flotillas which had left ports in southern Greece steaming for the island of Crete. It is the story of the ships of those flotillas and the Gebirgsjäger who sailed in them that we now relate.

General Ringel, commander of 5th Gebirgs Division, had been warned in a secret operational order, dated 3 May, of the part which his formation was to play in the battle for Crete. The 5th Gebirgs Division was to supply the back-up force to the paratroop offensive and was to take over the battle and bring the operation to a speedy and successful conclusion. Ringel was advised that there were insufficient aircraft to carry out both the initial assault and the rapid build-up which were essential to capture the island. Part of his division, he was told, would have to travel to Crete by boat and the operational orders gave him authority to requisition vessels to convey some of his men in two groups of ships. The total number of vessels which he commandeered amounted to sixty-three. Twenty-five were caiques, chiefly fishing vessels whose principal motive power was supplied by huge sails supplemented by a weak auxiliary engine. On those twenty-five wooden ships would be embarked 2250 Jäger who would be disembarked at Maleme. A further thirty-eight ships, including seven small freighters, were to carry 4000 men whose destination was Heraklion. Those orders were changed on 21 May, when Student made Maleme the main point of effort and both convoys were ordered to sail to the Maleme area.

The first flotilla was to leave at sunset in the evening of 19 May from the port of Piraeus and the second convoy, at dawn on 20 May, from the harbour of Chalkia. The first group would be escorted by the Italian destroyer *Lupo* and motor torpedo boats. The Italian escort for the second convoy would be the light destroyer *Sagitario*. In addition to the two battalions of Gebirgsjäger the ships were also to carry heavy equipment belonging to 7th Para and 5th Gebirgs Divisions as well as additional artillery and some armoured fighting vehicles. No mules were shipped or air portered.

The news that they were to travel by sea to their new battlefield caused a great deal of amusement to the men of the Jäger battalions and they had soon nicknamed themselves the "Air Landing Naval Mountain Division"! Many looked forward eagerly to the sea journey, for most had not seen the sea before the Greek campaign, coming as they did from the land-locked provinces of Germany and Austria. A sea cruise in the Aegean was, therefore, a new and exciting prospect. They were not to know that the ships in which they were to travel from the mainland to the shores of Crete were not designed either for comfort or for speed. Nor did the Jäger know that British Intelligence had anticipated that a build-up to the air landings would have to come by sea and had prepared accordingly.

Admiral Cunningham, the British naval commander in the Mediterranean, knew that an airborne invasion of Crete was to take place and he also knew that the German 11th Air Corps had only a limited number of transport aircraft at its disposal. It was logical for him to assume, therefore, that reinforcements would have to come by sea and he disposed three groups of ships to intercept the German/Italian convoys and to destroy them. In this way, reasoned Cunningham, the air landings, starved of men, would wither away and the German attempt to seize the island would fail.

On 19 May 1941 part of the first light flotilla left the harbour at Piraeus bearing men of 3rd Battalion of 100th Gebirgsjäger Regiment and followed by the remaining vessels of the convoy. The departure of the second flotilla was delayed, and it was not until the evening of 20 May that the ships left the harbour of Chalkia on Embos carrying 2nd Battalion of the regiment. The two flotillas sailed across a sea as smooth as a mill pond, making at best only 7 knots, and this speed, that of the slowest ship, determined the speed of the whole group. By nightfall on that first day the ships of the first flotilla had reached and had made anchorage in Milios, which they then left at dawn on 21 May. Their departure was premature for no reports had been received to say that it was safe for the convoy to proceed towards Crete. The first flotilla was, thereupon, returned to harbour and not until dawn on 22 May did it set out again with the expectation, indeed the need, to reach Maleme before last light. Daylight belonged to the Luftwaffe but by night the ships of the Royal Navy determined who sailed on the waters of the Mediterranean. Adverse winds, however, slowed the convoy's pace and it was clear that it would be midnight before the vessels of the first flotilla made landfall. The second flotilla was still held in harbour waiting to hear that the first flotilla had reached Crete.

As the afternoon of 21 May wore on without a sight or sound of the Royal Navy, the hearts of the Italian naval commanders began to lighten. Perhaps, after all, the Luftwaffe had driven the British ships away from the convoy's route. Soon the long hot day began to draw to a close; there remained only the dangerous period of a few hours' steaming after which the convoy would reach its destination on Cape Spatha. There a group of air-landed Jäger had already driven out the British forces and had begun to set up a disembarkation point illuminated by light signals which would guide in the flotillas.

Soon it was quite dark and on the vessels no light showed but the riding lamps as the ships chugged their way across the Aegean. The moon rose and the Gebirgsjäger lying on deck, enjoying the smooth crossing and the soft warm night, talked among themselves of the things that soldiers talk about. Only an hour to midnight, to Cape Spatha and the end of the journey. The Jäger began to dress and to fit on their equipment ready to disembark. The new battlefield of Crete lay to the south just over the horizon, but also just over the horizon waited the cruisers of the Royal Navy, whose mast top radar had picked up the shape of the convoy and the number of its ships, 15 caiques, about five sea miles north of the Cape.

At 23.00hrs the southern horizon was lit by gunfire and then by the searchlights. Within seconds the first British shells began to fall among the slow-moving wooden vessels. Three cruisers and four destroyers of the Royal Navy had intercepted the convoy and were now intent upon destroying it. The Italian destroyer *Lupo,* raising full steam, turned towards the British ships but was smothered in a salvo of shells. Lit by the searchlights of her enemies and hit several times she swung away out of control and moved back towards the convoy followed by fresh salvoes. Out of the night loomed the ships of the Royal Navy and began to destroy the caiques at point blank range. On board the *Lupo* the battle damage had been hastily repaired and she returned to the fight trying in vain to draw the fire of the cruisers and to cover the escape of the ships of the first flotilla as they fled northwards. For two and a half hours the Royal Navy hunted down the caiques, but then at 03.30hrs as the first light of dawn showed in the eastern sky, the British ships turned to the west, for with the sun came the Luftwaffe; and the Germans enjoyed aerial superiority.

Meanwhile a second group of British ships was heading northwards and, unusually, in broad daylight, in compliance with orders to enter the Aegean. Some twenty sea miles south of Milios they picked up on their radar sets the vessels of the second flotilla which were now heading south and prepared to engage them. This second group of German ships had sailed during the night and having received no orders to return to harbour was sailing directly into range of the Royal Navy's guns. The time was now 08.30hrs. Alerted by distress signals from the Italian escort ships, Luftwaffe headquarters sent its bomber squadrons to attack the British warships and, even as the guns of the destroyers and cruisers swung towards their targets, the first Heinkels and Junkers flew overhead. Admiral King, the British commander, realising that he had insufficient ammunition to carry out the tasks of firing an anti-aircraft barrage and of engaging the enemy convoy, broke off the engagement and turned away.

These details from official accounts conflict with the personal statements which tell of interception and destruction of the ships of the convoy during the morning of 22 May. I am convinced that the Jäger have confused time and date but their vivid descriptions have been summarised and included.

Soon after 10.10hrs, according to the Jäger, the *Lupo* and five small ships of the first flotilla, steaming northwards to escape from one group of British ships, came within range of the guns of the second group.

We were aware of the sinister significance of those, low, narrow, grey-painted ships that moved towards us and we knew that our slow-moving tubs could not outrun them. We were all crammed together on the deck and the order came for us to don our life jackets. We hauled down the rusty red sails of the caique and stopped her engine. Our officer told us that if it came to it and we had to abandon ship then at least we would be jumping into the hostile sea from a stable and halted platform and not moving one whose stern screw might cut us to pieces. I heard later that one company commander ordered all the non-swimmers on his ship to get into the life rafts which were then launched and certainly there were rafts full of men floating about, usually without direction, for there were no paddles. Our lieutenant gave orders for us to stand fast but to be prepared to jump overboard if he ordered it. We stood on deck facing outwards and our boat rocked violently as the whole sea was a turmoil. Destroyers raced about creating huge waves which threw our boats about while above them our Stukas dived down dropping bombs whose explosions raised geysers of water and all the time our caique wallowed about trying to avoid the gunfire and hoping to hide itself in the smokescreen which the Italian ship was trying to lay.

I was surprised to get out of the battle alive and thought that I must be one of a very small band of survivors. I am really astonished at how light our losses were. We were after all completely defenceless against an enemy whose ships had speed, armour and guns.

A few caiques were sinking and ours suddenly turned over. She had been hit by shells but these had hit high and had exploded in the rigging and masts. None, so far as I knew, had hit the actual vessel. But suddenly she went over and we were all flung into the sea. Now that really was frightening, especially when the British ships came steaming towards us. Some of our casualties were caused when Jäger were run down by ships. One body I saw had shocking damage caused to it. I cannot remember such noise, although there must have been a considerable amount of it. I do remember the concussion of exploding bombs, even far away ones, for they seemed to burst my whole body. I hauled myself on to some wreckage and found I still had my waist belt, water bottle and bayonet. I drank some water and felt a lot better for it. Some time later, an hour or two perhaps, a Ju 52 flew over the scene. It seemed to me as if I was the only living person in the whole area. The British had gone, some caiques were burning, there were lots of rubbish in the water and lots of German soldiers, chiefly Gebirgsjäger, all of whom seemed to be dead. Then another aircraft came along; a seaplane, and began slowly cruising about. When it came over to me I stepped from my wood pile on to the float and was helped into the body of the machine, where a couple of Jäger were already lying. So I hadn't been the only living thing. The aeroplane flew us back to Greece and to a divisional rest camp. I never actually set foot on Crete.

There were losses on both sides as the air and sea battle raged around the caiques. At long last the Royal Navy drew off and the battered convoy held course to the north, waiting until darkness fell when another attempt would be made. This next run was attempted during the night of 22–23 May, but was aborted when it became clear that the British were once again waiting for the German vessels. The convoy was intercepted and fired upon shortly after it set sail. A withdrawal to Greece was the only course left. A safe run home to the mainland and to embark the dispirited Gebirgsjäger into aircraft and a quick flight to the island.

How had the Gebirgsjäger fared during the night engagement of 21–22 May in which they could take no active part? They were men who had been under fire and to whom death was no new phenomenon. On terra firma a slit trench might offer some slight chance of escape from the worst effects of a barrage but on a ship there was no safe place, no place to hide. The Jäger stood or lay on the decks amid the rain of shell fragments which scythed through the air. Many jumped into the sea wearing full equipment and sank like stones. One group, a hundred or more swimmers, were formed into an organised detachment and towed life rafts, on which lay badly wounded comrades, four kilometres from the scene of destruction to the coast of Crete. This was an inhospitable coast, for when the swimmers approached the shore they found that they could not beach their rafts at the foot of its steep cliffs, and they were too exhausted to scale them. The survivors headed out to sea again where they were among the 178 men rescued by the air/sea rescue service aircraft. A further 64 Jäger were picked up by rescue launch. Some Gebirgsjäger did struggle ashore and the war diary of 5th Gebirgs Division reported the arrival of one group which reached divisional headquarters almost naked and suffering from exposure but each of whom, the diary added proudly, still carried his weapon.

The sea-borne invasion had failed and that with heavy loss of life. No further attempts to bring in troops by sea were made, at least not until the outcome of the campaign was assured. The build-up of reinforcements then became the responsibility of the Luftwaffe's Transport Command. Hundreds of Gebirgsjäger had been killed or wounded and one battalion, having suffered more than 300 dead, was almost wiped out. Of the two battalions of men who had embarked into the ships only 52 went into action on Crete. The strength of a single platoon was all that fought in the campaign, out of the regiment which had attempted the sea crossing.

On 21 May the ground situation became more clear. The paratroops at Maleme were the strongest of all the isolated groups that had been dropped. Maleme was, thus, a bridgehead, the base from which the eventual capture of the island could be undertaken. German success can, perhaps, have been said to have been assisted by the failure of the 5th New Zealand Brigade commander to carry out a strong, immediate and concerted attack to destroy the German forces on and around the airstrip while they were still weak and few in number. The many reasons for his seeming inaction cannot be gone into in this short account but it can be suggested that the brigadier, aware from documents which had been found on a dead paratrooper that the original German intention had been a major thrust for Canea, decided to stand firm in prepared defensive positions west of the town and to allow the Germans to run their heads against a strong defence. The New Zealand Brigade was thus disposed to meet a frontal attack down the west–east road and the battalions were deployed accordingly. The 22nd Battalion was concentrated around Point 107 and the Maleme airstrip. The 23rd Battalion was situated immediately behind 22nd Battalion, east of Pirgos. On the left flank of 23rd Battalion was the 21st Battalion. The 28th Maori Battalion was in deep reserve around Platanias.

The largest and most active of the German groupings faced the 22nd Battalion and the paratroops of No. 9 Company had, by vigorous patrolling, found the southern flank of the New Zealand battalion and had begun to work round behind this. The commanding officer of 22nd Battalion was faced with paratroops before him and on the airfield; with others turning his left flank and still others, in small pockets, behind him and dotted around the area of his command. There remained very little choice but for him to pull back from Point 107 and to insert his battalion between 21st and 23rd Battalions. His move, after all, was predicated upon the expectation of a German frontal assault. And so his battalion moved back and in this withdrawal lay the seeds of the eventual German victory.

During 21 May the paras had fought alone, buoyed up by the certainty that back-up troops were on their way. We have described how the ship-borne component of the relief force was doomed to be destroyed. There remained, therefore, only the air bridge, the shuttle service of Ju 52s to bring in the battalions of Ringel's Gebirgsjäger. On Tanagra airfield all was made ready and at mid-morning on 22 May the first machines lumbered into the air en route for Crete.

As the ships of the light flotillas set out on their ill-fated expedition there flew above them, shining in the bright morning sunlight, the transport aircraft carrying the first Jäger platoons. The Ju 52 was not the ideal vehicle to air-lift soldiers. To convey them the interior of each machine had had to be altered and despite this conversion the maximum number which could be carried was only twelve men. The Jäger sat on either side of the exit doors with their backs to the thin metal walls of the fuselage. They did not need to be told that the operation into which they were flying was a hazardous one. When the aircraft touched down they would have to deplane under fire and go immediately into action. For the pilots the experience was nerve racking. They had to land, avoiding the aircraft wrecks and then on the short and crowded runway they had to swing the big machine, rev the throttles to gain maximum power and, half blinded by the clouds of dust, take off pursued all the time by shell and machine gun fire. Above them other Jus waited to make their own run-in; waiting for the thick obscuring sand clouds to settle. The quickest turn-round time between two aeroplanes landing and taking off was ten minutes and each plane carried only a dozen men. To bring in a single battalion took more than four hours.

The aircraft flew at almost wavetop height towards the island and on crossing the coast those Jäger near the windows and looking towards the small jumble of white-washed houses that was Maleme could see among the low hills a red brick coloured rectangle which looked, according to Student, "like a tennis court". That was the airstrip and from the Junkers there was little to indicate the fury of the battle that was being fought below. As the slow lumbering Jus rocked along the strip to land they passed the wrecks, some of them still burning, of planes that had crashed. The jagged metal fuselages stood piled along the sides of the runway like tombstones. Even as the Ju roared along the short strip while it was still swaying from side to side as the brakes bit and were then released, the Jäger prepared themselves and before the aircraft had halted they had begun to leap from the doorway to hit the ground, roll over and run crouching under fire into the shallow ditch around the airfield perimeter; if they were lucky with nothing more than bruises. Others were not so fortunate. Their machines, the pilots killed or wounded by machine gunners on the ground who aimed deliberately at them, ran out of control to hit other aircraft littering the runway. Bright flames and clouds of black smoke indicated where planes had collided and Jäger lying wounded or unconscious from the crash and, inside the bellies of the machines, were burnt to death before their comrades could reach them. Some aircraft, their engines hit by anti-aircraft fire or by the machine guns of the occasional Hurricane making fast sorties over the island, caught alight in mid air and crashed flaming into the waters of the Mediterranean. There were, inevitably, some remarkable escapes from almost certain death. The Jäger in one Junkers which had been hit and was on fire sat calmly in their seats until the pilot had pancaked the aircraft on to the surface of the sea and just off shore. The Jäger climbed out of the fuselage and waded from the sinking machine on to the beach.

Waves of planes brought in fresh loads of mountain men and these were put straight into the line to relieve the paratroopers exhausted from battles fought without pause since touchdown on 20 May. The first companies of Jäger went into action manning the Maleme perimeter around the airstrip and found that their New Zealand enemies were at some places only 300 metres distant. More and more aircraft came in until by midday of 22 May the whole of 1st Battalion had been air portered. The small perimeter was now crammed full with troops and these worked their way forward across the sunbaked ground to take over the para positions on Point 107 where a night attack by 22nd New Zealand Battalion had been beaten off.

During 22 May Ringel assumed command of all forces in the Maleme area and was charged with the task of establishing contact with the German forces isolated in the central sector, of capturing Canea and Suda bay and of clearing British forces from the western part of the island.

There were more landings of 5th Division units during that day. The first of these was 2nd Battalion/100th Regiment followed by 1st Battalion/85th Regiment and then by 95th Pioneer Battalion. With this build-up there came a chance for the Germans to take the initiative and to make ground to the south, the east and to the west. To achieve this desired effect Ringel formed three battle groups. The pioneer battalion was not merely to cover Maleme against any British thrust coming from the west and thus into the division's back, but it was to clear the western part of the island and to capture Kastelli. The second group was made up of the paratroops under command of Colonel Ramcke. These were to be formed into fighting units and were to strike northwards to the sea and to protect the airfield along the coast road and extending eastwards. The third group, commanded by Colonel Utz, had the task of advancing eastwards with part of its forces while the second part were to carry out a march into the mountains and in a wide sweeping movement to turn the flank of 5th New Zealand Brigade's positions. This move would force the British field artillery, whose fire still dominated the airstrip, to withdraw to avoid encirclement.

The direction of this thrust, coming as it did out of the mountains, surprised the British Command for it will be remembered that the New Zealand brigadier had disposed his forces facing west to meet a head-on German assault coming down the coast road. The Gebirgsjäger advance across this difficult terrain confounded a defence plan based chiefly upon the fact that the mountains were impassable. It is with this outflanking group that we shall stay, for theirs was the vital move which led to the first major British retreat.

The first battalion of the outflanking group, 1st/85th Regiment, was sent on its march to Platanias during the afternoon of 23 May, traversing the mountains until it reached a point 2kms south-east of Modion. The tenacious defence put up by the New Zealanders in the area halted their advance outside the village, but the second of the outflanking battalions, 1st/100th, swung past the halted companies of the sister regiment and then turning northwards attacked Modion from the flank. The village fell at 10.00hrs but the British defenders although driven out were still not beaten and put in a series of counter-attacks, hoping to drive back the Jäger who had not had time to consolidate the gains which they had made.

Outside Modion stood Point 259, a dominant feature, possession of which was essential to the next stage of the advance. The 1st/100th was ordered to take the peak and 1st/85th was directed to cover the flank of the attacking force. At this stage of the fighting on Crete the heavy weapons with which to support the Jäger assaults were arriving in small numbers, and very few had moved away from the airfield perimeter. Thus the men had to carry everything needed for the attacks upon their own backs. Most of them were fighting as riflemen and carried their ammunition and weapons as well as belts of ammunition for the light machine guns. The struggle to gain Point 259 was thus a soldiers' battle: one set of infantrymen against another. The German battalion commander held a final briefing in a small clump of stunted olive trees growing on the south-western side of the mountain and then, in the harsh afternoon sunlight, the companies moved off. Under protective fire from 1st/85th the men of 1st/100th moved by bounds from cover to cover. The New Zealand positions were well camouflaged and sited with excellent fields of fire. The whole defence had been well designed and expertly constructed with interlocking fire zones, backed by snipers.

The heat was stifling and the mountain men were dressed in thick uniforms. Sweating in their clothes and with the exertion of the climb in the hot sun they moved forward through a rain of bullets, flinging themselves down as mortar bombs fell on the rocky ground sending out slivers of razor-edged rock with every explosion. It was not only machine guns and mortars which opposed their upward climb. In some places the determined New Zealand infantry charged forward in desperate counter-attacks and on those bare and desolate slopes there was a thrust and counter-thrust of bayonet fighting. But however determined were the New Zealanders the swing of the Gebirgsjäger advance was irresistible and by late evening the peak was in German hands. Two Jäger battalions, the first battalions of 85th and 100th Regiments, were now poised near the left flank of 5th Brigade but still it would not be budged. The arrival of a third German battalion changed the situation. The 2nd Battalion/100th Regiment arrived at last light. This unit had begun its march at 07.00hrs and had spent the day climbing heights and descending into valleys as it moved through the trackless terrain. It did not reach Stalos until 19.30hrs but then moved further southwards and round the British flank. There was now no alternative for the enemy but to pull back to avoid encirclement. In the hours of darkness the New Zealand guns moved back to positions south of Platanias. Maleme airfield was no longer dominated by enemy artillery fire.

The strain of this day was not yet over for the men of 2nd Battalion/100th Regiment. Against this tired unit the New Zealanders flung their heaviest barrages. Crouched to the ground to avoid the shrapnel and the rock fragments, the mountain men tried to dig slit trenches in the rocky ground or, when this proved impossible, erected primitive sangars. The blazing heat of day gave way to the bitter cold of night. There was no food for the men who had traversed and fought across those barren hills. There were no wells where water bottles, long since empty, could be refilled. Water shortage was a dreadful fact of life on Crete and a considerable portion of the supplies brought in by transport aircraft had to be drinking water, for the wells on the island were too few to meet the heavy demands which were being made upon them. Lacking hot food and water, but inspired by the leadership and example of their officers, the mountain men battled on attacking and capturing other peaks during the night. Ground was being gained. The stubborn British were being forced to pull back to a new line set up to protect Canea. Slowly but inexorably the situation was turning in favour of the Germans. They were being massively reinforced and the British were not. There were no properly constructed defences in front of Canea which might hold the Germans, and the New Zealanders could not counter-attack in force. Firstly, they were not trained for mountain warfare and, secondly, they were being outflanked. Against an enemy growing stronger by the hour and who was passing strong forces round their flank there was no alternative but to withdraw.

Only seventy-two hours earlier the first paratroop drops had been made. The survivors of those drops and of the glider landings had then gathered themselves into small, desperate groups ready to meet counter-attacks which, in fact, never came. The failure of the British to mount immediate and strong counter-attacks gave to the parachute troops the time they needed to regroup and to consolidate their positions. By the morning of 22 May air landings had begun to bring in the mountain troops and the arrival of these fresh, experienced soldiers had slowly altered the balance. Then the march through the mountains by the three Gebirgsjäger battalions had swung the initiative very firmly into German hands, and from a situation which only three days before had looked unpromising there was the definite feeling that victory might soon be gained. It is true that the paratroop groups east of Maleme were isolated but they were still holding out and were being supplied by air drop. Their resolve was strengthened by the news which was received on their radio that the Gebirgsjäger were en route to relieve them.

During 23 May twenty aircraft each hour had come in bringing artillery, anti-tank guns and other equipment. A platoon of anti-tank gunners was ordered to join the pioneer battalion and, as the pieces lacked prime movers, they were towed to Kastelli by teams of soldiers. The arrival of the guns into their firing positions meant that barrages could now be fired. In writing of the successes in the western part of the island the divisional war diary reported that during the day it had fought battles against partisans, including women and children. These local groups had carried out frightful atrocities on wounded and dead Germans alike. The eyes of some paratroops had been plucked out; others had had their sexual organs mutilated and on others even more appalling tortures had been committed. Division ordered that, for every Jäger or paratrooper who had been killed in that fashion, ten Cretans were to be shot in reprisal. Houses and farms from which attacks upon German troops had taken place were to be burnt down and destroyed. Hostages were to be taken from every village and town. The Luftwaffe dropped leaflets warning the civil population of the measures that would be taken against partisans.

That evening a welcome reinforcement to 95th Pioneer Battalion was received. This was a headquarters group and two companies from 55th Motor Cycle Battalion which were ordered to strike for the south coast at Paleakora and then to secure it. In fact most of 23 May was spent in concentrating and regrouping. There were bands of scattered paratroopers to contact, supplies to be brought forward and local actions to be undertaken against the British forces. The Germans were building up their strength preparatory to going over completely to the offensive. Action was soon to follow.

The plan for 24 May was not merely to hold the ground already gained at Platanias, but to use this as a springboard for a rapid sweep to clear the British from the whole east of the island. The most important task was to advance the centre of the line and the southern flank on both sides of the Alikianu–Canea road. Then to push forward to the Galatas heights and to gain touch with Colonel Heydrich's paratroops.

The successes achieved by 100th Gebirgsjäger Regiment were such that during the night of 24–25 May touch was gained with the western part of Heydrich's forces. Reconnaissance of Galatas showed it to be well fortified and strongly garrisoned.

On other sectors of the divisional front the airstrip at Maleme, no longer under artillery bombardment, saw the landing of the first German fighter aircraft which were flown in to give even closer support to the ground troops. Farther west still, Kastelli fell to the pioneer battalion after the town had been "softened up" by Stuka dive bombing.

The first task that had been given to 5th Division, that of gaining ground, had been accomplished and it was now time to undertake assaults against new objectives. The intention was to advance upon the British forces massed in front of Canea and to destroy them, then to go on to seize the island's capital and to gain the Suda bay area. Ringel decided to divide his forces. One group would advance along the coast road and attack Galatas, the key to Canea. While this force was moving forward a second group, Krakau Force, was to undertake an 80kms outflanking march through the high country. Speed was the important factor that Krakau Force had to consider for, until the group was in position behind the New Zealand front, the task of reducing Galatas could not begin. Krakau Force had as its objectives the Canea–Retimo road in the area east of Suda where it would cut the British escape route. The accomplishment of these several objectives would mean that the area vital to the British defence would have been taken from them and the mass of their forces destroyed west of Canea, or forced to retreat.

The two successful operations which began on Sunday 25 May, the one a thrust and the second an envelopment, began the string of small but important, and above all victorious, actions which ended with the capture of Crete. Each will be described separately although each was complementary to the other.

It is the account of the action by the troops making the east–west drive up the coast road and of the battle for Galatas which will be first recounted. For this operation Ramcke's paratroops formed the left flank. The two battalions of 100th Regiment—the third had gone down with the light ship flotilla—held the centre and on the right wing were Heydrich's paratroop soldiers, recently relieved from encirclement and incorporated into the German battle line. The task of the para units on both flanks was to support the main thrust which would be made by 100th Regiment. The aim of this combined para/Gebirgsjäger operation was to cut off Canea from the west and the south. The key to success of the whole operation was the capture of Galatas.

The village of Galatas lay 2kms inland and was situated on high ground dominating the two roads Agia Marina–Canea and Alikianu–Canea. Just as Galatas covered Canea so did that city, the island's capital, cover Suda bay, the retention of which was the only reason for a British presence on the island. Thus the defence of this natural harbour and naval base depended upon Canea and Canea's defence depended upon Galatas. Once that village fell there was no other natural defence line along which the British could attempt to hold the Germans west of Suda.

So important was the capture of Galatas that a frontal attack was ordered to capture it, for it could not be bypassed. The Germans realising the importance of the place assumed that so vital a sector would be held by picked troops backed by the strongest possible defence. Their unit war diaries indeed not only claim, but stress, that the defenders of that small Cretan village were soldiers of the British Empire's elite units. The truth was that most of the New Zealand troops in the Galatas sector were men taken from a great number of miscellaneous units and grouped into what was termed 10th Infantry Brigade. Many of the men were without previous experience of infantry warfare but, in the fighting in which their splinter groups had been involved since Heydrich's men had dropped over them, they had given a good account of themselves even though their inexperience had caused them grievous casualties.

Their stout defence was smashed on 25 May. In the late morning men of the New Zealand Petrol Company, from whose positions there was excellent observation, saw the signs of a German build-up on the Brigade's right (that is, northern) flank. This was a sector into which 18th Battalion had recently arrived. To contest the German advance there were few back-up troops and the principal support to the defence of Galatas consisted of three old Italian 7.5cm guns, none of which had sights and for which there was only a limited supply of ammunition.

It was against the "scratch" force of Kippenberger's Brigade, short of every sort of supply and equipment, that the now rested, regrouped and re-equipped paratroops and Gebirgsjäger of Ringel's eastern thrust came in. Only in one respect did the units of the New Zealand Brigade have the advantage: they knew the ground for they had held it for days. Their own weaknesses did not permit them to make an assault against the Germans but they could make a solid defence when the Jäger came in, as they must, across an open plain and up the harsh ridges which dominate Galatas. Secure in their slit trenches the New Zealanders could pour rifle fire upon the mountain men toiling up the slopes and if the Germans came too near then the Kiwis were still men who believed in carrying the bayonet to the enemy.

For his attack Ringel disposed two Jäger battalions; 2nd Battalion/100th Regiment on the left to attack the village itself and 1st Battalion/100th Regiment on the right to capture the high ground north of the village. The highest point in the area lay south of the village and was known to the New Zealand troops as Ruin Hill and to their adversaries as Castle Hill. To gain that high ground was essential to the success of the frontal assault whose flanks were to be guarded by the paratroop units.

Throughout the night the German units brought forward the heavy weapons, mortars and artillery pieces and this build-up continued well into the late morning of a hot, airless and sticky day. The infantry assault would be preceded by Stuka dive bombing and to ensure absolute accuracy by the Luftwaffe pilots directional markers were laid out on the ground to mark the Jäger forward positions.

Just after midday in the blazing, searing heat the Jäger companies moved forward to their form-up lines to the accompaniment of the screaming sirens of the Stukas and the thunder of a properly concerted barrage of artillery fire which had begun some hours earlier. At 17.00hrs with the sting of the sun diminishing and with its light behind them, thus shining into the eyes of the defenders, the set-piece attack to capture Galatas opened.

The pace of 1st Battalion's attack across the flat ground covered with olive and orange plantations was very slow. The No. 3 Company on the battalion's right flank had the greatest distance to cover and passed through a shallow valley whose principal feature gave its name to both sides alike: Prison Valley. The road fork, some 500 metres south of the prison, was held by Heydrich's men who were pouring a barrage of machine gun fire into the New Zealand positions between the cemetery chapel and the Petrol Company's positions on Castle Hill.

Under cover of this indirect support fire No. 3 Company wheeled left, pivoting on No. 1 Company and thus, abreast and advancing on a generally north-eastern line the 2nd, 1st and 3rd Companies of 1st Battalion, with TAC headquarters to the rear of No. 1 Company, began to make the slight ascent towards the village. No. 3 Company had soon crossed the narrow road which enters Galatas from the southern side and began to push towards Cemetery Hill. No. 1 Company started its ascent of Castle Hill and No. 2 Company covered the left flank of the advance.

The defenders struck back at the German thrust. Most of the New Zealanders were men who had used rifles in their civil life and were expert marksmen. They were also masters of camouflage and in laying out a closely co-ordinated defence. Concealed in tree tops and firing from well concealed positions they began to inflict casualites upon the Gebirgsjäger at quite long ranges. Then the Brens opened up and in the crossfire of the slow but accurate Bren guns the Jäger advance faltered. As the pace slackened and the mountain men reeled back a scant 50 metres in front of the British first line positions, the Colonial troops sprang from their slit trenches and drove forward in a bayonet charge forcing the mountain men to withdraw. The platoons on the right wing of No. 1 Company began to conform to the slower pace and this slackening of tempo began to affect both the attacking companies. Battalion headquarters put in No. 2 Company to boost the assault but Regiment halted the advance and called back the Stukas. Punctually at 18.00hrs the Ju 87s screamed down upon Galatas laying their bomb line only a short way ahead of the Jäger as they lay exposed on the open hills. A Very light fired to indicate the end of the dive bombing flared white in the sky and the Jäger of No. 2 Company rose to their feet and moved off, passing through the machine gun line set up by battalion HQ, from the muzzles of which weapons streams of tracer floated across the valley and into the village. No. 1 Company, led and inspired by the regimental commander, Colonel Utz, who marched with the leading groups, charged in with the bayonet on to Cemetery Hill and to a smaller rise some 500 metres south of Galatas. The capture of these now put one company of mountain men in the rear of the New Zealand defenders.

No. 3 Company also gave supporting fire and upon the southern side of the village two dozen machine guns poured bullets in support of No. 2 Company's assault. By 19.30hrs the Jäger had penetrated into the first houses and had gained a foothold. But at what a cost. Behind them on the slopes of Castle Hill lay sixteen of their number killed in action. These sixteen Jäger lay in the comradeship of death with the paratroops and British who had been killed in the five days of fighting which had taken place around the small rural village.

The battle was confused and bitter. Once again, as so often in the Cretan campaign, it was a soldiers' battle, man against man, with determination to win and sharper reflexes deciding who lived and who died. The advance was contested by snipers and Bren gunners who opened up at point blank range. A house in the village would be taken and cleared but then lost again as a group of New Zealanders stormed through the door hurling the British 36 Grenade whose tremendous blast effect was increased by the squares of heavy casing which tore through living flesh, ripping and gouging.

On the edge of the village the fighting swayed to and fro with neither side strong enough to win the day, until late in the evening men of No. 1 Company thrust past the Jäger outposts on the south-west road, drove for and captured the ridge upon which stood the chapel and the cemetery. The two companies then combined forces and pushed up the narrow village streets towards the centre of Galatas. Behind them came No. 3 Company as battalion reserve bringing with it the anti-tank rifles and mortars whose fire would support the attack upon Castle Hill.

But Galatas was not to be taken that easily and at last light the New Zealanders counter-attacked with two light tanks leading the advance. There were minutes of confusion as streams of tracer from the machine guns in the armoured fighting vehicles ricocheted from walls and cannon fire smashed German machine gun posts. Quickly the anti-tank rifle team went into action firing into the thinly armoured side of one machine and knocking it out with a succession of well-placed shots. Behind the tanks the New Zealand infantry charged through the village streets and in the dark night there were hasty and whispered challenges, sudden bursts of firing, the flaring and deafening detonation of grenades, screams and shouts as opposing groups met in alleys and fought hand to hand. Men from both sides coughed out their lives, their bodies riddled with bullets, torn by shrapnel or else with their life blood pouring from bayonet thrusts or from gashes inflicted by entrenching tools used at close quarters. Around the church standing in the centre of the village the fighting was particularly bitter and across the small village square Jäger fired at British infantry whom they could not see, aiming at the muzzle flashes from the Bren guns. A sudden sortie by one side would be driven back by a hurricane of fire from the other and the number of dead soldiers grew as the battle continued. Towards dawn a strong thrust by the British troops forced the Jäger of 1st Battalion out of the village and sent them racing down hill and across the open slopes upon which their dead still lay. For the moment the 1st Battalion's attack had been flung back and the survivors regrouped on Castle Hill.

To the north the thrust by 2nd Battalion had also moved off at 17.00hrs, with two companies up: No. 6 on the left and No. 7 on the right. No. 8 Company lay behind the battalion TAC headquarters on the reverse slope of a hill directly facing Galatas. The advance of 2nd Battalion was critically dependent upon the capture of Castle Hill for from this summit enfilading fire could sweep into the right flank of the advancing companies.

Shortly after the Stukas flew away at 17.00hrs, the two companies of 2nd Battalion moved forward across the open country. The first hundred metres brought them losses. Snipers, hard to detect in the olive trees, fired at those whose collars or shoulder straps marked them as being of NCO or officer rank. The leaders began to fall and then the leading section of the battalion came under sustained and heavy rifle and Bren gun fire. Although the Stukas had bombed and bombed thoroughly, even though fighter bombers had swept the New Zealand positions with machine gun and cannon gun fire, the echeloned slit trenches had suffered little damage and it was from these defences that the bursts of accurate fire were coming, driving the men of No. 7 Company back to their start line time and time again. As often as they were forced back they stormed forward again, going in with bayonet and grenade, losing Jäger with every thrust but making no impression upon the rock-like British defence.

No. 8 Company came forward to support the attack and with its help the slow, the very slow advance continued. The regimental commander, returned now from leading the advance of 1st Battalion, grouped every machine gun that he could lay hands upon and from his headquarters, a wadi at the base of a hill facing Galatas, directed a concentrated fire upon the high ground. Mountain guns began a barrage, even anti-tank guns were brought in to knock down the stone walls and houses. Under this bombardment the New Zealand defence began to give way. Late in the afternoon the surviving officers and NCOs of the 2nd Battalion's Jäger Companies brought their men on to the high ground to the north-west of the village and from that point into the narrow, broken streets of Galatas itself. The battalion's companies, like those of 1st Battalion within the village, then came under the New Zealand counter-attack which has been described above and 2nd Battalion's Jäger, too, were expelled from the village.

The battle died away as both sides broke off the fighting in which they had been involved without rest for over 12 hours. Tired bodies could find no rest as nerves, stretched taut, held many of the soldiers awake. Without food, water or blankets the Jäger spent a cold night on the ground comforted only by the thought that the enemy infantry were sleeping no easier with the realisation that full daylight would bring back the Stukas and a renewal of the German assault.

The first Jäger patrols went out while it was still quite early and had soon penetrated into the village. In the cold grey light they could find no trace of the enemy but his unburied dead and some discarded equipment. The patrols drove deeper into Galatas. There was no sound, not even a dog barked and of the New Zealand infantry, whose counter-attack only hours before had driven them from the

place, the Gebirgsjäger found not one man alive. The Kiwis had
slipped away eastwards in the night. Galatas was a slaughter house.
In every alley, every street, in the village square and in most houses
were the dead. Jäger, paratroops, New Zealanders all were there;
some corpses with mutilations wrought after death by shells which
had exploded in the streets. The smell of death hung heavy over the
little Cretan village and the Jäger losses had been heavy but they had
won and the British had been driven out of the defences which covered Canea. The road to the Cretan capital and to Suda was open.
The Royal Navy's base on the northern side of the island would soon
pass into German hands and when Suda fell the British forces on
Crete, already sub-consciously preparing for evacuation, would be
isolated and would have no other choice than flight or surrender.
Freyberg had conceded as much to Churchill days before. The battle
for Crete, as he clearly saw, was nearly over.

While the men of 100th Regiment were fighting the battle for
Galatas other Gebirgsjäger of 85th Regiment had begun their march
to turn the flank of the New Zealand defences based upon Canea and
Suda bay. The regiment had grouped around Alikianu, south-west of
Galatas, and from that place had begun the task of passing along the
British flank with the greatest possible speed, avoiding where possible
any conflicting with the defenders for until the 85th was in position
the attack upon Canea could not begin.

War diaries are, of necessity, sober documents and battle reports
written by unit commanders after a particular battle are equally as
solid and factual. Such reports err on the side of understatement, seldom allotting either praise or blame but leaving the officers at headquarters to draw their own conclusions. Thus, in the report of
the Krakau Group which follows, and which describes the march
through the mountains, very little is said of an air raid by Dornier
aircraft upon the units of 85th Regiment. The commander's post-
battle report states baldly: "Air attacks by our own aircraft upon us,
unfortunately, delayed the advance by 1st Battalion for two hours."

The bombing of one's own troops by air forces is not an unusual
occurrence in war and, even though most units of the German Army
had Luftwaffe liaison officers on attached duty, co-operation was frequently faulty and on this occasion, as well as on the same day
against 100th Regiment, seems to have failed completely. It is one of
the most serious blows to troop morale for soldiers to be bombarded
by their own forces, whether this bombardment is carried out by ar-

tillery or aircraft, and the effect upon the Jäger of 85th Regiment can be best imagined.

In accordance with standing orders direction markers had been laid out, swastika flags displayed and flares fired. All these had no effect and the Dorniers as they passed over the battalion's positions at 13.40hrs carpeted the area with high explosive, the smoke from those explosions falsely indicated the target to the following groups. Despite the long and furious bombardment when the aircraft flew away they left behind them men shaken with rage but without casualties.

Even the expanded version of the attack given above can only be an indication and an outline of the tragic error and yet this raid is described in eighteen words by the battle group commander, Colonel Krakau, in his report which now follows. This is a straight translation of one of 5th Gebirgs Division's battle accounts written only days after the battles. It has, therefore, a freshness and an immediacy and is quoted in full.

Copy

Gebirgsjäger Regiment 85   Heraklion 3.6.1941
1A

Combat Report

on the outflanking attack by Gebirgsjäger Regiment 85
south of Canea against the British routes of retreat
at Stylos.

The 1st Battalion of Gebirgsjäger Regiment 85, which was the first unit of the regiment to be emplaned, landed under heavy artillery fire on the airfield at Maleme. Placed under the command of Gebirgsjäger Regiment 100, it was ordered to take out the enemy artillery which was in position near Ag. Marina and to gain touch with the hard-pressed paratroops. To accomplish this it was to undertake an envelopment to the south but was given no details of the enemy situation. In addition the advance was to be carried out across steep and trackless terrain.

The battalion drove into the flank and rear of the enemy south-west of Ag. Marina. Carefully controlled attacks led to hard fought battles during which the enemy, who was in superior numbers, suffered serious losses and was forced to withdraw. The battalion's task had been accomplished. The commanding heights of Ag. Marina, which were vital to the enemy for his defensive operations west of Canea, were torn from his grasp and contact was made with the paratroops.

To cover the right flank of the Gebirgsjäger Regiment 100 and the paratroops who were fighting along the coast, the battalion renewed its drive and then struck southwards against a strong resistance backed by partisans. After a number of separate and successful battles the positions which had been allotted to the battalion in the Alikianu area were reached and secured.

On 24 May regimental headquarters and 3rd Battalion/85th were landed. These debarked forces concentrated south of Modion and in the area north-east of Kouvos. On 25.5.1941 elements of 2nd Battalion/85th and No. 16 Company/85th with 6 guns arrived on the Maleme airstrip. These elements, together with regimental headquarters were then concentrated in an area 4.5kms south of Platanias. On the evening of 25 May, after assessing the situation at Alikianu, the regiment was ordered to prepare to undertake an attack in an easterly direction.

The orders for the attack, which was to be carried out on 26 May, were: "To attack eastwards across the mountains south of Canea and to drive on Retimo to liberate the hard-pressed paratroops."

To enable the regiment to carry out its given task three battalions were assembled. None had anti-tank guns or artillery pieces. No. 16 Company of 85th Regiment could only follow along the road south of Canea and leading to Stylos, once this had been cleared of the enemy.

After strenuous physical efforts the 3rd Battalion, moving via Alikianu, reached the heights south-west of Varypetron against only weak enemy resistance. The regimental commander's plan of attack was for the regiment to go over to the assault only after the high ground east of Alikianu had been gained by 3rd Battalion.

During the outflanking operation carried out by 3rd Battalion/85th, it became clear that the enemy who had occupied the heights south-west of Alikianu and south of Episkopi up to the afternoon of 25 May, had withdrawn southwards during the night of 25–26 May.

In order that no time would be lost in getting into the rear of the dogged English defence in and south of Canea, the regimental

Command changed the battle plan. This then read: "1st Battalion/85th will form the point of the Regiment's advance in the direction of Malara. The 2nd Battalion which was in the area of the reservoir [at Hagia], will follow immediately behind the 1st Battalion."

Air attacks by own aircraft upon us unfortunately delayed the advance by 1st Battalion/85th for two hours, but after beating down determined enemy resistance the battalion attacked the heights immediately south-east of Pirgos during the evening of 25 May. One of the companies of 1st Battalion carried out a most difficult climb and followed this with a bitter battle to break the enemy's resistance on Point 542. This allowed the battalion's eastwards thrust to be maintained. The 2nd Battalion/85th followed closely behind, while 3rd Battalion was given the task of protecting the right flank.

In suffocating heat and across steep, broken and trackless mountain terrain the 2nd Battalion/85th (on the right), reached Point 507.50 at 12.15hrs. The 1st Battalion/85th reached the road across the pass 4kms south of Canea at about 11.15hrs having overcome enemy resistance and fought against partisans.

Calling upon every ounce of effort the men of the regiment, encouraged by the personal example of their officers and non-commissioned officers, reached Points 610.40–284–444, possession of which was vital to the resumption of the attack on 28 May. Enemy resistance was smashed everywhere. *Thus the regiment was deep in the flank of the English still fighting around and south of Canea by the evening of 27 May 1941.*

During the course of the day the regiment took 300 prisoners (English and Greek). A few civilian snipers were liquidated.

Led from the front by commanders who brought out the best from the regiment, *the encirclement of the hard-fighting British around Canea was successfully completed.*

At dawn on 28 May, the regiment's eastward attack was continued. No. 3 Company acting upon its own initiative did not halt on its given objectives but took Point 231.73, as well as reaching the bridge 2kms south of Kalami. The explosive charges which had been laid were removed and a bridge vital to our intended pursuit of the enemy was taken intact. The main of 1st Battalion/85th soon reached the road south of Point 194 and east of Point 284.

The 2nd Battalion/85th, fighting on the regimental right flank, advanced as far as Stylos and took the height, Point 76.1 north of the town during a swift advance in which it had had to beat down strong enemy resistance. The enemy, in force around Stylos, was surprised by the thrust against roads down which he would have to retreat. Exceptionally heavy fighting then developed. Much of this consisted of bloody hand to hand combat during which 2nd Battalion/85th finally succeeded in seizing from the English the vital retreat roads as well as the commanding heights immediately to the west of Stylos. Unfortunately, the regiment had no artillery with which it could have taken under effective fire the enemy groups seen retreating in the direction of Neon Chorion.

The 2nd Battalion/85th destroyed in the fighting two modern British Medium tanks. The enemy suffered heavy losses and the booty included a number of lorries and a large ration dump. About 2000 Italian prisoners of war were liberated.

As a result of the regiment's outflanking manoeuvre through difficult and steep mountain terrain south of Canea, by the determined breaking of any enemy resistance, by the drive into the rear of and against the British roads of retreat, the strong enemy position in Suda bay was finally smashed. The advance guard which the division sent out to pursue the beaten enemy was able to move forward along those roads. The regiment had taken a decisive part in smashing the enemy's strong positions in the Suda bay area.

To carry out the destruction of the enemy's resistance in front of the Advance Guard in the area 3kms south-east of Neon Chorion, the 2nd Battalion/85th was put into a pincer attack on either side of the road and this caused the English severe casualties.

On 29 May, the Advance Guard was once again able to take up pursuit of the enemy in the direction of Retimo.

During these battles the regiment took over 500 prisoners (English and Greek).

Own losses were : 1 Officer killed
3 Officers wounded
30 non-commissioned officers and men killed in action or wounded (not including the losses suffered in the light ship flotilla).

Signed: Krakau

The dispassionate words of the report give no true indication of the strain that the outflanking march had placed on the Jäger. It will be remembered that no pack animals had been brought across to Crete so that everything for living and fighting in the trackless jumble of mountain peaks through which the Jäger advanced had to be carried. The machine guns, their tripods, ammunition, tents, mortar plates, barrels, the rifles and mortar bombs all had to be portered by the Jäger. These had been heavy enough but also they had had to break down into loads and to carry the little mountain guns and the ammunition which these fired. These heavy loads had to be portered through the mountains in temperatures which rose above 90° in the shade, except that on those empty, eroded, scorching, knife-edged slopes there was no shade. The blinding sun shone down out of cloudless skies for ten hours of every day and was unbearably hot for six of those hours.

On the slopes there were no orange plantations whose fruit would quench the agonising thirst. There were no trees just as there were no people, no houses and, therefore, no wells from which the Jäger might fill their emptying bottles.

For Colonel Krakau and his staff the terrain difficulties were added to by a shortage of reliable maps of the area which they were traversing, nor could he keep in touch with divisional headquarters by wireless; all communication with his superiors came to him through aircraft. The light Fieseler Storch machines flew into the mountains searching along crests and through valleys for the serpentines of Jäger moving slowly across the glowing rocks, ascending into the barren hills and descending into the sterile valleys. From the aircraft dropped white-streamered message containers giving the latest intelligence and fresh orders. Part of one of these instructions was to detach the 141st Gebirgsjäger Regiment which was following behind 85th and to send it northwards to a point where it would take up a position between 100th Regiment and Heydrich's paratroops. The right wing of the extending German battle line, now past Galatas and nearing Canea, needed to be thickened if the imminent attack upon the island's capital and the Suda bay area were to succeed.

The 85th's battalions struggled on eastwards, sweating in their thick woollen uniforms. These were men experienced in climbing. Behind them lay the recent experiences of the campaign in Greece, but this outflanking march tested them almost past the level of endurance.

I have never in my life been so depressed as on that terrible
march. Mountains are empty places but even on our tallest peaks
at home there is sometimes a patch of grass, a clump of flowers;
something homely. In Crete the mountains were forbidding and
dreadful. Never had I seen such a hostile terrain. There were no
paths, not even animal tracks along which we could have moved.
There was nothing. The point group had to cut a trail for the rest
of us to follow and that path led uphill and downhill.

As part of the machine gun group I had, at times, to carry the
tripod of the gun. Even without it my knees were trembling with
the strain of the climb within only a few hours and, when we
rested at midday for a three-hour rest, I was almost unconscious.
My comrades were all the same; we were exhausted. The column
stopped and we flung ourselves down where we were. I slept immediately for more than half an hour and woke up with my face
burning. I tried to find shadow to keep my face out of the sun and
lay with my head behind my rucksack. It was a cloudless afternoon, not one little shadow to hide that burning golden disc. The
area was a desert of mountain peaks and on the very few occasions when we stopped the air was as hot as a greenhouse. It was
as hot as the desert and about as lifeless and as inhospitable.
There were no wells from which we could top up our water bottles
—my battalion's march discipline was very strict and we had not
drunk more than a couple of mouthfuls of tepid water from our
bottles since dawn.

The afternoon march was worse. Our rucksacks dragged on our
backs, the ammunition cases seemed like lead, each of us carried
30 kilos of weight on his back. The tent half was appreciated when
we stopped for the night but we cursed it by day for its weight. I
cannot tell you how much we longed to throw everything away
and to march unencumbered by rucksack, ammunition cases and
all the heavy bulky and bruising equipment.

The only good thing about the afternoon march was that the
sun was behind us and did not shine into our eyes. Also it shone
on to our rucksacks and not on to our backs. Many of us fell out
with a sort of heat stroke or exhaustion and lay there almost
paralysed. The stretcher bearers moved them into whatever cover
there was and left them to rest until the cool of the evening made
their march easier. For myself I had a terrible headache, my vision

began to go and I stumbled repeatedly. I cursed everything and everybody, including the inhabitants of this miserable island. We were lucky that the English were not mountain men for just to cross the White Mountains was terrible enough. To have had to fight across them would have been impossible. In the mountains the defender has the advantage and a handful of determined English and a few machine guns could have held us off for days. As it was we saw nobody and nothing except for a few birds.

When we did meet the Tommies they fought very hard to hold us and several times attacked us with rifle and bayonets. I think they were desperate men, knowing that if we won it was a prisoner of war camp for them. Their attacks cost them a lot of men and I remember Crete as the place of black corpses. Usually, we had advanced so quickly that the dead were often only a day or two old and had not begun to decompose. But the bodies on Crete, left lying for days in the hot sun, had all turned black and had swollen. Most of them were covered with greenbottles and the stink of decay was everywhere.

Night was bitterly cold and we lay shivering in our tents which were weighted down with stones. We could not bang the tent pegs into the almost solid rocky ground. We had no hot food because the soup kitchen had not come up with us. Nothing on wheels could have kept pace with us even though our slowest speed was one kilometre an hour and our fastest only four.

When we started out that first morning we had been in good spirits and looking along the trail both backwards and forwards I could see the long grey column as it wound its way up and down the slopes. By evening we didn't care who was in front or who behind. The big question was how soon could we rest. About an hour before last light we stopped and bivouacked. Everything had to be done quickly for once the sun went down it was soon totally dark and no lights were allowed. A slow sort of gargling with a mouthful of water, swilling it round and round the mouth. Allow a little trickle down the back of the throat and then swill the rest of the water round again to cleanse the inside of the mouth. I didn't feel hungry and I certainly did not want to eat the dry ration bread as it would have been too hard to swallow in throats which seemed somehow to have become constricted.

We were up at dawn and marched immediately. There was no

breakfast and no spare water to wash. Then we marched again, going on and on and on. Sliding off the narrow paths with tiredness and almost crying with exhaustion. I hated Crete and I've never been back; the memory of that three-day march has never left me.

Back on the sector facing Canea the battalions were drawn up waiting only for the intelligence that 85th Regiment had reached Stylos and that news came on 27 May. The first move then made against the town was that by 141st Regiment, now part of the forces outside Canea, when the battalions advanced in the direction of Suda bay. At first the forward movement by these relatively fresh troops made good ground but then, at a point only 2kms from Suda, close fire was opened upon the lead battalion spread out and moving across the sun-baked ground through the olive and orange plantations. The companies, caught in the rapid rifle fire of the New Zealand infantry, halted and went to ground. With the momentum gone the Jäger were ripe to be counter-attacked and the Kiwi infantry rushed forward in a bayonet charge. The Jäger of 141st broke before them but the impetuous New Zealand thrust overreached itself and was caught in the cross fire of massed machine guns. But the fury of the charge was upon the British and ignoring losses, perhaps not even seeing them, the survivors came on as if this single charge would drive the German invaders of Crete back into the hills, into the sea, anywhere; or if it did not then they would cover the fertile plain with the bodies of German dead.

It was, however, the British who fell, cut down in groups as the bullets struck them, their glistening bayonets shining from the ground on to which they had collapsed. Soon the khaki tide had melted into the ground and across the New Zealand dead the Jäger of 141st Regiment, shaken at the ferocity of the charge, returned to their own advance. This was then contested by small groups of New Zealand infantry who held out and scorned offers to surrender. The German war diaries pay tribute to the heroism of rearguards which fought to the last. By tea time the 141st had its battalions astride the main road at Metochi–Chatsalli and had consolidated their positions. The success of this drive had cut off the British forces in Canea. With no escape route open the only choice was to fight or to surrender; and from their behaviour it was clear that they had chosen to fight.

On the sector held by 100th Regiment the assault went in to seize the Yellow hills and the New Zealand opposition was once again based on rapid rifle fire at close range and this by men, many of whom used a rifle at home as farmers, and were thus first class shots. In the face of their fire the Jäger went to ground but were lifted on to their objectives by the mountain guns, the skilfully deployed mortars and the indirect fire of machine guns; to say nothing of the Stukas, the flying artillery, whose skill had been demonstrated so often during the campaign. This firepower brought the Jäger forward, overrunning the well-camouflaged slit trenches, skirting the open, using the dead ground until through a combination of fire and movement they had driven the Kiwis from the crest.

The Gebirgsjäger of the 100th Regiment then swarmed downhill, captured intact a bridge in front of the town and penetrated the outer environs of Canea. Patrols sent out at night gained touch with outposts of 141st Regiment to the south-west of Suda, holding fast against severe and frequent British counter-attacks. These were the last major efforts by the Imperial troops, and the Cretan capital as well as the Suda bay were found to be deserted. Leaving only weak rearguards to hold back the aggressive Jäger, the main body of the British troops had pulled back, but not eastwards as Ringel had anticipated, but southwards to Sfakia from which the ships of the Royal Navy began to embark them.

On 27 May the men of 85th Regiment came down out of the high mountains and descended upon Stylos, another important village on the road to Vrases and eventually to Sfakia. It was still not quite certain to Ringel in which direction the British would withdraw. At that time the Germans held less than a sixth of the area of Crete and the whole of the eastern part of the island was still in Imperial hands. To Ringel it seemed logical to suppose that the British would pull back eastwards intending to hold the German advance along any of the natural defence lines which existed rather than submit themselves to long and tiring marches through the mountains and along less than a handful of minor roads and cart tracks. The intention of the commander of 5th Gebirgs Division was, therefore, to maintain his advance in an easterly direction and aware that British resistance was slackening he decided to form a pursuit group, a spearhead detachment, a fast advance guard whose task it would be to make ground with all possible speed towards Heraklion and the east of Crete. A second group would thrust southwards towards Sfakia but before they could move the village of Stylos would have to be taken and it was obvious that at that tactically important place the British would make a determined stand.

To carry out his plans Ringel had the 85th to hand, for at dawn on 27 May their point units had reached the final spur and had begun to move down towards the little village lying quiet and white in the early morning sunshine. The Jäger battalions, increasing their pace at the thought of fresh water and an escape from the burning mountains, began their careful descent down the trackless steep mountain sides and then as they neared the road came under the fire of artillery, infantry and tanks. The British rearguard had allowed them to come up close before opening upon them a heavy and destructive fire. On small pieces of flat ground and behind quickly piled-up sangars the mountain guns were assembled, the ammunition prepared and the barrage began. To the left and right the Jäger bounding downhill went into action, crashed across the road and began to ascend the hill to the east of the village from which the fire was coming. The rifle and machine gun fire of the first Jäger groups held down for short periods the British defence and then with the arrival of an anti-tank rifle group the Jäger began to stalk the British armoured fighting vehicles. Approaching one of them from the flank the gun team fired into the suspension and the lightly armoured flanks of the machine and with a few quick shots had soon immobilised it.

The first British counter-attack came in at that time, 06.00hrs, against 2nd Battalion and the fury of the British charge drove the Jäger back across the narrow country road. But from the mountains the battalions were now sending down their companies and these were put straight into the line. As the first British bayonet charge was destroyed another succeeded it and then a third. This rearguard was determined not to let the Germans take the Stylos–Mega Chorafia road and came forward across the dead of earlier assaults without hesitation.

The Gebirgsjäger trying to break into the village were forced back, but on either flank the mountain men stormed forward and raced for the high ground from which they would be able to dominate the battle. No. 6 Company at the approaches to the village was flung back with shocking losses and every available man was put into the gaps in the line. The lightly wounded were patched up by stretcher bearers and went back to the fight, for possession of the village dominating the road was vital to the future course of operations.

The last groups of artillerymen carrying the heavy parts of the mountain guns and the mortar men bearing the broken down parts of their important weapons had, by this time, arrived and set up their weapons. On the hills opposite no movement could be seen, no defences made out for the British had concealed their positions well and only came out of their slit trenches to make another bayonet charge. Aiming blind the guns and mortars set up a searching barrage on obvious and likely places under cover of which the Gebirgsjäger climbed to the assault. The closely co-ordinated infantry and artillery attack smashed the British defence forcing the defenders southwards and along the south-east road. The British withdrawal was paced and orderly. As one rearguard moved back the eager attackers were held up at other places and by other groups of British seeking to gain time for the sea evacuation to continue for, by this time, the Royal Navy's evacuation was in full swing and the Imperial troops were heading for Sfakia.

Late in the evening of 27 May Ringel set up his pursuit group and gave his instructions to Colonel Wittmann, whom he had selected to command it. "You and your group will first open the way to Suda bay. You will give the enemy no rest and will advance eastwards to Retimo where you will liberate the paratroops encircled there. You will gain touch with the 85th Regiment's group under Colonel Krakau who is heading for Stylos. Other divisional units will follow you to Vrases and to Vramos." Colonel Wittmann's report on the role played by his group now follows:

Copy

Advance Guard Detachment 5th Gebirgs Division

Regimental HQ 1.6.41

Combat report by the Wittmann Advance Guard Detachment

27.5.41   During the afternoon of 27.5.1941, 5th Gebirgs Division gained a decisive victory in the fighting for Canea. It was clear that the enemy had begun to pull back and during that evening Division issued orders to 95th Mountain Artillery Regiment headquarters for it to take command of an advance guard group whose task it would be to pursue the retreating enemy and to move as quickly as possible towards Retimo and Heraklion to relieve the paratroops who were cut off there.

Troops composing the advance guard

Headquarters Mountain Artillery Regiment No. 95
Motor Cycle Battalion No. 55
Mountain Reconnaissance Battalion No. 95
Two platoons of the Mountain Anti-Tank Battalion No. 95
4th Battalion of the Mountain Artillery Regiment No. 95
One battery of the para artillery
One platoon of heavy infantry guns from the 100th Gebirgsjäger Regiment
Two tanks
One pioneer detachment.

28.5.41   The advance guard was ordered to leave the area of Platanias at 03.00hrs, but elements of the battalion which were en route from the western and southern coastal sectors were not able to reach the start line in time. Accordingly, at 03.50hrs the move forward began with only the reconnaissance battalion, the artillery and the pioneer detachment taking part. An officer guide was left behind near Platanias to direct the other units. The march began without a point detachment, but one was eventually made up from the mountain reconnaissance battalion. The advance continued without hindrance until Suda. The road some 3 to 5kms west of that place was broken in two places by explosions. Using all available personnel, including men from the rear of the column, the road was reopened shortly after 09.00hrs.

Motor Cycle Battalion No. 55 and one platoon of anti-tank guns joined the column while work on repairing the road was still being carried out. The intent to form a strong point detachment could still not be carried through as the head of the column then came up against enemy resistance, located on the heights running parallel to the road and at a point past the road fork on the far side of Stylos. The enemy dominated the road junction and the road had also been made impassable by demolition.

Before any attempt could be made to remove this road block it was essential to seize the passes to the southern heights near Mega Chorafia. For this purpose the lead unit (a motor cyclist squadron of Mountain Artillery Regiment No. 95) carried out an outflanking attack from the right. The heavy squadron of Mountain Artillery Regiment No. 95 first opened a defensive fire on the southern slopes of the road and the remainder of the artillery was then brought into position to beat down the enemy. Effective fire by mortars, PAK and mountain guns was opened on the road junction and those parts of the road which had been destroyed were then skirted around. Protected by the fire of the heavy weapons detachments, the lead company of the Motor Cycle Battalion No. 55 broke through the southern passes at about 12.00hrs. Apart from single rifle shots no other enemy resistance was encountered. It is likely that these were from an enemy rear guard group protecting the back of the enemy battalion which was locked in battle with the 2nd Battalion/85th Regiment to the west of Stylos. Alternatively, it could have been resistance put up by elements of an enemy battalion which had become detached from the main body as a result of the attack launched by 2nd Battalion/85th Regiment. The losses suffered were quite high when considered against the brevity of the fighting. Simultaneous advances carried out by the Krakau Group and the reconnaissance battalion helped to bring this thrust to a rapid and successful conclusion.

Following this breakthrough an advance guard was made up of the following units:-

One reinforced motor cycle company
The pioneer detachment
One platoon of para artillery
One anti-tank platoon from the mountain anti-tank battalion
The heavy squadron from the mountain reconnaissance battalion.

The other detachments then formed the main body and remained together except for a cycle squadron which, reinforced by a platoon of anti-tank guns, undertook a separate thrust along the Kalami road to Vamos, near the road junction east of Alikampos.

In Stylos touch was gained with the leading elements of 2nd

Battalion/85th Regiment. In hot pursuit and generally without any interference from the enemy, except for single shots, the advance continued via Neon Chorian towards the road crossing south-west of Kaina. On the ridge 1km north-west of the road crossing west of Kaina the leading elements caught up with the rearguard of an enemy battalion retreating in front of 2nd Battalion/85th Regiment. The enemy had taken up position on the heights and commanded a good field of fire which was supported by a cross fire and numerous snipers, all of which force dominated the road forward. On the road itself at least one enemy tank inhibited any advance.

An attempt to break through the enemy by deploying while on the move did not succeed and, indeed, brought the lead platoon into a difficult situation. To hold the ground already gained and to establish the situation took up most of the afternoon and consumed the combined strength of both the advance guard and the main body. The enemy's reactions to the move indicated that he was likely to hold his position with every means at his disposal and certainly until the evening with the probable intention of then withdrawing under cover of darkness. Indeed, he made a number of counter-attacks, many of which resulted in close-quarter fighting. As our artillery could not be used to its best advantage because there were no good observation points and, because the armoured fighting vehicles had not yet come up, our attack could not be resumed for it would have resulted in a heavy loss of life. It was also anticipated that the effects of the encirclement operation which was being carried out by the Krakau Group, in conjunction with Esch's battalion, would soon make themselves felt. This indeed happened at last light. The left-hand company of that battalion extended to the left and captured a commanding height from which it was possible to pour an enfilading fire upon the enemy. Some hours later, at 22.00hrs, on the right flank another company reached to within a kilometre of the cross roads. Reports received after 23.59hrs from reconnaissance patrols on the road forward showed that the enemy had withdrawn and by 03.00hrs the road fork 2kms south-west of Kaina was reported clear of the enemy. The following losses had been suffered during the day:

3 officers
27 other ranks

At first light on 29 May the pursuit was taken up again. The advance went well until a point 2kms north-west of Episkopi even though a number of road blocks had had to be cleared and mines lifted. It was found that suspected mined areas turned out often to be false fields. The bridge at Episkopi was badly damaged and this delayed the advance until 11.00hrs, when it was finally possible for motor cycles to cross it. The drive to Retimo met only scattered rifle fire and the advance guard passed through the place at 13.00hrs. After clearing the resistance put up by Greek soldiers as well as driving off the enemy from the heights south of the town, the advance guard pushed on until contact had been established with the westernmost group of paratroops in Retimo, at a cross roads some 3kms east of the town. After sweeping the southern slopes of the hills with anti-tank and artillery fire, as well as their being combed by patrols, a group of some 100 Greek soldiers came in to surrender.

From reports received from the paratroop commander as well as from personal observation it was clear that in the area east of Retimo the British had at least three guns and a great number of machine guns in position. It could thus be assumed that the enemy held the heights running parallel to the coast road in some strength. British artillery, mortar fire and machine gun barrages fell continuously in the paratroop area and, as there was no artillery or heavy weapons of ours with which an attack could have been supported, an assault did not seem practicable. After discussion with both Division and Corps the attack was postponed until the following day by which time two armoured fighting vehicles and two heavy infantry guns would have been brought forward. The whole of 29 May was, therefore, spent in clearing up in Retimo, making moves to clear the southern flank and in carrying out the necessary reconnaissance for the morrow's attack as well as in collecting more prisoners. (In Retimo alone there were about 400 and others were being brought in out of the mountains.)

The object of the attack planned for 30 May was to dominate the enemy by bringing heavy artillery fire to bear along the road flanking the heights. Under cover of this our advance would begin led by the armoured fighting vehicles. In addition the troops engaged were to be supported by heavy weapons and a platoon of artillery. These guns had the task of laying a creeping barrage some two to three kilometres ahead of the advance and to continue laying this until a successful penetration of the enemy's positions had been made.

At 05.00hrs the advance guard moved into the attack. At this point the enemy was bombarding the approach road, the road junction and the exits out of Retimo with three guns. Our own artillery was soon able either to dominate two of the enemy guns or to force them to change their positions. It was also able to bring effective fire upon the heights on the river bank, which were set about with olive trees, and from which we could have been enfiladed. By 07.00hrs the point group had pushed forwards a further 4kms. The heavy weapons groups and the guns which had been brought forward were now put into action and bombarded the heights on our flank. The effect of this barrage was soon apparent. First individually, then by groups, more and more British soldiers were observed with raised hands or waving white cloths. A cease fire was ordered and by waving a white flag of our own and by beckoning signs we conveyed the information that they could approach us without danger. Within a quarter of an hour the point company had assembled several hundred Australian soldiers, including a colonel. After leaving a small detachment to guard the prisoners and following a discussion with the colonel on how to bring in the other British soldiers still scattered about the hills (according to the colonel this amounted to a force of about 1100 Australians and Greeks), the advance was continued at 07.30hrs.

At about 08.30hrs the point group reached the eastern paratroop group at Retimo and was greeted with enthusiasm. The advance was then pushed forwards with best possible speed. At three or four places the group was fired upon. Several civilians who were captured with weapons in their hands were summarily tried and shot. Suspicious houses from which rifle fire had come were set alight. Individual unarmed soldiers were met. Numerous stone barricades slowed down the tempo of the pursuit. Nevertheless, towards 11.45hrs, shortly after crossing the pass 10kms west of Heraklion, touch was gained with a reconnaissance patrol from Colonel Bräuer's paratroops.

Towards 13.30hrs the advance guard rested its vehicles on the airfield at Heraklion. Those squadrons which, in the morning at Retimo, had been given the tasks of flank protection or of collecting prisoners, were of course not able to join us. The Lepperding

In the German Army senior NCOs were the ensigns. This sergeant, wearing the neck gorget which indicated his duty, is seen here with soldiers of a guard of honour.

Taking the oath. Six Gebirgsjäger recruits, representing their comrades, forming hollow square, take the oath of allegiance on the regimental Colour. Bavaria, April 1938.

Pre-war training for Gebirgsjäger. Pupils at a Hochgebirgs school receiving their instructions before setting out on a Langlauf, a cross-country march on skis. Bavaria, 1938.

One of the techniques used in mountaineering in the high peaks. A soldier of a Hochgebirgs unit demonstrating the use of ropes in rock climbing. Berchtesgaden area, 1936.

Training the pre-war Gebirgsjäger. Two Jäger, dressed in white camouflage caps and suits, undergoing snow training. While one man keeps guard with a rifle his comrade constructs a simple defence of a snow wall.

Pre-war training for Gebirgsjäger. This soldier of a ski-ing detachment has adopted the position taught when firing a rifle on skis. The wearer sits to fire his rifle. He cannot kneel or lie down and if he stood the recoil might unbalance him. He is wearing the white camouflage overalls and hood.

A Polish officer offers to surrender the town of Lemberg to a Staff Officer of 1st Gebirgs Division. Although Lemberg was at that time technically part of the Soviet occupation zone, the Polish commander chose to offer the capitulation of his forces to men of the Gebirgs Division of the German Army.

After the campaign in France had been brought to a successful conclusion men of the 1st Gebirgs Division were trained to take part in the invasion of England, "Operation Sealion". Here men of a pioneer unit practise their part in the planned invasion in an assault boat.

Gebirgsjäger of 1st Gebirgs Division with a barge converted into a landing craft during the exercises they undertook in preparation for "Operation Sealion", the invasion of Britain, summer 1940. The men in the dark jackets are sailors.

Gebirgsjäger of General Dietl's force crossing one of the primitive rope bridges across a Norwegian river in the Narvik area, spring 1940.

Men of General Dietl's force manning a machine gun post in the Narvik area. The campaign in Norway's northern regions was fought to secure the iron ore supplies which were vital to the German economy.

Pioneers of 1st Gebirgs Division carrying an asault craft onto the bank of the river Drau, during the invasion of Yugoslavia in 1941, before undertaking the river crossing.

After fighting their way through the Metaxas Line in Greece the Gebirgsjäger advanced through the mountains which run along the Struma valley. The picture shows a machine gun post in position on the heights overlooking the river.

battery (from 2nd Battalion of Mountain Artillery Regiment No. 18), reported in at Heraklion and replaced the para artillery for the resumed march to Iarapetra, together with Kauffmann's battery. The advance continued again at 16.00hrs. The only obstructions were found to be street barricades. No more resistance from civilians was encountered. From the pass to west of Neapolis the march was led, for reasons of security, by the armoured fighting vehicles. From that point the advance guard was led by the reinforced motor cycle platoon which moved at great speed to reach Iarapetra, which was the day's objective. During the advance to Iarapetra and west of Kalo-Korea, at the road junction Sitia–Iarapetra, touch was gained with Italian troops. Shortly before the arrival of our point group Italian motorised reconnaissance troops had taken up position at the junction to guard it during the night. After greetings and an exchange of intentions the advance guard continued its journey and reached Iarapetra at 22.00hrs. The remainder of 55th Motor Cycle Battalion, excepting No. 1 Company, arrived by 23.00hrs. No. 1 Company remained in Kalo-Korea. No more enemy troops were met with. The place had been totally destroyed. The only signs of life there at the moment were Greek policemen. The following troops were also left behind in Kalo-Korea: the reinforced Heavy Mountain Reconnaissance Battalion No. 95 as well as Lepperding's battery. The Kauffmann battery reached Aj. Nicholas during the night.

The number of prisoners and the amount of booty captured cannot be measured as the point unit had had insufficient forces available to collect the material and to guard the prisoners. Losses to us during our break through the enemy's positions were surprisingly low. The enemy's fire, particularly that of his artillery, did not exploit the terrain advantages nor was it sufficiently mobile. In addition, the enemy's infantry counter-measures were smashed by the concentrated fire of our artillery and that of the heavy weapons groups. During this one day the point detachment and the main carried out a drive of 80kms to Heraklion airfield, during which it fought a battle and then drove 110kms to Iarapetra. In the areas allotted to us local defence positions were taken up and the troops then retired to rest. The course of this operation had demanded of them, but particularly from the advance guard and its component units, the ultimate in perseverance and ability. In this connection the efforts of the motor cycle battalion are worthy of particular mention.

The battles themselves were purely ones of pursuits. Advances after penetrations had been made demanded sustained effort and watchfulness as the terrain was more suited to defence. One dominating crest after another opposed our advance. In the interests of maintaining a fast pace it was not always possible to consider the safety factor and the risk that there might be a sudden and surprise attack upon the advance guard had to be accepted.

The course of the advance was a testing time for the equipment on issue. My experience was that, by and large, the equipment proved satisfactory in every respect. It would assist mountain troops and particularly mountain artillery units if they were issued with motorised carriers such as those already supplied to para artillery units. This is no new claim. The need for a vehicle of this type by Gebirgs units has been apparent for years. If anything else led to the success of this operation then it is the highly developed skill at improvisation shown by our soldiers. The ability shown by nearly every man made the course of the whole operation on Crete that much easier.

Wittmann. Lieutenant Colonel

While Wittmann's men were carrying out their pursuit of the British eastwards and towards Heraklion the other regiments and units of the division had been set a southward course. It is now clear to Ringel that the mass of the British forces were withdrawing through the mountains and heading for the south coast from whose ports they would be evacuated.

At 08.50hrs on 29 May the 1st Battalion/100th Regiment was ordered forward to clear the Armei–Sfakia area and to clear the coastal sector around Lutra. The other battalions of 100th Regiment and of 85th Regiment were stood down from their fighting activities and were put into service as supply columns in order to assure a steady and regular flow of ammunition to the 1st Battalion.

Throughout the morning the companies of that unit had been pushing south through the mountains. The tactics which they used had now become established as a routine. The drive was made, where possible, along the narrow road but where resistance was encountered from a British rearguard then the point company would halt and the other companies would sweep through the hills outflanking the British troops and forcing them to withdraw. By 15.00hrs the leading troops of 1st Battalion were south of Alikambos and to strengthen the assault 2nd Battalion was taken from its portering duties and put back into the line. The two-battalion advance then moved smoothly forward until at 18.00hrs, north-east of Askifos, a very strong and determined rearguard refused to be moved. There was little that could be done by night and the leading elements consolidated and waited for the follow-up troops to arrive.

At first light on the 30th the 100th went in again and by 05.00hrs had taken the Askifos pass and were striking southwards towards the Imbros pass which was stormed four hours later. Slowly but steadily the mountain men pushed down upon the British concentrated now around Sfakia for by the evening of 30 May the whole of Crete, with the exception of the Lutra–Sfakia sector, was in German hands.

The rearguard effort put up by the British forces covering the evacuation at Sfakia held the two battalions of 100th Regiment some 4kms distant from the coast and at 09.00hrs it was clear that the regiment was heavily engaged with British troops supported by armour. Every effort was now made to support the Jäger and, during the afternoon and early evening, bombers were directed against the scattered groups of British still holding out at Komitades and the troops at Sfakia. Just before midnight a message from Regiment to Division stated that about a thousand English with some tanks were still offering a desperate resistance in the olive groves at Komitades, and that the outflanking moves by other companies of the regiment had not influenced the battle.

By the following morning this resistance had been broken and at 09.00hrs the British forces began to surrender leaving the Gebirgsjäger to occupy Komitades, Cora Sfakia and Lutra. The war diary of 5th Gebirgs Division recorded that at 16.00hrs the last English resistance was silenced in the mountains north of Sfakia by units of the division after very heavy fighting.

The struggle for Crete was over and with this victory the Germans had established themselves in the eastern Mediterranean. But, as it was stated in the opening paragraphs of this section of the book, this was a victory which was never exploited strategically and it was, in the words of Student, the paratroop commander, "the swansong of the airborne forces". At a more personal level the Gebirgsjäger had lost 20 officers and 305 other ranks killed in action. Those wounded had included 13 officers and 274 of the rank and file. Among the missing were those who had gone down with the light ship flotilla and the numbers involved were given as 18 officers and 488 other ranks.

To conclude this section of the book which deals with the actions fought by the Gebirgsjäger of 5th Division on Crete during May 1941 are the final lines of the report which their Commander, Ringel, wrote on 4 June 1941:

> My brave Gebirgsjäger fought for twelve days in bitter battles carried out across the most difficult terrain, in conditions of terrible heat and against an extremely tough and capable enemy backed by native partisans. The Jäger had to carry all their equipment, particularly the heavy weapons, on their backs and for great distances through the mountains. They were supported by the Luftwaffe and by the paratroops who fought with them as far as Canea and together victory was achieved. Heavy losses were suffered. The deeds of each individual were great and great was also the victory.

Russia 1941

At 03.30hrs, dawn, on 22 June 1941, the German war against the Soviet Union opened. It ran for nearly five years and the high hopes with which it had begun ended in the bitter despair of total defeat in the ruins of Berlin.

During the course of that war the German Army was to advance as far as Stalingrad in the east, to the Caucasus mountains in the south; it was to invest Leningrad for years, was to carry out operations in regions as disparate as the Arctic Circle and the deserts of the Kuban. It was to reach a point on the crest of a hill in a Moscow suburb from which the towers of the Kremlin could be seen shining in the pale December sunshine. Ne plus ultra.

The German successes of the first months of battle in the new war were enormous. Four million soldiers of the Red Army lay dead on the battlefields and a further three and a half million were prisoners of war. By far the greatest number of those had been rounded up during one or the other of the vast battles of encirclement which were carried out by the Germans during the autumn battles; it is a description of one of those pockets which forms the subject of the next account. How the Germans were able to carry out such manoeuvres that they could capture millions of men I shall explain, but I would stress that the explanation is only a lead into the next account and in no way a history of the conduct of operations in the first year of the war.

"Operation Barbarossa" was based upon false premises, and included among those errors of judgement were the vital factors concerning the strength of the Red Army and the Russian potential for supplying all the weapons of war required by a mass army. The task ahead of the German Supreme Command was to destroy the mass of the Soviet Field Army before it could retreat into the vast hinterland of a country which occupies one sixth of the world's surface area. Concurrently, the Russian centres of production and her economic wealth were to be seized and the advance east continued until a line was reached so far away from the cities of Germany that they could not be reached by any Russian bomber. The territory thus captured would, of course, include all the economic prizes for which "Barbarossa" had been planned. German Intelligence had, however, failed to alert the High Command to the existence of the new, vast industrial region east of the Ural mountains, an arsenal and a supply depot which was outside the bombing range of German aircraft.

The OKW time-table for this destruction of the Red Army and the seizure of the economic prizes was a matter of months only. All things had to be accomplished before the onset of winter and the summer was already far advanced. The German Army was to attack along an initial battle line running from Finland to Romania, a distance of well over 2600kms, and this line would expand as the armies drove farther eastward, until it would be over three and a half thousand kilometres in length. Excluding the allied, foreign contingents who had come to fight on Germany's side, the forces to man that vast front consisted of three huge Army Groups: North, Centre and South, each of which, it may be said, had a major objective: Leningrad, Moscow and the Ukraine respectively. Three quarters of the German Field Army marched into Russia on 22 June; a total of some 136 divisions facing a host, in Western Russia alone, of 154 infantry divisions, 25 cavalry divisions and 37 brigades of tanks.

The disposition of the great mass of the Red Army along the western frontier, the strategy of the STAVKA (the Soviet High Command), and the field tactics of the Russian forces seem, when seen in retrospect, almost to have been designed to allow their easy encirclement and destruction. Theirs was a linear defence and the whole ethos of Red Army training was to hold ground, the soil of the Soviet Union. If any had to be given up then immediate counter-attacks had to be launched to regain it and those attacks had to continue until the order had been carried out. Russian signals procedures were not designed for the rapid transmission of orders, for the Red Army operated under a dual system of control and command. This hierarchical method had a political officer at each and every Command level. The Commissar's order was final and was law. No military action could be initiated without his sanction and his philosophy was always to attack the enemy. Officers authorising a retreat which might preserve their units from destruction could have their orders countermanded and could be degraded or even executed on the orders of the Commissar. This need to have orders and instructions approved by a political officer slowed the speed of Russian reaction to German moves and often left units completely bewildered by the speed of the panzer thrusts.

Since this cumbersome system of duality operated from the front line units to the highest echelons of command, and since each officer stood in danger of the firing squad if he failed to achieve a set objective, it is hardly surprising that the Soviet armies were not handled in so flexible a fashion as were the Germans. They, with four successful campaigns behind them, had mastered the craft of moving armour in mass and even though the more adventurous plans of the senior panzer commanders were affected by the decisions of conservative-minded superiors, the operations they did conduct were far-ranging and successful.

By fast advances, pressing on regardless of uncovered flanks and by striking deep in the enemy hinterland the panzer carried out one pincer operation after the other, closing within the panzer jaws the slow-moving, slow-reacting Russian armies. In the first year of the War in the East there were a great number of encirclement battles. The earliest major ones included Minsk where 324,000 men, 3342 tanks and 1809 guns were taken. Smolensk which yielded another 310,000 men, 3205 tanks and 3120 guns followed. The Vyazma with

663,000 men and Gomel with 84,000 Red soldiers taken prisoner. The encirclement battle with which the next account deals is that fought around Uman where 17th Army's 49th Gebirgs Corps, with 1st and 4th Divisions under command, helped to capture over 60,000 of the total of 100,000 prisoners of war taken during that operation.

The very success of the encirclements was a danger, for they offered a quick tactical victory, to achieve which drew off the strength which should have been used in the pursuit of strategic objectives. The encirclement in the Kiev region during the autumn of 1941 can be considered as one such case. Hitler halted the advance upon Moscow and the destruction of the main Red Army grouping in front of the Russian capital, in favour of a pincer operation in the south which certainly destroyed the Red Armies around Kiev and led on to the capture of the Ukraine, but also gave the Russian armies the breathing space which they needed to regroup, to prepare defences in front of Moscow and to form new divisions to oppose Army Group Centre when it resumed offensive operations once again at the end of a two-month spell of inactivity.

The Red Army's losses in the first months were appalling and would have destroyed any nation which did not have the vast reservoirs of manpower of the Soviet Union. That the Russians could lose so vast a number of men and still field millions of others soon became clear to Halder, Chief of the General Staff, for his diary note of 11 August 1941 says: ". . . increasingly plain that we have underestimated the Russian colossus, which consistently prepared for war with that utterly ruthless determination so characteristic of totalitarian states. This applies to . . . economic resources . . . and most of all to the strict military potential. At the outset of the war we reckoned with about 200 enemy divisions. Now we have already counted 360 . . . if we smash a dozen of them, the Russian simply put up another dozen . . .".

Halder saw that it was going to be a bitter war and for the Gebirgsjäger, whose establishment was to rise to seven divisions during the first year of the Russian war, those gloomy forebodings of one of their principal military leaders were to be fulfilled. Let us not anticipate the turn of future events but follow the men of the 1st and 4th Divisions who, after successful battles of pursuit, were told as they lay at rest for the night around Vinnitsa that the next principal objective was the town of Uman, some 130kms away in a direct line.

Uman 1941

The German infantry has always been able to march tremendous distances; 50 kilometres per day was not an unusual achievement but a normal one which was carried out often day after day for weeks on end. Despite the propaganda pictures and stories which were put out regarding Germany's armed might it cannot be accepted that its

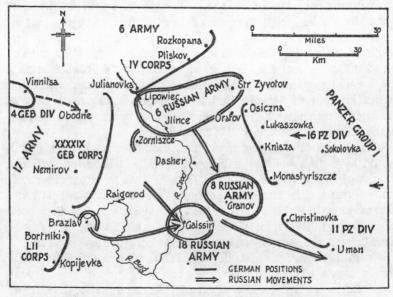

The encirclement at Uman. Situation at 22 July, 1941

Army of World War II was a modern, that is a motorised force, for the movement of the great mass of its units was on foot or hoof and thus the main moved little faster than it had under Kaiser Wilhelm during World War I.

In the campaigns between 1939 and June 1941 the German infantry's marching capability had been amply demonstrated, but in every case those campaigns had been against countries with easily reached boundaries. Once the German Army turned east, as it did during

June 1941, and attacked the Soviet Union, it had invaded a territory which had no geographical location nor easily attainable point at which the new war might have been considered to be won. The size of Russia was daunting: it covered one sixth of the world's land surface. The principal cities, and therefore the primary targets, Leningrad, Kiev and Moscow, lay enormous distances removed from the frontier. The initial battle line ran north and south for nearly two thousand kilometres and it was across vast expanses of Soviet territory that the infantry of the German Army was forced to march on foot.

There was no other means of transport. Had the railways been left intact then, perhaps, part of the distances which had to be covered might have been made by train, but the Russian railway system was underdeveloped and the small amounts of rolling stock that the Germans had captured were hardly sufficient to bring forward the huge supplies of ammunition, food and other material which were needed daily to nourish the advance. There was no spare space for foot soldiers to be carried en masse, at least not in the early days of the new war.

The road network was scant and poorly maintained. As the distances lengthened from home-based depots in Germany to the front in Russia, wheeled vehicles of the supply services had farther to travel and their journeys were made on surfaces that were always poor and frequently almost impassable. The terrible roads brought about an increase in petrol consumption, the result of which was to create quite serious shortages of fuel, even as early as the first months of the Russian war. Those shortages, in turn, seriously limited the amount of ammunition which could be brought up for the guns and thus reduced the artillery's support of the infantry. If there was insufficient space for essential ammunition then there was certainly none to transport infantrymen. So they foot-marched. Some units had begun to trek to the front from concentration areas hundreds of kilometres removed from the German/Russian frontier and continued this throughout the summer, the autumn and into the winter, often with only one day's rest for every six spent on the road.

This ability to cover great distances on foot was common to all German infantry units and even the Gebirgsjäger, whose principal skills were surely not intended to be employed in covering long distances on flat terrain, were capable of sustaining a daily marching rate of over 45kms per day throughout many succeeding days.

The attack by Germany upon Russia, "Operation Barbarossa", opened late in June 1941 when three German Army Groups, North, Centre and South, struck across the frontier. One of the main objectives of the first offensives was to destroy the great mass of the Red Army in southern Russia, and this was to be carried out west of the Dnieper river by Army Group South aided by elements from the southern wing of Army Group Centre.

Von Rundstedt's Army Group South disposed three armies: 17th, under Stülpnagel, with thirteen divisions; the 6th, commanded by Reichenau, having six divisions and the 11th, under Schobert, with seven divisions on its establishment. Attached to this Army Group was Panzer Group 1, under Kleist, a combination of armoured and motorised divisions which was intended to be the cutting edge of Army Group South's sword.

The unit with which this narrative is concerned is 49th Gebirgs Corps of Stülpnagel's 17th Army and the period of action is a few short weeks from 20 July to 13 August. The 49th Gebirgs Corps had two mountain divisions, 1st and 4th, on its establishment together with one or more infantry divisions. During this particular operation the 97th Light, the 125th Infantry and the 259th Infantry Divisions all served. The reason for the inclusion of standard infantry units within the establishment of 49th Gebirgs Corps can be traced back to the organisation of mountain divisions. In earlier chapters it has been shown that such divisions were composed of two Jäger regiments. Standard infantry divisions had three regiments. For warfare in the mountains a two-regiment establishment had proved to be the most efficient organisation, but when fighting in normal terrain lack of a sufficient infantry force was soon apparent. A Gebirgs corps could not meet the demands of, or cover the length of, a conventional corps front without adding to its strength by drawing upon neighbouring infantry divisions.

The terrain in the western republics of the Soviet Union was flat. So far as the mountain men were concerned it was a tragedy that there was no high ground, during that first year of war, anywhere along the thousands of kilometres of battle line, no mountainous area in which their special skills might have been more gainfully used. As it was they fulfilled the role of line infantry carrying out exhausting marches across the Russian steppe and fighting on flat ground an enemy who, although retreating or encircled, was fanatical in his will to resist and totally aggressive in his counter-attacks. Not until 1942 and late in the German summer offensive of that year did the Gebirgsjäger at last have an opportunity to demonstrate their ability in the really high mountains; a short account of the part played by 49th Groups in that offensive, the advance into the Caucasus, follows this one. For the main part, however, the Gebirgs units in Russia served in terrain unsuitable to their abilities and it is to the credit of Ringel, commander of 5th Gebirgs Division, that he once demanded of Hitler the removal of his men from the swamps of the Kuban, in which they were at that time fighting, and their re-deployment in at least an area of high hills.

This story of the 49th Gebirgs Corps fighting to hold encircled the Red Army's forces in the Uman pocket, opens towards the end of the third week of July when the opening offensives by Army Group South had smashed through the Russian border zone, had captured Galicia and had gone on to break the Stalin Line, a Soviet defence system. By 18 July Corps had established itself across the Bug river at Vinnitsa and was preparing to push its advance eastwards in pursuit of the Red Army.

The situation as seen at High Command level was that the left flank of Army Group South, Reichenau's 6th Army, was pushing towards Zhitomir and Kiev, drawing Soviet strength towards those places to defend them. Kleist's Panzer Group 1 on the right flank of 6th Army had ruptured the weak front south of Reichenau's army. The panzer forces had been unleashed and were pouring eastwards overrunning all opposition, to cut off the retreating Soviet forces between the Bug and the Dnieper rivers. The 17th Army, advancing more slowly in foot marches, was also heading east towards the great bend of the Dnieper river, while to its right units of Germany's allies, Hungary and Romania, together with Schobert's 11th Army, formed not only the right flank of Army Group South but also that of the German Army's battle line in Russia.

By 18 July it had become clear from reports received from panzer and motorised units of Kleist's group that a dramatic breakthrough had been made and this thrust had thrown a northern pincer arm around a group of Russian armies, to the south-east of Kiev. If a

southern pincer could be flung around these Soviet forces then a
great part of the enemy's strength in the Dnieper bend would have
been encircled and could be destroyed at leisure. It was the task of
17th Army and of its several corps, of whom 49th Gebirgs was one,
to ensure that this ring was cast and that the Russian forces did not
escape.

This pincer operation might have been nothing remarkable, for
there had been earlier encirclements and there were to be others of
greater importance in the course of that first autumn, had not an
order issued by Army Group South, which failed to maintain the expected direction of the attack, given to the Russians an escape route
which they were quick to exploit. The closing of the gaps by the
marching and counter-marching of the Gebirgs divisions and the ability of their men to fight and to hold back the massed break-out attempts by the Soviet forces are the burden of this story.

During the evening of 19 July, Corps issued orders to its divisions
for them to maintain the pursuit of the retreating enemy so closely as
to bind him frontally. By holding him that tight he would not be able
to fling eastwards against the thin panzer ring which had now begun
to surround the mass of his trapped units. This pursuit and battle
with rearguards was carried out by 4th Gebirgs Division and 97th
Light, while 1st Gebirgs guarded bridgeheads which it had established
across the river Bug. During the following day Lanz's 1st Gebirgs was
brought forward and given the task of gaining the road from Vinnitsa
to Nemirov and of driving along this while 97th Light pressed its advance towards Obodne and 125th Infantry advanced upon Voroshy-
lovka.

Conscious of the need for speed, Lanz divided his forces so as to
achieve greater mobility and sent its components racing eastwards.
Around each of his two Jäger regiments he formed a battle group
and reinforced this with an artillery battalion. In addition to Battle
Group Kress (99th Jäger Regiment) and Battle Group Picket (98th
Jäger Regiment) a third battle group was organised as the advanced
or point unit. This was Battle Group Lang, made up principally of a
motor cycle battalion, an anti-tank detachment, an artillery battery
and a heavy group: self-propelled guns and 8.8cm Flak.

The direction of the division's advance was towards Nemirov and
the first stages of the drive upon that place were fast, carried out as
they were against only moderate opposition. By mid-afternoon the

leading units of Kress Group had drawn close to the objective and following the capture of two bridges outside the little town, the point group roared on to capture it. The direction of the thrust then changed from east to south-east as the Lang detachment moved down upon Brazlav. The lack of good roads in the Soviet Union forced the German troops and vehicles into predictable routes of advance and ones which could be easily and strongly defended. The country across which the advance was being pushed consisted of heavily wooded heights between which lay valleys of swamp and marsh created by the numerous tributaries of the Ssod river. A road which skirted this difficult ground was the main traffic artery and thus a sector which the Soviets would defend bitterly. This road ran from Tultshin in the south, via Brazlav, Gaissin, Mikhailovka and Ivangorod to Uman in the east and it was Corps' intention to pass 1st Gebirgs Division along that road. At each of the towns and villages named, as well as those whose names do not feature in this account, it could be anticipated that the Soviets would put up a strong rearguard to hold back the thrusting German units; but of all the places the town of Gaissin was the most important and, therefore, the one most likely to be tenaciously defended.

Gaissin was a land bridge: dry ground in a region of swamp. This topographical accident was responsible for the fact that the little town stood at a junction of four roads running north–south, east–west. The map shows how important was the possession of such a place for both sides. But if the Germans were to take Gaissin they had first to capture Brazlav and the Russians had prepared it for defence. Its large garrison was augmented by units which were withdrawing from the west and which were re-organised until the Soviet defenders were sufficiently strong in number and determination to hold back the thrust of 1st Gebirgs Division. These came in throughout the whole of 22 July and were principally from the north and from the west.

The length of front held by Corps now extended for over 45kms. Difficult terrain and the lack of adequate roads separated not only the battle groups but also the divisions from each other. A concentration of maximum strength at one point was not possible. All that could be done was to select a number of objectives and to battle in order to wrest these from the Soviet troops who were determined not to relinquish them.

By late in the evening of 22 July it had become clear that the northern pincer of armoured and motorised divisions had advanced so far eastwards that its units had outflanked the great masses of 6th, 8th, and 18th Red Armies which were defending the ground in front of 17th German Army and who were obstructing its advance upon Uman. Kleist's forces now having pressed eastwards and having outflanked the three Soviet armies, changed direction southwards and by this movement came down behind the Russian force. The armoured fighting vehicles of 11th and 16th Panzer Divisions were now more than one hundred kilometres away from the Gebirgs Corps; they then turned back to drive westwards and thus to constrict and to drive the Red units on to the infantry divisions of 49th Gebirgs Corps. The panzer divisions thus formed both a shield and an anvil. The shield held back the Soviet troops outside the encirclement and the anvil was the iron mass against which the Russians were to be crushed by the advance of the main of Army Group South, whose units were pushing from the north-west, the west and from the south-west.

Under this pressure the Soviet forces began to give ground and to seek four routes along which they might escape. The most obvious direction was to the east or to the south-east and, obsessed by the fear that the Reds might rupture the fragile armoured ring to the east of the encirclement, Army Group issued orders for an even closer grasp by 49th Gebirgs Corps of the enemy in front of it. Corps was to hold the Russian forces committed even more firmly to battle and if these were, somehow, to detach themselves then, by relentless pursuit, the Corps was to bring them to battle again. In vain did the Soviets fling rearguard groups, one after the other, into the path of the storming men of 1st Gebirgs Division, hoping that behind each sacrificial screen the main force might escape, but as each rearguard was set up the relentless advance of the mountain men smashed it down. The Soviets tried other measures to stem the advance.

Heavy and repeated counter-attack by lorry-borne infantry throughout 23 July sought to slow the pace of Lanz's thrust across the Ssod river to gain the main roads: the one northern via Ilince and Granoy and the southern one from Brazlav via Gaissin. Both highways met at Mikhailovka and headed eastward to Uman, now less than 60kms distant. That night the Corps war diary reported that although fighting was bitter along the whole length of its front the ad-

vance of the Gebirgs division had outstripped that of the 97th Light
whose opponents had struck back in attacks so suicidal in nature that
they had halted that unit's advance through the wooded uplands. In
an effort to strengthen the northern wing of his Corps and to push
this forward to gain touch with the panzer divisions in the east, General Kübler brought 4th Division back into the line. He ordered it to
move during the night of 23–24 July and to head for Obodne. This
march from the rest area around Vinnitsa, where the division lay re-
laxing, was to take the best part of six days across appalling terrain.
To maintain the tempo of the pursuit the 1st Gebirgs was then set
against the little town of Brazlav.

From the north the advanced guard group Lang of 1st Gebirgs Division struck down to seize the bridges across the Bug, but each attempt failed against severe and desperate resistance of the Russian
rearguard, backed by armour. Daring efforts by engineer detachments to cross the river using rubber assault boats were smashed.
Towards midday one group of engineers carried out a successful attempt which seized a bridgehead, but this was soon driven in by
persistent Russian motorised infantry assault. One officer's report
stated:

> The Soviet infantry were brought forward in lorries and these
> attempts were to smother the defence by use of mass. Their lorry-
> borne attacks were made by waves of vehicles in which the infan-
> try stood firing all the time. Where we had an SP up with our
> troops of an FOO [Forward Observation Officer] then we could
> destroy them with little trouble, so long as we had spotted their
> approach at distances above 800 metres. I saw one SP, firing from
> the halt, smash every vehicle of the leading group of about 18 lor-
> ries in less than three minutes. Fire; a direct hit. Fire; a direct hit,
> fire, fire, fire and so on. Under the detonation of the 7.5cm shells
> the Red infantrymen were flung out of the trucks. It was a scene of
> wild confusion with burning lorries, Russian infantry running in all
> directions and almost continual mortar fire.

In the Bug bridgehead the Russian mass attacks had overrun the
German engineer bridgehead and had flung back yet another attempt
to drive on Brazlav. It was clear that any thrust from the north
would meet the strongest defence but a feint assault, followed by a

quick thrust from the west while the defence was facing northwards, might at least have a chance of making the enemy divide his forces and might lead to the capture of the town. The 99th Jäger Regiment fought its way across the Bug at Astapkovchy, then swung eastwards and forced the advance into Brazlav. The street fighting was short but hard and it was not until last light that the war diary could record that the regiment not only held the town but stood on the heights to the south. The 1st Gebirgs Division was then given a short rest, while on the right wing 125th Infantry Division now formed the spearpoint and carried the advance towards Gaissin. The 97th Light Division, on the left flank, was deeply and heavily engaged withstanding heavy Russian counter-attacks against its units.

Tactically the Corps situation was unsound. The infantry divisions were separated from each other by terrain which being naturally strong favoured the defence. Whether the Soviets were in the wooded hills which parted the two spearhead divisions, and in what strength his forces might be, were factors which made for unease at Corps HQ about open flanks. The 97th Light was then ordered to drive southwards to force any groups which it encountered on to the guns of the 125th Division, while to thicken the line 4th Gebirgs Division, whose leading elements had reached the area, was put straight into the front sector. Corps needed more men in the line and a further infantry division, 295th, then came on to strength and was put on the northern flank: the area of maximum effort. The pressure which Corps now exerted forced the Russians to take a generally south-eastern line to avoid defeat. With the 295th Division advancing down the line of the eastern bank of the Ssod river and sending out patrols to gain contact with 16th Panzer Division, Corps placed 97th Light, followed by the 4th Gebirgs Division, aiming for the capture of Granov and Mikhailovka. When they were captured the 97th and 4th Divisions would be in the rear of Gaissin, upon whose strong defensive positions outside the town the 125th Infantry Division was advancing on a western line.

During 25 July the men of 49th Gebirgs Corps encountered seriously for the first time two of the natural conditions which were to make the campaign in Russia so difficult for the ordinary German soldier to endure. These were weather conditions and its effect upon terrain. Throughout the fighting rain had fallen, chiefly during the evening and only intermittently, hindering military operations to only a certain degree. But during that day torrential rain fell, washing away roads and producing deep mud which held the vehicles fast and turned the infantry assaults upon the forested hills into a misery of slow-moving advances uphill, against an enemy concealed in well-designed pillboxes which dominated every avenue of approach.

For the attack ordered for 26 July both Gebirgs divisions were brought forward and both were placed on the right wing, to which flank the Corps' maximum effort had been switched. The 4th Division was given the objective of Nemirov, while the 1st was given two separate objectives; the capture of Teplik by Battle Group Lang and the seizure of Gaissin by the main of the division. The Corps commander's intention to fling his strong right wing deep into the Red forces opposing it would be followed, once a breach had been gained, by a swing north-eastwards towards Novo Archangelsk. This would be the southern encircling pincer.

The continuing bad weather confined the German advance to the main road and thus against the strong Soviet forces which were using it to escape towards Uman. It was, therefore, an advance which was contested bitterly by the Russian detachments but despite this opposition Teplik fell to the men of Lang's group during the late afternoon. It says much for the confidence of the German units of those days that a single detachment could be allotted such a task. Lang group had fought its way forward in isolation, through difficult country, including an area of marshy lakes into a region held in strength by an enemy whose forces outnumbered its own. With scant concern for threats against their flanks the units of Lang group had reached their objectives, and, when these had been attained, the whole group was isolated and separated by more than 45kms from the main body of its parent division, and by more than 20kms from the divisions on its flanks.

Although the Red resistance was still determined and counter-attacks were mounted with ferocity and regularity, there were growing signs of disarray in the Soviet host and the divisions forming Gebirgs Corps were able to carry out small encirclements of their own as they drove farther and farther eastwards, forming a wedge which struck deep into the Russian mass facing them.

The situation maps at Corps headquarters on the night of 27 July showed that the 49th Gebirgs Corps formed a front which resembled a clenched left fist with projecting index and middle fingers. The clenched fist was formed by the left-wing divisions, 97th Light and 295th Infantry which, now firmly linked, had gained contact with 125th Division, holding the centre, at Granov. One projecting finger was part of 125th Division which was reaching out towards Ivangorod and Gorodka. The other finger was that made up of the right-hand division, 1st Gebirgs, which had gone on from Teplik to reach Sserebriya, Ternovka and Ladyshinka and whose crooked finger was encircling Uman from the south.

The day had been marked with frequent and heavy deluges of rain which worsened the already terrible road conditions. These seemed to have less effect upon the movement of the Russian units but they severely influenced the German conduct of the battle. While the German troops floundered in the mud the Red Army soldiers went over, along the whole Corps front, to counter-attacks, often carried out solely by infantry but frequently supported by armour. The Lang battle group, exhausted by the continual combat and the clinging mud, was able to reach no nearer to Ternovka, its given objective, than a point some distance from the small town where the units laagered or dug in to await the arrival of the foot-marching Jäger regiments. On the front of 125th Division early gains were lost to the furious and repeated Soviet counter-attacks around Granov and when Corps TAC Headquarters moved into the Gaissin it was bombarded with frightening accuracy by Red artillery. The 295th Division made no progress at all during the day due to the bad terrain. The 97th Light was removed from the line and taken into Corps reserve.

Despite the setbacks of the day, during the evening of 27 July the feeling grew that the Soviets were beginning to break and Corps resolved to pursue them so closely that the Red rearguards would have no time to form fresh defensive lines. The German rearguards were, by their own unaided effort, too weak to harry the Soviets and to close any gaps which might be created by any mass escape of Soviet troops through the German line. More infantry was needed and in large numbers if the enemy was to be contained. The nearest Jäger regiments were far away and there was no transport to bring them forward. Ordinary marching would be too slow to bring them to the critical points in time and to maintain touch with the thrusting advance guard detachments. The Jäger would have to come on in forced marches and at the conclusion of each day's effort might then have to fight an infantry battle. The maximum effort was being demanded of the mountain men.

The compression of the Red forces had now reached a dangerous point. The trapped Russian troops were superior in number to the Germans at all points around the perimeter and, working on internal lines of movement, could switch the point of their maximum effort from flank to flank with greater ease than could 49th Corps. Given the masses of men and vehicles over which the Red Command still had control, STAVKA could launch repeated and severe counterattacks to breach the ring. They could conduct a battle of attrition, wearing down the Germans by continual assault and subjecting them to a steady flow of casualties. This they certainly tried to accomplish but their handling lacked flexibility. Their infantry attacks, light or heavy, whether supported by artillery or not, whether by day or by night, were conducted upon rigid principles and did not vary in pattern or in timetable. From Ternovka, where the Soviets struck back in a frontal attack against 1st Gebirgs Division, to Ivangorod where they launched flank attacks against 125th Infantry Division, the method did not change and this rigidity enabled the Germans to exploit the situation by resting their men, refuelling or bringing forward new supplies of ammunition, confident always that the next assault would come in at a precise time and at a certain place. Rested and rearmed the Jäger waited until the khaki lines came on and then the slaughter began again. Kipling wrote that "when it comes to slaughter you do your work on water and you'll lick the bloomin' boots of him what's got it". The mountain men may never have heard of Kipling but they knew the truth of his words. They were fighting in a region deficient in proper water supplies. There were streams in plenty and marsh abounded. But this brackish, tepid, bitter-tasting liquid, the product of thin, slimy soil, did not quench the thirst like the foaming, ice cold, glacial waters of their own Alpine homeland. In 1939 they had slaked their thirsts with melons as they trekked across Poland, but the melons were still green and unripe, unsatisfactory fruits with which to slake a terrible thirst. Lacking proper wells there was nothing else for them other than to fill their bottles with the muddy marsh water, to which the water-purifying tablets gave an even more unpleasant taste.

The heat by day was oppressive; the rain, which fell heaviest in the evening between 19.00 and 21.00hrs, produced thick mists, a humid steamy atmosphere which the mountain men found difficult to breathe. And in this close, airless atmosphere, on roads that were more than ankle deep in mud, without adequate water or proper food the Jäger marched for hour after hour, day after day in pursuit of the Soviets. After hours of marching a sudden flurry of shots would rouse them from the hypnosis of the route march and indicate that another Russian rearguard was opposing their advance. Then the weary limbs, given new strength by the imminence of action, would carry them into set piece attacks against the entrenched enemy whose retreat was only a matter of time. But every rearguard defeated still brought a blood loss in dead and wounded Jäger, reducing the fighting strength of the companies and placing a heavier burden on those who remained.

The advance of 49th Gebirgs Corps had thrust a salient into the Soviet area and thus the Red units were surrounding the German divisions on three sides. The important task, to gain ground eastwards and to reach the panzer and motorised divisions forming the eastern wall, had still not been accomplished, despite this salient, and haste was needed to achieve it. Concern for flank protection was less important than to gain touch, so that as the advance guard groups of each division probed forward the Russians sensing their opponents' weaknesses on the wings flung against these a succession of assaults. One main group of Red Army units sought for and found the junction between 1st Gebirgs and 125th Infantry Divisions and as the German units drove eastwards they were forced to divert from the main eastward thrust units to hold firm their threatened flanks.

By 28 July the Soviet forces, now a hotch-potch of more than fifteen divisions, were completely encircled. Some elements of these shattered units trickled through the loosely held German line, moving south-east, but the great mass was still seeking to move eastwards via Uman to Korovgrad and Kremechug and thus towards the line of panzer divisions. STAVKA's control over its formations was becoming flabby and little central direction was evident in the Soviet conduct of operations. That the main of the encircled Soviet forces was moving into a German trap, and was not concentrating to carry out mass attacks in a south-easterly direction through the weakest part of the German ring, shows how total was the Russian defeat and how complete the breakdown of firm control. Indeed, German wireless intercepts showed that there was little traffic between corps and that

Gebirgsjäger hoist the German War Flag above the Acropolis in Athens after they had taken a successful part in the campaign in Greece, April 1941.

Gebirgsjäger fighting on the airfield at Maleme take cover behind a Ju 52 which had brought them across from airfields in Greece. The men of this group were among the first mountain troops brought into Maleme.

General Ringel congratulating men of his 5th Gebirgs Division during a presentation of decorations after the campaign in Crete, 1941. The man to whom the general is talking is an Oberfeldwebel and has on his breast the edelweiss badge of a mountain guide, and the small black badge which indicates that he has been wounded.

General Ringel, General Officer Commanding 5th Gebirgs Division, bestowing decorations on men of his Command after the campaign in Crete, 1941. The paper which can be seen carried in the hands of the two men in the front rank is the certificate of authorisation which proved the soldiers' right to wear the decoration. German awards were not marked with the recipient's name and number.

The German military cemetery at Maleme, Crete. The graveyard contains the bodies of 4,465 members of the German Armed Forces who were killed or died in Crete and included not only partroops but Gebirgsjäger, sailors and airmen.

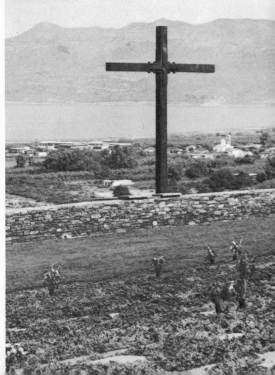

Gebirgsjäger used local means of transport. During the fighting in the Caucasus and the advance into Asiatic Russia Bactrian camels were often used as substitutes for mules and horses.

The crew of a divisional anti-tank gun detachment blew-up a Soviet tank in the fighting around Uman, summer 1941. The weapon is the standard 3.7cm gun of such poor performance that it was nicknamed the "door knocker" by the German gun crews.

Russian troops, who had carried out an attack against the Gebirgsjäger positions during February 1942, lie dead in front of the Jäger positions.

Two-man shelters erected by Gebirgsjäger in the extensive woods which cover the Caucasus. This picture is of men of 4th Gebirgs Division and was taken in the early months of the summer offensive of 1942.

Another shot of a Gebirgsjäger encampment along the Sukhum Army road in the Caucasus some ten kilometres above Sukhum in the valley of the Klisch river.

A ration column made up of Gebirgsjäger and Russian prisoners of war bring food to the front line positions in the Caucasus mountains, during the German summer offensive.

Mountain artillery of the 4th Gebirgs Division marching from the Kluchor Pass to the valley of the river Klisch. The 7.5cm pieces have been broken down and are being brought forward on mule back. The Caucasus, summer 1942.

even at divisional level there was an almost complete lack of communication.

The advance of 1st Gebirgs Division was temporarily threatened by a great mass of Russian vehicles which aerial reconnaissance had reported and which the Luftwaffe had begun to destroy with dive bombing attacks. Nevertheless, this grouping was a menace which threatened the flanks of Lanz's division and aggressive patrolling was needed to establish whether the motor mass was seeking to break out or not. More patrols were sent out to sweep south of Ternovka–Donovka road and this switch of strength to the division's right flank weakened the left wing. Between that wing and the right flank of 125th Infantry there was an unpatrolled gap and in order that the Soviets might not find and exploit this weakness the 4th Gebirgs Division was ordered to move with all haste and to insert itself between the two sister divisions of its Corps.

It will have been noticed that 49th Corps frequently switched the point of its maximum effort along its front. On one day it was 1st Gebirgs Division on the right wing which forced the pace, but then the emphasis swung to 125th Infantry in the centre and thence to the left wing, each blow confusing the Soviet defenders and separating their units from each other. For 30 July the main effort was carried by 125th Division but then, in the evening of that day, orders from Army swung the emphasis back on to the right wing. The reason for this change of emphasis was that Panzer Group Kleist had begun a new offensive towards Pervomaisk, a town on the confluence of the Bug and the Ssinyucha rivers and located about 100kms west of Uman. To stem the expected reaction to this German move it was essential to seize and hold Golovanevsk, through which town aid would flow to the Russian units under attack by the panzer divisions. The 1st Gebirgs Division's right wing, Battle Group Lang, was ordered to turn due south and to strike towards Golovanevsk while the main of the division continued its drive towards Dubovo. This was an order which took the division by surprise for it divided its strength at a time when concentration of force might have been the logical and expected order. This new move extended the Corps front and consequently weakened the eastern drive. At Army HQ, however, the picture seen was a different one and it was thought that a dangerous grouping of Soviet forces building up around Golovanevsk was likely to try and link with other main groupings of the Red

Army west of Uman. Army considered it more important to smash these cohesive and possibly virile Red Army units than to continue the pursuit and encirclement of the shattered Russian divisions around Uman. The task of the Lang battle group was to form a shield and to prevent a junction of those two Soviet forces.

In vain did Corps, condemned to fight through trackless woods or along roads of liquid mud, seek to carry out its task of gaining ground to the east and to the south. Its weak infantry force was depleted by 17th Army's order and it is not surprising, therefore, to learn that not one division reached its objective that day. Each of them was repeatedly counter-attacked by waves of Russian infantry and armour, and Battle Group Lang, en route to Golovanevsk, ran up against field defences which the Red Army had erected around the town. These were sufficiently strong to halt the group's attack dead in its tracks and the baulked German force was then bombarded with a massive concentration of guns and counter-attacked by infantry masses which seemed to grow out of the ground.

The speed with which Ivan built up his strength was incredibly fast. By ones and twos he would filter across a crest, seemingly without any sort of organisation. Within a very short time surprising numbers had crossed the heights and had descended into the valleys from which, directly in front of us and out of dead ground, would charge whole lines of them; whole lines where only a short time before there had been a scattered rearguard. The time taken from observing the seemingly random infiltration down the forward slope of a hill to their charging at us with their thundering "OOray", was always terribly short. They could conceal themselves like deer in a forest and dig like moles. A pocket of them uncleared at last light would be a battalion in well-prepared defensive positions at first light next morning. Theirs was the patience of the hunting animal. In the Caucasus [in 1942] parties of them would conceal themselves for days in the snow of recent avalanches and wait until our patrols came out to blaze new trails. Around Uman it was more than usually difficult to dig them out because of the almost incessant rain and the thick white mist which was produced as a result of the damp ground and the high day temperatures.

The hill tops were usually clear of mist for this hung in the valleys and along the water courses. Visibility was often measured in metres around daybreak and Ivan could move without making a sound or being seen. Then at the last moment would come their battle cry and they would stampede out of the mist shoulder to shoulder, wave after wave. We shot them down in batches but always there were more to storm forward. Of course they were encircled and were sent forward to break our line. Sometimes they succeeded and hundreds would escape. Little did they know that echeloned behind us were other regiments and divisions waiting for them. As they flooded through the gaps which had been created and fanned out they would, quite often, begin to relax thinking that they had escaped and were safe. The units positioned behind us killed them as they relaxed, as they moved in groups down the roads singing and laughing like schoolboys given the day off. They fell in swathes to our weapons, but ours were not the only weapons which killed them.

At one place we found groups of bodies, hundreds of them lying with their wrists tied. It was our belief that this was an NKVD execution area because some of the bodies were over a week old while others had been there only a day or two and not one of the fallen had a weapon with him, not even a bayonet. We had read in Intelligence abstracts that under the pressure of our encirclement, the pounding from our guns, the nerve-shaking Stukas and our infantry attacks there had been cases of mutiny in some Red Army units and that commissars and officers had been murdered by their men. The dead we saw with their wrists tied were probably the victims of NKVD detachments who restored discipline by Draconian methods. The whole Uman battlefield, as I recall it, was one huge graveyard.

During the day the first elements of 4th Gebirgs Division pushed themselves along mud tracks and into the gaps in the encircling ring. The leading units had barely settled in when a fresh massive and general assault was launched by several trapped Russian divisions. From the front of 295th Division and running southwards across the Uman highway along which 125th Infantry was driving, to the right flank of 4th Gebirgs Division at Ossitna, the Soviet attacks came in seeking to drive back the Gebirgs Corps now dangerously close to Uman. In the north the Red counter-blows were accompanied by armour and artillery, the intensity of whose fire drove back the men of 295th Division. The situation was critical. No German panzer could manoeuvre in the thick morass of mud which covered the battlefield and even the Soviet armoured fighting vehicles, normally mobile even in quite bad ground conditions, could move only with difficulty. The Red infantry flooded across the muddy flats covering the ground with their numbers, trudging forward through the pouring rain, sweeping down out of the woods, striking at a dozen different points and forcing the men of 49th Corps on to the defensive where a stalemate situation might have developed but for the timely arrival of two fresh German divisions whose attacks halted and then flung back the Russian thrusts. But even with this fresh accretion of strength Corps was still unable to achieve the long term objective which had been given it, the capture of Uman, for its divisions stretched over a distance of 65kms and lacked the power to advance eastwards. Then came the order for the whole of 1st Gebirgs Division to strike southwards and to support the Lang battle group. The divisional commander raised the strongest protests but the order stood that his division was to cut the roads and paths in the Golovanevsk sector and to deny their access to the enemy. Corps promised that all available reserves would be sent to reinforce the division whose attack, timed for 14.00hrs on 31 July, to take out the town and to threaten the 50,000 trapped Russians around it, would go in from the north and from the south.

At mid-morning the Stukas flew in and dived vertically bombing the Soviet defences and gun positions. For an hour the chains of Junkers aircraft fell and climbed and when they flew away westwards they passed over the small groups of Jäger who, forming one arm of the assault, were emerging from the great forest to the north of Golovanevsk and pressing the advance on either side of the main road into the town. These had soon fought their way through the mass of Russian soldiers and then from the west a second arm, that of the Kress battle group, drove forward, swung left round the southern edge of the woods and sealed off the town from the south. The third blow to fall was that dealt by the Picket battle group which came down to close the gap that existed between the northern and southern pincers and to guard the backs of those detachments.

The advance by the Gebirgs Corps had now almost cut off the town of Uman even though the Russian counter-attacks on that sector were as furious and as regular as ever, and even though the Soviet rearguards put up a stubborn, not to say fanatical, defence. This staunch resistance still held off the Gebirgs Corps from the objective of Uman, even though 17th Army's eastwards advance had gained touch with certain of the panzer divisions and had cut every road out of the city.

On other sectors of the Corps front parties of Red Army men escaped by filtering through the vast woods, using forest paths and deserted tracks. The familiarity of the Russian soldier with the vast forests allowed him to move through these more easily than the Germans so that the last thing many German sentinels saw as they peered through the curtains of pouring rain was the sudden appearance, only an arm's length away, of lowering and menacing khaki figures who, looming out of the murk, struck quickly and killed swiftly. Then through the gap the silent files of Red Army men would pass, flitting from one tree to another, or crawling flat on the ground where sights and sounds indicated the presence of a large party of Germans. However, often and quite suddenly, a hoarse challenge would ring out and in the shocked silence a German light machine gun would fire and the bodies of another group of would-be escapers would lie dead under the sombre, weeping trees.

In many places strong and furious counter-attacks came in against the Germans, the weight and fury of these increased by the desperation that encirclement had bred, but many of these suicidal assaults were smashed by Jäger who were convinced that victory, total and utter victory, was only a hairsbreadth away. Little did they know that ahead of them lay days of all-out battle, far more demanding than any effort they had made that far.

Inspired by the fear of captivity, or of the NKVD execution squads, the Red Army units flung themselves in reckless assault against the panzer divisions in the east and also against the infantry divisions in the west. Rearguards fought to the last man or pitted their strength in vain attempts to halt the Jäger advance. The ring was drawing tight around the Red units. The 16th Motorised, 9th Panzer, 16th Panzer, 25th Motorised and 11th Panzer Divisions formed a roughly shaped half ring east of Uman, while to the west other divisions of the Gebirgs Corps made up the matching half ring. Neither ring was a continuous and firm line and touch had not yet been made with all the armoured forces, but aggressive patrolling covered most gaps and shepherded back into the confining ring those Russian troops who sought to escape it.

The left wing of Corps was more solid and firm than the right flank where the absence of 1st Gebirgs Division, still engaged on its southern drive, not only left a gap but compelled Corps to weaken its main effort. Then occurred the crisis which General Lanz had foreseen. His division in its advance formed a salient pointing southwards towards Golovanevsk and then came under attack along three sides of that salient from troops of the Red Army's 17th Infantry Corps moving down the great south-easterly road from Uman. These troops had escaped the city before the Jäger/panzer link up had cut it off completely and had formed into a massive wedge determined to force their way out of the encirclement. The Corps commander, realising perhaps that he had over-extended his front, recalled 1st Gebirgs back to its former place on the right wing. Once in position it was to launch an attack eastwards so as to take in flank the great mass of 17th Russian Infantry Corps and to halt their escape attempt.

This was an order which could not be immediately complied with, for the efforts by the mountain regiments to disengage themselves from the Soviet troops brought an astonishing response. The Russians presumed that the 1st Gebirgs Division was in fact retreating and put in against it wave after wave of attacks so as to destroy it utterly. Even when the battalions had broken off the battle and were heading back to their original positions they found that many of the villages on the road back had been re-occupied by Russian troops who, by defending these tenaciously, forced the mountain men either to undertake long and difficult diversions across poor country or to make costly frontal assaults to recapture them.

As an example of the difficulties faced by the whole corps let us examine the Battle Group Lang which, first to disengage itself from the Soviets, then began its drive shortly after 08.00hrs. So often was its advance impeded and by so strong a defence that it was not until 21.30hrs that it had returned to its former sector. Then came the attack eastwards to cut the Uman road again. The fighting, already bitter, then flared to new heights of fury and the men of Lang group and of the Jäger regiments battled through fields and woods, losing men to snipers, machine gun fire and in close quarter fighting. Or else they battled to capture low hovels which formed the villages of this region of the Soviet Union. The wooden huts were crammed with

Red Army riflemen; in the dust roads, not turned to sloughs of mud, were freshly laid mines and from trenches outside the villages streams of bullets poured out from machine guns upon the attacking mountain men. Despite the most strenuous efforts to maintain contact with each other uncaptured villages and uncleared woodland stretches left wide gaps between the 1st and 4th Divisions; one of these was more than 30kms wide, too great a distance to be adequately covered by patrols. To close the breach the Corps commander ordered detachments of 97th Light into the gap. This was a unit which during this particular operation was fated seldom to fight as a whole. Rather was it used by the Corps commander as a milch cow supplying strength, the strength of its battalions or regiments, to other units and being put piecemeal into the line to close gaps. It was during one such operation that the advance of detachments from the 97th met head-on another mass break-out attempt. As the German companies came into the line they were hastily allotted areas and took up all-round positions. No properly co-ordinated system of defence was possible for the Soviet soldiers were everywhere. The tactics which the rifle companies and battalions of the 97th Light employed that day were as old as formal infantry warfare. To reach the positions which had been allocated the groups moved forward on foot with patrols on either flank maintaining contact with other units on the wings. The left and right flanks of 97th were covered by patrols of motorised infantry who pushed forward seeking to gain contact with the two Gebirgs divisions, and thus to establish firm shoulders to support the slower-moving infantry whose progress through swamp and across the hills of the region was naturally less fast than that of the lorried infantry.

It was against the foot soldiers that the heaviest Soviet attacks came in. Russian artillery observers on one high ridge after another directed the fire of massed artillery upon the small groups, but gun fire alone could not deter or obstruct the advance. Cossack cavalry formations, their riders bent low in the saddle, swept down upon the lines of German infantry trudging across the open fields. At a command the lines would halt and prepare to receive cavalry; light machine guns would hold the front and the corners of a hastily formed square and then, as the black horses rushed down and the riders rose high in their stirrups to slash and cut at the infantry groups, German fire would sweep them and within seconds, although it seemed like hours, there would be the heaped bodies of horse and rider motionless upon the ground or else riderless horses careering across the plain. Under cover of the Cossack charge, and while the concentration of the German infantry was upon the cavalry, the Red infantry would begin their assault and then on the open steppe it was a question of how well and accurately one could fire if the lines, succeeding lines one after the other, were to be beaten back.

There were times when the wireless equipment functioned so well that a battalion under attack could inform Regiment and through them Division of the critical situation and that Luftwaffe help was needed. Then to the aid of the hard-pressed German infantry would come the hunting aircraft: dive bombers peeling off to smash the concentrations of the enemy with anti-personnel and high explosive bombs, or else the lean and shark-like fighters which, roaring low over the Russian detachments, strafed them with machine gun fire and dispersed them.

But more usually the temperamental wireless sets could reach no higher formation and then it was upon the infantry that the burden of the fighting fell to battle on unsupported. If the Russians fought bitterly for love of country, through fear of captivity or of the execution squads then the battle fought by the Germans was no less so, for many of these men appreciated that Russian soldiers attempting to escape from encirclement would have no time to escort prisoners of war, and that captivity might be very brief and end with a bullet in the back of the head. It was that fear which made the men of the German regiments around the Uman pocket fight with a desperate fury and along most of the line of the 97th's detachments the infantry held the Red assaults and forced the units back into the confining ring.

The efforts of 49th Gebirgs Corps were at last meeting with success for during that day the city of Uman was captured and by evening the units which had seized the Corps objective stood ready to resume their advance at first light on 2 August. A spirit of optimism, false though this turned out to be, animated the mountain men who thought with the fall of Uman that the objectives of the offensive had been attained. At Corps the situation on the battle maps still showed that in the south, that is on the Corps' right wing, touch had not been made with 9th Panzer and that between the leading elements of the armoured division and the forward patrols of 1st Gebirgs there still yawned an open space which needed to be quickly and firmly closed.

To fill this gap General Kübler directed both Gebirgs divisions to maintain their tasks of containing the Reds and ordered that part of the reconnaissance battalion from 97th Light should be used to block this escape hole. The unit began its march across roads which had long since ceased to have a surface and which had deteriorated into slow-moving rivers of liquid mud. Hour after hour the men of the 97th pushed and pulled their vehicles out of one pot-hole after another, and for hour after hour the marching troops of the reconnaissance group trudged doggedly along through the hindering slime to reach the Lang battle group. No sooner had the detachments arrived when they were given orders to support the attack which Lang intended to mount in the early evening. The men lay down in the mud and slept where they fell, totally exhausted. There was little time for rest for now reinforced and strengthened by these infantrymen Lang began his attack eastwards.

The road eastwards was one long line of burning lorries. Whenever we were forced to halt, which was often even though the point unit was moving at a very fast speed, we would look into the trucks. Not merely out of curiosity but because in some we found wounded men. The sights in the burning trucks were horrible. In some there would be whole rows of Russian soldiers sitting on the floor of the vehicles and burnt to cinders. The drivers still sat, blackened to charcoal, at the wheels of the trucks and everywhere there was the terrible smell of bodies burning, a stink that was even able to override that of burning rubber from the tyres. The fields were strewn with bodies, so were the roads and the crops. Some of us went into the maize fields to gather something to eat although, of course, the cobs were generally still unripe. Even in those fields we found fallen Russians. These had probably been wounded on or near the roads and had crawled into the crops to hide themselves in the maize. There were Russian dead everywhere.

Late in the evening of 2 August, Lang group's rapid thrust had driven a wedge into the Red forces and had pushed these aside in its endeavour to gain touch with the leading elements of 9th Panzer Division reported to be near Dogyanka.

As we drove up the roads a DR came by and ordered us to dismount and to prepare for imminent action. The 9th Panzer were said to be ahead of us and it was certain that the Ivans would fight hard to hold us apart. As we stood on the road making the last-minute adjustments one of the comrades pointed to white flares shining brilliantly in the eastern sky. These were followed by another group of white flares which Lang group fired off. We were told to wait and then about ten minutes later new sets of flares were fired. We were then told that the Lang detachment had driven up to the western bank of a river and had found the panzer waiting for them on the eastern bank. We had gained touch.

As a result of this meeting, contact had been made in the south as well as in the north of the pocket but the hold was still tenuous and there were not sufficient troops to hold the southern gate in great strength. There were still unclosed sectors and two of these were in the sectors of the Yatrani and the Ssinyucha rivers. Patrols went out to seal these gaps and both battle groups of 1st Gebirgs Division set out to complete the task of making the ring solid around its whole perimeter by closing the gap in the south very firmly. All night the Jäger marched through intermittent rain, the myriads of mosquitoes which plagued them and against surprisingly weak Russian attacks. By dawn the two battle groups and Lang group stood united and on the main battlefield ready to meet the challenges of the new day.

On the northern front 125th Infantry had achieved successes of its own and in a rapid advance down the Uman–Novo Archangelsk road forced a river crossing and crushed the Russian defences in that area. Patrol reports and aerial reconnaissance indicated that the main group of the Soviet forces, including nearly fifteen hundred vehicles, were compressed in the area Novo Archangelsk–Okssanino–Dubovo and Ternovka. With the enemy thus located and contained the sole task was to destroy him and with every confidence of success on the morrow the Corps commander issued his instructions for the annihilation of the invested host. The prizes of war were not to be so lightly gained, however, and the mountain men did not know that ahead of them lay four days of the bitterest fighting they were to encounter throughout the whole war, and that the casualties which they were to suffer during those four short days were to exceed those sustained in the previous two weeks of hard fighting.

The chief reason for the false optimism which Kübler felt was that he was of the opinion that Panzer Group 1 was co-operating with his drive to crush the Soviet pocket. Not until quite late during August 3 did he become aware that the role of the panzer divisions of Kleist's group was passive and that it was upon his men that the burden would fall. In vain did the Corps commander protest and he appealed to army group command, but the officers at that echelon refused to involve the panzer group in what were considered to be essentially infantry battles. It was in fact this refusal to use armour which had left the southern sector of the ring unclosed, just as it was the continued denial of armoured fighting vehicles in the next stage of the operation that led to crisis conditions in the battles during that first week of August. Lacking armoured support the Jäger had to hold fast the seal in the ring in the face of pressure by 60,000 trapped and desperate Russians and it is the struggle of the mountain men to hold firm against those blows that forms the final chapter of this account.

An encircled enemy will, of course, seek to find a weak place within the ring against which he can concentrate his forces and by exerting pressure try to smash a breach through which his forces can flood and break out to freedom. On the southern and south-western side of the German ring there was such a weak area. Viewing the pocket from the north to south the 125th and 9th Light Divisions had long since joined hands with the panzer units holding the eastern wall and the front along their sectors was fairly firm. In any case there was no point in the Reds attempting a strike to the north for that whole area was now strongly held by the German Army. To the east lay the armoured formations of Panzer Group 1 now backed by the infantry divisions which had caught up after long and tiring marches. The Soviets had found out in unsuccessful assaults how firm was the eastern panzer wall. However, to the south lay the Dnieper bend which was still in Russian hands. Barring access to this Russian-held sector lay the southern sector of the ring held by two hard-fighting but almost fought-out mountain divisions. A thrust against this weakness might gap the line and permit a mass escape of Red Army units to join with those Soviet forces still fighting west of the Dnieper river. This junction had to be prevented but the problem which faced the Corps commander was the usual one of lack of infantry. He had committed all his reserves and no infantry could be spared either by army or by army group. It was upon him and his men that the outcome depended.

He knew his men. They were confident of victory, they were tough and good soldiers and they could march. He would switch them in small detachments from one threatened point to another. They would have to march and counter-march, sealing the ring where it showed signs of giving way. It was their strong nerves which had to hold them in action against an enemy more than twenty times their number. To hold and then to march and fight again. To counter-march to meet some new thrust by the Soviets and to continue this until any infantry which could be spared from the northern sector of the ring had come down in forced marches to strengthen the southern flank. Trusting in the ability, the undoubted ability, of his men to win a defensive battle, General Kübler also expected them to attack, pushing the Soviet troops into killing grounds where their destruction could be more easily accomplished by gun fire, by Stuka bombardment and by panzer assault. Fired by his knowledge of the sterling qualities of the Jäger, Kübler penned the orders for, as he thought, the final destruction of the two Red armies in the pocket around Uman.

These efforts, those prodigies of marching, fighting, digging in, patrolling, marching again and fighting afresh were not restricted to any particular regiment or division. Each of the formations of the Gebirgs Corps suffered them as did each unit in all the corps which were enclosing the Red forces. There was along the whole perimeter the possibility that the troops holding part of the line would come under such heavy attack that they could neither withstand the protracted assaults of the Soviet troops nor hold back the fury of the break-out attempts without appealing for help. That help was given without qualification and frequently alarm units would be ordered to march away to help a neighbour leaving their own regimental sectors depleted and in possible danger.

So great was the length of the perimeter and so few were the numbers of soldiers to hold it, certainly in the first days of August, the period about which I am writing, that responsibility devolved upon quite junior officers who carried out their duties on an almost autonomous basis. To have such charge was nothing new for the junior mountain troop commanders; their whole training had in fact been based precisely upon small unit actions carried out independently, and in this type of operation they proved the excellence of that training.

Just as divisions had loose contact with each other based upon patrols maintaining touch, so did this situation apply at regimental and battalion level and the men in the line spent much of their time on reconnaissance patrols to determine the enemy's positions or intentions; in standing patrols to deny him some tactically important area or feature, or on fighting patrols to seek out and to destroy the Soviet enemy. Each patrol had as its chief objective the dominating of the Russian forces, a psychological as well as a military battle, for it was imperative to control the areas of no-man's-land and to make these "no-go" sectors for the enemy.

The strains of patrolling are many and are borne by each patrol member from the commander to the junior rifleman.

We were all very deeply aware of our numerical inferiority *vis-à-vis* the Russians. The Red Army as a whole numbered far more than did the whole German Army so we were outnumbered from the start. Then, of course, there was their local numerical superiority which was very great and we all knew that in any engagement only our ability and determination to win would compensate for our lack of numbers.

At that time we were confident of victory. We were winning. Our organisation was better, our operations more flexibly conducted, we were familiar with our weapons and we were, in a word, dynamic. The enemy was not. His control functioned spasmodically usually ineffectually. His supply system failed often and left his men hungry. His wireless channels were choked with traffic which when translated turned out to be exhortations from Stalin and his Staff to attack and win. Whole hours of air time were taken up in transmitting and receiving this gibberish while urgent requests to higher headquarters were held up. Orders would go out demanding attacks at some stated point. Rhythmically the Russian assaults would begin and continue at the stated time intervals, irrespective of the tactical situation and carry on because no countermanding order had come through on a network blocked with propaganda exhortations.

As a junior officer, at that time, most of my waking hours throughout this period were spent on patrol. . . . There was little excitement, only a deadly tiredness which paralysed us mentally. Individual days or attacks I cannot honestly say I recall with complete accuracy. An unusual incident, a particular corpse brings back the memory but whether that patrol occurred on one day or another cannot be recalled with honesty. The days of the week ceased to have any special significance; the dates meant nothing. Nights and days were dominated by patrols, marching or digging. Tiredness enveloped us all like some huge straitjacket and held us fast.

Standing patrols were the worst for they were the most boring, even though they involved less walking. Arriving at the patrol's objective, usually a bridge, we would take up all-round defence and would jump into the slit trenches which we had dug and occupied on previous occasions. Familiarity breeds contempt. On our third night the first men to jump into the slits had their feet blown off by the small green anti-personnel mines which Ivan scattered about so freely. The Russians planted them in perhaps only a couple of trenches but no one wanted to test the other slits and, while we were still dazed mentally by the shock of the explosions and our concern for the wounded, Ivan attacked us. Luckily we were able to beat him off but thereafter we were never so careless. With Ivan as an enemy death was the inevitable price one had to pay for a single second's lapse from total alertness.

Reconnaissance patrols were usually boring even though dangerous. Our small numbers could attract the attention of a Red group which would attack us. Recce patrols in woods were the worst. Fighting in those damned trees and through that tangled undergrowth exhausted us completely. Woods were the very devil to clear. I have known Russian snipers tie themselves to tree tops so as to leave both hands free to aim and fire. Or there would be a machine gun post hidden in the wide-spread roots of an old and large tree. These posts were almost indistinguishable from the undergrowth and Ivan would hold his fire until point blank range.

We learned his tricks and when we began to use them against him we enjoyed a great measure of success. Even in the Kuban swamps Gebirgsjäger were better at flushing out the partisans than the line infantry because we fought as Ivan did, with cunning and in small, well-commanded detachments.

On one fighting patrol, for which I was 2 i/c, our commander chose a position which gave us a tactical advantage because he had read the spoor correctly and had drawn the right conclusions. We had seen a large Russian group, not a patrol but probably some men hoping to slip through our lines, and it was clear that this group would hold a course which would take it along a forest track descending gently to the valley. A stream ran parallel to the path and about 10 metres distant from it. There was a large open space. It was more than just a forest clearing and was about the size of a football field. It had been raining and we were all soaked. Steam began to rise off our wet clothes and this perhaps gave our commander the idea. He recalled that after rain and towards evening a mist would form and hang above the streams. Russian patrols had often caught us this way by firing out of the fog.

He decided to make the large open space the killing ground and we were ordered to hide in the stream and to keep our heads below the river bank. This meant being immersed up to the chest for at least fifteen minutes. We took up position with MG groups at each end of the line. A whistle blast from an observer in high ground to our rear would let us know that Ivan was in the killing ground. Other blasts from either end of the line would show that the whole group was contained. We were then to open fire.

Then suddenly the mist which our commander had expected began to form and soon hung over the stream effectively concealing us from the Russian soldiers. We opened fire upon the whistle blasts from either flank and after the first fusillade came out of the stream into visibility so as to give aimed fire. We killed them all and lost only one man slightly wounded. Surprise had been total even though there had been some return fire and the whole episode was about 3 minutes. We had used LMGs, MPs and hand grenades. We had no time to bury the dead but left them as a warning that we were alert.

Let us, at this point, recapitulate the events of the past days, and consider the results of the various moves which had been made. In the north of the pocket the German divisions were firmly in position and in control. The pressure they were exerting upon the troops of the Soviet armies was such that these were beginning to concentrate in an area immediately to the north of the weakest part of the German line. For a short period, in some sectors only of hours, there had been a lessening of Russian counter-pressure which could be interpreted either as a weakening of their offensive capabilities or, more sinisterly, as a concentration of forces ready to drive through the weak sectors of the ring. The German troops, confident of a quick victory, were preparing to launch a general move to break up the Soviet forces into smaller pockets and to destroy them.

On the weak sector of the German line stood the 1st and 4th Gebirgs Divisions and it was upon this latter that the full pent-up energy of the Soviet break-out attempt was to fall. The 4th, under its commander Englseer, had been given three days rest at the opening of the offensive and then had been brought back into action by way of forced marches from Vinnitsa where it was resting. For six days the Jäger had marched and even though each day had had its difficulties that of the last day had been the most demanding for it had been well over 45kms and had been made carrying full kit and extra ammunition.

On reaching the line, 4th Division had been put into the gap between the Yatrani and Ssinyucha rivers and had been ordered to seal the breach. The first attempts had failed but when the divisional reconnaissance battalion reported that it had established a bridgehead across the Yatrani, the divisional commander swung the 91st Jäger Regiment round and ordered it to exploit this success. This was no easy move to make across a soaked and muddy country cut with waterways and dense water forests, but by 13.00hrs the leading elements of 91st began to cross the Yatrani river bridge near Polonistoya after a forced march of more than 25kms. A cloudburst then fell upon the area washing away what remained of the roads and turning their surfaces into mud in which the mules sank to their knees. In such conditions neither machines nor beasts could continue but the Jäger, the eternal infantry, maintained their march and kept going for a further 25kms until they had gained touch with the men of the reconnaissance detachment who had by that time reached an important crossroads 5kms south-west of Podvyssokoya.

To the north-east of the sector held by 4th Gebirgs Division lay a large tract of wooded country and the principal town in that region was Kopyenkovata which lay to the east of the forest. It was in those great areas of trees that the Soviet troops pulling back from the pressure of 125th Division had begun to concentrate where they joined other Red Army units already in position and preparing for an all-out drive to smash through the sector held by 4th Division. Among other sensitive areas in the critical but decisive battle which was about to break was the village of Podvyssokoya, certain high ground, Points 196 and 193 and the largish village of Peregonovka. From the map it can be seen that the weakest sector of that whole weak front was between Peregonovka and Polonistoya some 8kms due south of it. A mass attack passing through that gap could be into an area weakly held by German troops and gain access to open country.

This was indeed the Soviet plan and it was their intention to mount a snowball type of operation. Units already hidden in the great Kopyenkovata woods would strike to smash the breach, and their assault would gain impetus and strength from the force and power of the formations withdrawing in front of 97th Light and 125th Divisions. Like some human snowball the attack would gather strength and roll, irresistibly, through the German line, held by the 91st Jäger Regiment.

The Corps plan was for an assault to be launched during 3 August to carry the front farther towards Podvyssokoya but during the advance by 4th Gebirgs Division furious Russian counter-attacks came in against both regiments. The Soviets, acutely aware that Peregonovka and Podvyssokoya were the keys to their own imminent breakout attempts, were determined to retain their hold on those places and met the German advance with counter-thrusts by infantry and by armour. Five times masses of tanks and infantry swarmed out of the forest roaring down towards the thin Jäger line but each of the major assaults was crushed. The smaller infantry attacks were more numerous and eighteen were launched against one battalion of the 91st. The sister regiment, 13th Jäger, succeeded in forcing a crossing of the Yatrani and established a bridgehead at Peregonovka.

Throughout the following day, 4 August, the regiments of 4th Gebirgs struggled to form a firm front while against them poured an almost unbroken succession of attacks by Red Army units fighting to keep open their escape routes. In the face of such furious opposition the 91st made little progress and the 13th failed to take its given objective, the village of Kopyenkovata. The reason for this failure to achieve the tasks given can be attributed to the lack of infantry strength suffered by Gebirgs divisions when fighting on the flat. To support the division during the forthcoming general assault and to close the gap which existed between the 2nd and 3rd Battalions of 91st Regiment, the 477th Regiment of 257th Infantry Division was temporarily taken on to the strength of 4th Gebirgs Division. The whole of 4th Gebirgs Division now prepared itself for the fight which would, once and for all, smash the enemy in the pocket and while 91st Regiment with its attached infantry regiment made ready to go against Kopyenkovata. To support those assaults and to lift the infantry on to their objectives, the additional power of ten batteries of artillery was made available.

All was now ready and while the regiments and battalions were forming up to begin the assault, the first assaults of the Red Army's own offensive to break out opened to a thunder of artillery. The Russian blow had been the first to fall and the Soviets had gained the tactical advantage forcing the Germans on to the defensive. The fury of the Russian assaults shattered the Jäger battalions. Wave after wave of Soviet soldiers formed the mass for the first attacks and flung themselves upon the German trenches. By the light of alarm flares which the 91st fired into the air other Red columns could be seen moving towards these areas which their patrols had found to be less strongly held, tramping solidly forward hoping to gain open ground while the attacking waves, screaming their battle cry, struck repeatedly at the Jäger positions. At times the Russian masses reached and then flooded over the thin German trench line; then the men of the companies of the 91st stood to and fought their enemy in close combat. The antagonists, fired on the one side by the need to escape and on the other by the belief that victory was only hours away, fought with fanatic desperation. The Red soldiers came in with the bayonet and were fought back with entrenching tools, shovels and hunting knives. At times groups of Russian soldiers, having driven back the defenders, escaped into the darkness but then the Jäger alarm companies, alerted and vigorous, struck hard, re-occupied the trenches and fought on firing like demons into the masses still pressing forward until at last these broke and ran.

By now the fighting was general along the whole of the western edge of the pocket. Along the front held by 125th Division one of its regiments fought for seven hours to capture a wooded concentration area in which Soviet forces had been reforming and was assaulted by a succession of Soviet attacks supported by tanks. On the left wing of 4th Gebirgs the high ground around Point 193 held by a battalion of 13th Regiment was bombarded by heavy Russian guns, many of them of 18cm calibre and followed by massed infantry assaults. Under this pressure the men of 2nd Battalion were forced off the hill but reformed and went back in again to seize the height and to hold it.

The morning brought no respite as attack followed attack. Blackened with the smoke of explosions, half mad with the noise and the fury of the battle, the Jäger of the 91st stood, soaked through with sweat and rain as across the ground in front of them, churned now by many marching feet into a lake of thick mud, tramped more and more Russian regiments, determined to force the breakthrough which STAVKA had ordered. Every assault wave was driven back by men whose own casualties had been so heavy that fifteen metres was the usual distance between one occupied slit trench and another. But still the men of the 91st battled on. They knew that the blood-soaked mud on which they stood was the point at which the Reds were determined to smash through and this post of honour they, the Jäger from the southern provinces of Germany, were determined not to give up. Rather were they still under orders to attack and the Russian assaults had delayed but not cancelled those orders. At 11.30hrs the assault by both regiments of 4th Division went in.

Corps was still optimistic that victory was imminent and the attack opened with the commander taking a calculated risk confident that his optimism was justified. Supply difficulties had reduced the number and variety of shells reaching the divisional artillery and, indeed, a crisis in supplies had been evident during the Soviet assaults of the previous day. Despite the very low stocks Kübler ordered that the last reserves of shells should be used to support the attack which he claimed, in an Order of the Day, would bring victory that day.

Just as the mountain men had been determined that they would stand fast to win or die, so did the Russian infantry, in like fashion, contest the German advance. The area was one in which the Soviets had had time to construct extensive trench systems fronted by barbed wire and backed by artillery. Against these deep field fortifications and with the assault weakened by a too-short bombardment the Jäger assaults were baulked and made little ground, while the men of 1st Battalion of 477th Regiment, temporarily attached to the division, suffered so heavy a loss and were so shaken by the tenacious Russian defence that they withdrew to their start lines and gained not a metre of ground. During the afternoon, the Jäger of 13th Regiment after battling unsuccessfully for the greater part of five hours halted the attack and began to dig in on the saturated battlefield but came under almost immediate assault of fresh regiments of Russian infantry storming out of Kopyenkovata.

It is a measure of the respect that fighting soldiers have for each other that German war diaries recording the events of the day paid tribute to the heroism of the Russian soldiers who, whether in attack or defence, had fought bitterly and often to the last man. Whatever the politicians and propagandists may have claimed in far-away Berlin, the Jäger of the Eastern Front recognised and lauded the valour of their opponents.

Both sides were now facing a crisis in supply as the roads, impassable through rain and mud, halted the movement of wheeled and even tracked vehicles. The Russians with their greater numbers of aircraft began an air drop of essential supplies to their troops; the Germans relied upon the portering power of their Jäger.

The battle was reaching a climax and Russian pressure was growing but however determined the Russian attacks or staunch their defence, the line around them was becoming more solid and gaps, formerly covered only by patrols, were tightly closed. The 477th Regiment and the men of the 91st now formed a solid front facing eastwards, but on either flank of the isolated 2nd Battalion of the 91st Regiment there were areas of seemingly impassable terrain which had been left uncovered. Behind the main front of 91st stood the divisional reconnaissance battalion which, together with elements of the divisional artillery and the 2nd Battalion/99th Regiment, formed a long stop to intercept and to capture any groups of the enemy which might filter through. Behind that group was another reserve, made up of a few companies of pioneers who, equipped with heavy weapons, were given the task of destroying any who eluded the first long stop unit.

Still anticipating that enemy resistance was crumbling, Corps passed a confident message to 17th Army during the evening of 6 August. "All the divisions of Gebirgs Corps are at this moment going over to a general and all-out assault to administer the coup de grâce to the enemy around Podvyssokoya." This confident message

found no similar response in the hearts of the Jäger. The marching
and counter-marching exhausted the men who saw no point in reaching one place only to be marched back again to the starting point. The
trenches in which they spent their time when not on the march were
deep in water. They were soaked through. Little hot food was coming forward to them for the roads were as impassable to mules as
they had been for days past to wheeled traffic. The Corps commander, conscious of this lowering in the high spirits of his men,
gave orders that each man was to be told of the great strategical
prizes for which they were fighting and which the constant marching
would help to bring about. The Jäger, heartened by the concern
which General Kübler showed, then marched and fought with renewed confidence.

On 3 August there had been the first Russian probes to find
weaknesses in the German line. On the following day the first snowball attempts were made to roll over 91st Regiment, pre-empting the
all-out Corps assault which then went in only to meet head on the
great Russian break-out attempt. During the fighting which followed
the battle swayed at one time in favour of the Germans and then to
the advantage of the Soviets. There was confusion and chaos as
masses of Red Army troops flooded across the countryside impelled
by the pressure of other troops behind them. None knew from minute to minute whether the sound of tank tracks heard through the
darkness meant that the Russian armour was moving forward in
waves against them. The Red enemy was everywhere at once and
struck at a great number of places simultaneously.

The artillery fire which heralded the Russian offensive was taken
by the Jäger in their trenches to be nothing more than a rather heavy
early morning barrage and they, therefore, showed scant concern at
its severity. Then instead of the gun fire halting, as it usually did after
half an hour's bombardment, it continued and even grew in intensity.
From the northern end of the pocket the line of fire flickered down
the perimeter to encompass the whole front and when it reached the
area of the Gebirgs divisions it grew to be a deafening roar. At other
points along the sectors held by the mountain men the sound of tank
engines presaged armoured assaults upon the exhausted Jäger and
then at 02.45hrs the 13th Regiment reported a mass movement out
of Kopyenkovata striking at its 3rd Battalion. Fifteen minutes later
an artillery battalion reported that its position was under attack by

tanks and then at 04.00hrs the heavy howitzers, deep in the rear of the division, signalled that they were under heavy and direct assault by Russian infantry. It was clear that the enemy had broken through in massive strength and at a number of places. Some of these were the seemingly "impossible" terrain areas and the whole of these groups had bypassed some of the Jäger positions. Less than two hours after the howitzer report had come in divisional headquarters came under assault. Now it was no time to claim that an orderly's duties or a signaller's task exempted one from having to take up arms. Now it was a matter of fight or die and each man of the headquarters, including the staff officers, went out to battle against the swirling hordes of Red Army men who flooded through the narrow streets of Peregonovka. The houses of that little town, poor in construction though they were, offered some sort of rallying point around which an all-round defence could be formed. Each hovel became a little fortress from which bullets poured in streams of bright-coloured tracer to strike the Soviet groups.

Intending to exploit the gap which it seemed had been torn in the Jäger line, a convoy of lorries bearing Red Army headquarters staffs and infantry roared through Peregonovka's narrow streets. A hail of shells from guns of the anti-tank battalion struck and set alight some of the vehicles. The lorries were head to tail and two abreast so that those in the village could not manoeuvre and those outside could only bypass the blazing barricades by bouncing across the fields where they came under fire from other anti-tank guns. More and more lorries went up in flames. Men jumped and ran from them. Explosions showed where some of them had been carrying fuel or ammunition and the Russian death ride to smash through Peregonovka and to cross the Yatrani river was thrown back with heavy loss. The lorries withdrew into the darkness, reformed and then changed the direction of their break-out attempt heading for Polonistoya. In that place there were other groups of German infantry, Gebirgs pioneers and men from the Flak batteries who met the Soviet storming drive and flung it back not once but a succession of times.

Each detachment of 4th Gebirgs Division was now fighting its own individual battle. Telephone lines had been cut; it was suicide for runners to attempt to cross the battle zone but the wireless was still working, although subject to distortion and interference. It was by means of wireless messages that the divisional commander ordered his major units to create hedgehog defence positions around the villages which they were holding until the situation had been restored and relief could reach them. It was accepted that this might take some time as the divisional reserve had long since been committed. Across the whole of the southern sector of the ring fierce battles raged as companies of Jäger fought off attacks by whole regiments of Russians, the Jäger standing almost back to back in the houses or shoulder to shoulder in the open firing into the khaki masses toiling across the sodden ground towards them.

Along the front of 1st Gebirgs Division the fighting was no less severe. One assault begun at 07.00hrs on the morning of 6 August was the first of a series of infantry and armour attacks intending to take the village of Podvyssokoya and the crossroads to the south-east. In their efforts to capture the village the Soviets poured out men in hopeless and suicidal attacks. The first houses fell to the storming Red assaults and then a few more. Fighting went on in the small gardens and above the houses smoke rose where houses were set alight by shell fire or deliberately to force the Germans to evacuate. The fighting went on and on without pause or let up and the garrison holding the village suffered more than one hundred dead to hold it. The Lang battle group was also heavily involved and the fighting against its detachments was frequently hand to hand, man to man. Ammunition began to run short, two company commanders fell at the head of their men, casualties among NCOs were abnormally high, but still the Jäger fought on and none either left his position or retired. It was battle at its most ferocious and its most basic. There was only victory or death.

Slowly Corps HQ began to form a clear picture as the confused situation began to resolve itself. The Soviet attacks had at some points in 4th Division sector by-passed the defensive line and the long-stop units of the reconnaissance battalion and the artillery regiment. The main Soviet effort had been made in a gap which they had located between 3rd Battalion of 477th Regiment and 3rd Battalion of the 91st Jäger. Although the other divisions and regiments of Corps had fought hard, nowhere had the battle been heavier or bloodier than between Peregonovka and Polonistoya, and the fighting for those two gateways to freedom was still continuing as assault followed assault. The Corps flanks had held firm but in the centre the situation was still fluid and uncertain for the Red Army had made such deep penetrations that the danger of a complete Russian break-through seemed very possible.

Not until midday was this uncertainty cleared to a great extent when, as a result of aerial reconnaissance, the interrogation of high-ranking Red Army commanders who had been taken prisoner, and confident wireless messages from surrounded German units, a whole picture emerged. This showed that everywhere the massive Russian effort had collapsed. The offensive had been launched from a starting point in the woods to the north-west of Kopyenkovata and from the area of Podvyssokoya. Despite a succession of major assaults by units from Soviet 6th Army, mainly from units of 16th and 2nd Tank Corps, two armoured and two motorised divisions, the breakthrough attempts had been held and flung back with heavy loss to the at-tackers. The dangerous situation wherein a wedge had been driven between the two Jäger regiments of 4th Gebirgs Division and a com-plete rupture had threatened was no longer a threat, for the units which had escaped had been intercepted and destroyed by rear eche-lon units of Corps. As an example of the efforts made by such units is the story of one battery of 4th Division's artillery regiment which alone and in an open position destroyed 110 lorries, a tank and six-teen guns as well as taking over 800 prisoners. The battery hastily unlimbered outside Slyessaryenko and had had no time to choose better firing positions than those which it took up in a field of maize. The ground had no rise from which observed fire could be directed and the nearest Jäger company was more than 2kms distant. Scarcely had the guns been unlimbered when the Russian offensive began and within hours the first Soviet assaults had begun to infiltrate through the Jäger lines and to reach the artillery's positions.

Throughout the night small arms fire and the occasional shrapnel shell had held the Soviet soldiers in check but with daylight their at-tacks grew bolder as they saw how isolated the battery was. Then the gunners worked at a frenzied pace to destroy the enemy who began his series of assaults with infantry, continued with cavalry and ended with a lorried attack spearheaded by armour. At times the gun layers had to reduce the range to less than 250 metres, that is to say they were in effect firing over open sights. When the final Soviet attack had been crushed and the battery was stood down an ammunition check showed that its guns had fired more than 1150 rounds, which represented a greater amount of ammunition fired off during that one offensive than had been fired by the battery during the whole campaign in France during 1940.

Wherever it had been baulked the Red flood had turned and twisted seeking an escape route. At one point the Soviet drive deflected by artillery fire turned westwards hoping to avoid the gunners but ran onto the flak guns of 1st Battalion of the anti-aircraft regiment and was smashed in the quick destructive fire of the 88s. Following groups found a gap between the field guns and the flak battalion and by reaching Lyebidyinka succeeded in escaping from the trap but this last bolt hole was then quickly closed by an alarm company and subsequent attempts by other Soviet troops to use that route were halted.

Towards midday the fighting died down and across the wide fields around Uman there was a sudden quiet. The battle was over and the woods and valleys were full of Russian troops wandering about hoping to surrender or trying to hide. The whole area was littered with groups of abandoned lorries. Many of these had been smashed during the fighting, others had been set alight by their drivers while others had been the victims of a general conflagration as fire had jumped from vehicle to vehicle. The dead lay everywhere in groups. In those areas of the bitterest fighting the Russian fallen were piled one upon the other as fresh waves of attackers had been shot down as they clambered across the bodies of the already fallen. In places the dead were piled in layers three or four deep. Then there were the horses, their bellies swollen, legs stretched stiffly in death, covered with greenbottles and bluebottles which fed upon flesh decaying in the heat. Whole squadrons of Cossacks and their chargers lay where they had been cut down, horse and rider, in the fire of machine guns. For as far as the eye could see the signs were those of a broken army: rifles with their muzzles pushed into the soil, equipment abandoned and left, rows of boots which the Russian soldiers had, for some unknown reason, removed from their feet and left along the road sides. Empty shell cases, artillery horses dead in their traces, calcined bodies in the cabs of burnt-out lorries and the black oil slicks where flame throwers had destroyed some particularly determined Russian resistance.

The scene, dismal though it was, represented a German victory, but it needed still to be crowned and consolidated and this could only be achieved by continuing to attack. At midday the 13th Regiment went into the assault to destroy the last organised resistance on its sector and within hours had forced its way through the masses of Red Army men wandering aimlessly about and had gone on to capture Kopyenkovata. German units, cut off and encircled during the Russian offensive, were freed from their temporary encirclements and joined the general eastward movement. As the ring contracted it thickened and became more solid. Some battalions of the 91st Jäger Regiment which had, during the battle, been placed temporarily under the control of 1st Gebirgs reverted back to their parent unit and the drive continued on all sectors throughout the whole day.

Although there had been some surrender of Russian troops there were still major detachments with stronger powers of resistance and in the woods around Podvyssokoya there were units still determined to fight on with the hope of escaping. These last groups began their drive during the night of 7–8 August but it was a last gasp attempt and by early morning of 8 August the Soviet troops still uncaptured began to come over, many of them driving trucks filled with their comrades and passing down roads filled with other marching prisoners heading for the temporary prison camps which had been set up. As an example of the prisoner masses which had been taken the Corps war diary reported: "In the streets of Podvyssokoya and extending to the woods which lie outside the town are hundreds of Russian corpses who fell as they charged in wave after wave. Burnt-out tanks and lorries lie abandoned in the fields, the remnants of breakout attempts carried out during 5 and 6 August. In Kopyenkovata there are masses of artillery pieces of every calibre . . . the prisoners march in an unbroken column, eight abreast, on the road and the column stretches across the rolling countryside for a length of more than 10kms".

On other sectors, however, the desperate resistance continued and Russian troops still fought to the last man using all their native skills to ambush German patrols. It is no easy task for soldiers to fight on when on other sectors of the front the battle has stopped. Along much of the perimeter of what had once been the pocket around Uman the guns had been silenced and the Jäger were busy tending the wounded and counting the booty. But chiefly in the sector held by 4th Division the pockets of determined Russian infantry held out and needed to be brought in or destroyed. The great woods had to be cleared and sweeps by the Jäger through the dark green silences of the forests had nightmare qualities. The woods themselves were hostile territory and when to the natural obstructions were added the tricks of camouflage and patience, in which the Russian troops were expert, then the hatred of the German soldiers for this type of warfare becomes understandable. The Jäger losses in such operations may not have been enormous but they were a constant drain upon companies already much reduced in number.

Hating the woods and the dangers they concealed; fighting a skilful enemy who gave no quarter nor asked any, sniped at, wearied and plagued by the myriad stinging insects which infested the trees made the Jäger more determined to root out the Russian groups, and the fighting rose to peaks of ferocity unknown hitherto. Death was present in a number of hateful disguises. Little mines which blew off the feet of unwary Jäger, sharp-staked pits carefully camouflaged to trap the careless, snipers in tree tops, gloomy copses which became killing grounds for so many German patrols and seldom a sight of the enemy who moved silently and struck mercilessly. On the few occasions when he was brought to battle and the fighting was hand to hand, as it was in such close country, then the sharpened edges of entrenching tools would be blunted and bloodied as their wielders frenziedly clubbed their opponents, taking revenge for the miseries they were suffering in the dank woods. The task of clearing the remnants of the Red armies lasted until 13 August when the last organised groups were destroyed or captured. Whether other survivors of the shattered Soviet forces withdrew deeper into the forests and there formed the nucleus of later partisan detachments is unknown but is probable. For the tired Jäger the threat of guerrilla warfare was of less concern than the immediate need to rest and to recover from the ordeal through which they had passed. Temporarily at least, the days of fighting and marching were at an end and the whole corps rested upon the battlefield of Podvyssokoya.

The commander of 17th Army was well aware by 9 August, only three days after the massive Soviet offensive, that a great victory had been won and his Order of the Day reads:

Army Order of the Day

From the GOC 17th Army   Army HQ 9.8.1941

The Army, in collaboration with Panzer Group 1, has encircled and destroyed in the fighting around Uman, the Russian 6th and 12th Armies which opposed it.

The number of prisoners taken is more than 100,000 of whom more than 62,000 including the GOC of Russian 6th Army, were brought in by 17th Army. The enemy has suffered a bloody loss.

More than 100 tanks, 450 guns and masses of war material have fallen into the Army's hands. This victory has brought the Army's operations to a successful conclusion. The losses and effort have not been in vain. The 17th Army has, since the beginning of the war, brought in 90,000 prisoners of war, 780 armoured fighting vehicles and 950 guns.

All my officers and men may look back with pride on their achievement. To them all I send my warmest thanks and deep appreciation.

Stülpnagel

The final tally showed that on the field of battle lay more than 18,500 dead Russian soldiers and that in addition to guns and tanks over 4700 lorries and 4000 horses had been taken. Two Red armies, consisting of four infantry corps and three armoured corps, a total of twenty-five divisions, had been destroyed.

All this had been achieved for a total loss to the 49th Gebirgs Corps of 145 officers and 4861 men. It had been a hard-won victory.

The Year 1942

The Soviet winter offensive of 1941 finally petered out leaving the Red Army disappointed and low in morale. The Soviet soldiers had been indoctrinated with the slogan promises that revolutionary élan could not be resisted. They had believed that the great offensive would drive the Germans from the soil of Russia, but when spring came the men who had suffered so much and borne so much during the weeks of bitter warfare realised that for all their sacrifices they had failed in the objective of destroying the German Army in Russia. True, they had won back huge areas of Soviet soil from the invaders but Leningrad was still encircled; on the Central Front their capital was still threatened and in the south the riches of the Ukraine were still in German hands. The Red Army lost heart and it lost faith in itself. Harsh discipline was needed to restore the trust in the Party which the common soldier had lost and which was manifesting itself in large-scale desertions.

For its part the German Army had been frightened by the power of the Soviet offensive, its duration and by the ease with which the Soviets had overcome the problems of supply and reinforcement during the battle. When the Russian assault finished, the German Army in the field was in a disastrous condition. Out of a total of 160 divisions only 8 were capable of undertaking any type of operation. Seventy-three could not be considered for anything other than a defensive role and a further 29 so badly destroyed that they were fit for only limited defensive action. Two were completely burnt out. There were sixteen panzer divisions on the German Army establishment at that time. Between them they had only 140 "runners". Thus low had the German Army been brought within only eight months of the opening of the war. The summer of 1941 had indeed been the high water mark of German military might. Its élan was smashed in the winter of 1941 and never again was the Army to recover from the losses which it had suffered.

For the summer campaign of 1942, which Hitler insisted upon, there were over a quarter of a million fewer German soldiers in the line than there had been in 1941 and there was, therefore, a greater dependence upon the armies of Germany's allies to man the gaps in the battle line.

Of the seven Gebirgs divisions on establishment in 1942, the 2nd, 6th and 7th were in Lapland or Norway, the 3rd and 5th were in the Leningrad sector of the Eastern Front and the 1st and 4th were with Army Group South. Of all the Gebirgs divisions only two, the 1st and 4th, were to fight in the mountains and it is the account of their part in the summer offensive which forms the next account.

The Caucasus 1942

The first opportunity for the men of the 1st and 4th Gebirgs Divisions to fight in the high mountains for which they had been trained did not come until late in the German summer offensive of 1942, and this short account deals with the fighting carried out by 49th Corps of 17th Army in the Caucasus mountains of the Soviet Union during that operation.

To understand the background to the drive for the Caucasus it is necessary to go back to the middle months of 1942. The horrors of the first winter of war against Russia had shaken the German Army. The confident enthusiasm of the first months of "Operation Barbarossa" had died during the first terrible cold, but the failure of the Russian winter counter-offensive restored hope and some degree of confidence to the German soldiers. By the time that the Soviet offensive had been called off the Germans, still in occupation of vast areas of western Russia, were planning for a summer assault.

The Military were not happy at the prospect of another all-out effort and indeed had hoped that 1942 might be a fallow year, during which the armies could be built up to strength and equipped with new and proven weapons, ready to undertake the decisive offensive against the Soviets during 1943. Adolf Hitler, the Supreme Commander, had, however, decided to regain the military initiative and had conceived an ambitious plan. This was outlined in his Directive No. 45, which laid down the guide lines for the new offensive. This was a two-pronged assault to be opened by Army Group South. That host would divide shortly after the operation began to form Army Group "A" (List) and "B" (von Bock).

Army Group "B" was to drive eastwards towards Stalingrad and the Volga while Army Group "A" was to drive into the Caucasus. The first result of the successful execution of those tasks would be, as Hitler saw it, the paralysis of the Soviet war effort through the seizure of its principal oil fields. His directive laid down that the task of 17th Army was to occupy "the entire eastern coastline of the Black Sea . . . while a force composed chiefly of mobile and fast-moving units (Panzer Group 1) will capture the area of Grozny. . . . Thereafter the Baku area will be occupied by a thrust along the Caspian coast." The second result of the summer offensive would be the encircling by Army Group "B" of the enemy forces which had crossed the Don and their destruction; this to be followed by the pursuit of, and final elimination of, the Russian left wing somewhere in the Stalingrad sector and along the line of the Volga river.

It is not the task of this account, or of this book, to analyse the strategy of either side but the intentions of Adolf Hitler can only be described as wildly optimistic. He seemed to be unaware that as the Army Groups advanced each would move farther and farther away from the other, rendering them incapable of giving mutual help, and that this divergence would weaken the main drive. As examples of the Führer's inability to grasp the concept of space in strategy can be cited the distances that Army Group "A" would have to cover. Grozny, one of the objectives of Panzer Group 1, was more than 260kms from the Black Sea. From Rostov to Baku was 880kms (in a direct line), and the width of the Caucasus was over 1000kms. These distances and the vast area of front had to be covered and held by inadequate forces whose final objectives, hundreds of kilometres removed from the start lines, lay on the far side of the highest mountain range in Europe.

Hitler's decision prevailed against the logical, safe and, as he saw it, negative advice of his military commanders. The advances *would* be made and it is with the south-east drive into the Caucasus that we are principally concerned. The eastwards thrust concerns us only in that it became a running sore draining away from the thrust into Asiatic Russia the troop strength necessary to sustain it. Then, when the Russian offensive against Stalingrad destroyed the German 6th Army, the battle line on the left flank recoiled, drawing back with it the forces of Army Group "A" and taking them out of the Caucasus completely.

The operations in the Caucasus are interesting for a number of reasons. Firstly it was, as already stated, the first opportunity for the Gebirgsjäger to fight in that terrain for which they had been trained. In this connection is the second interesting point; that the Caucasus was the scene of a piece of typical Gebirgsjäger braggadocio, the raising of the German war flag and the planting of both divisional insignia on Mount Elbrus, the highest peak of the Caucasus. Thirdly, had the offensive succeeded not only would the war, on that sector, have passed out of Europe and into Asia, but the vast deposits of lead, silver, oil and timber would have been lost to the Russians and gained by the Germans.

The opening moves of the summer offensive of 1942 found 49th Gebirgs Corps holding the line of the Mius river, positions which its divisions had held since the Russian winter offensive. In July the Corps was ordered to prepare for an operation which would break out of the river line and spearhead the eastward drive. By 26 July all was ready and the units, back in the front line, had crossed the Don at Rostov and made good progress against the delaying actions of Russian rearguards.

On 6 August Corps, which had been marching eastwards through the Kuban steppes, was ordered to move southwards and by forced marches to reach the Caucasus mountains, there to seize and hold the passes in a fast assault. The regiments marched most of each day in blinding heat, plagued by thirst, mosquitoes and the insistent demands of the higher staff for a faster rate of march: for greater speed.

By 9 August the foothills had been reached and during that day Maikop, some 280kms south-east of Rostov, and Piyatigorsk, 187kms south-east of Maikop, had fallen to 17th Army's storming advance. The Jäger were nearing their natural habitat and already the sights and sounds of the high country were welcoming them. The wind that blew brought with it the coolness of the mountains whose shapes, lying low and unclear on the far horizon, grew clearer and taller with every kilometre that their weary feet marched.

The sudden decision to divert the advance of the Gebirgs Corps southwards, although a welcome but surprising one, was one fraught with difficulties. Corps was preparing to cross the highest mountains in European Russia and had neither information about the range nor the equipment to carry out the orders which it had been given. There was a shortage of pack animals to form the trains which would be needed to supply the fighting troops, to say nothing of a lack of the specialist clothing and weapons which were essential. Far more important than either of those two factors, however, was the absence of the many experienced Jäger who had been killed during the fighting years of the war and particularly in the battles with Army Group South in the Ukraine. Their loss was to be grievously felt.

Accurate intelligence is one of the keys to victory and in order that he would be in possession of every scrap of information about the new battlefield, General Englseer, commander of 4th Gebirgs Division, sent a staff officer to Munich to study books and to gather details on the Caucasus: its mountains, its peculiarities, peoples, fauna and climate. He could then return to division fully equipped with the knowledge needed for the 4th Gebirgs to play a decisive part in the forthcoming battle. His short, intensive study showed that the Caucasian mountains form the natural barrier between European Russia and the Near East, and include Mount Elbrus, the highest peak, rising to 5633 metres. In addition to the major range, higher than the Alps of Central Europe, there are secondary ranges which cover a large area and are made up of peaks, some of which connect immediately to the main features but most of which are separated from each other by valleys of great depth and length. The foothills of the whole Caucasus range spread north to the upper course of the Kuban and Terek rivers and in the south descend to the plains of Georgia.

The climate is of warm Riviera-type along the Black Sea coast with a drier and hotter climate, rather like that of southern Spain, in the region of the Caspian Sea. Although so different both types of climate have a common link of long periods of rain in the spring and autumn. The heaviest rainfall is on the Black Sea side reducing to only a tenth of that region's precipitation on the Caspian side. In

their east–west journey the rain clouds deposit nearly 4000 milli-
metres of rain upon the high mountains.

Dry weather is the rule in the central Caucasus during the summer
months and long periods of bad weather are rare, but even then there
is seldom a continuously fine spell. Changes, when they occur, do so
rapidly. The area is notorious for the thick mists which form and descend during the afternoon into the valleys, but the winds which
sweep through the passes dispel these quite quickly. Another phenomenon are the cloud masses which appear out of the south towards midday and cover the mountain crests.

That rain which falls on the northern side of the central Caucasus
massif often takes the form of snow which does not always thaw
quickly but remains for long periods in the steep valleys. The treach-
erous summer weather means that the high passes which are open in
February cannot be negotiated during May or June, except by men
issued with special equipment. Above the 3500-metre line is the region of perpetual snow and beginning in that frozen wilderness glaciers descend and often extend far down into the valleys.

Summer midday temperatures in the region of the highest passes
do not rise above 10 degrees centigrade and these can sink to minus
15 degrees during the night. In winter the temperature which is usually minus 25 degrees can sink during periods of severe storm to
minus 50 degrees. The strong winds for which the Caucasus is notorious create snow-drifts which can pile up to four metres deep in seconds. Thus there is on the steeper slopes of the range always the
danger of avalanche.

The conditions found on the Caspian side differ very markedly and
the rain which falls does not always turn into snow. The danger of
avalanches is, therefore, less but precipitations can turn the mountain
streams into raging torrents within a very short time.

The abundant forests of the northern foothills provide one of the
economic assets of the area. Then there are the oil fields at Maikop,
coal in the Kutaisi region as well as silver and lead mines.

The reports which the officer studied were very old, many of them
dating from before World War I. The information given was, in certain respects, not totally reliable, but summarised it showed that the
area was deficient in roads which brought the conclusion that possession of these means of communication was vital to the progress and
success of the campaign. The first of these roads was the military or

Army road to Sukhumi which crossed the 2800-metre-high Klukhor pass and which, although difficult, could be negotiated by transport. The main pass roads were of better design and construction. They included the Pseaskkha (2000 metres), Adzapsch (2500 metres), Chmakharo (2500 metres), Marukhskiy (2800 metres), Nakhar (2900 metres), Chiper (3200 metres) and Azau (3400 metres). The two most famous military roads in the area, the Georgian, to Tiflis via the Daryal pass, and the Ossetian, to Kutaisi over the Mamisson pass, do not feature in this account for they are outside the region held by the mountain corps.

When General Englseer's staff officer returned to divisional headquarters he found that Corps had been directed to thrust into the Caucasus and that the commander of 1st Gebirgs Division intended to send a party of his most experienced Gebirgsjäger to climb the summit of the highest mountain, Mount Elbrus, and on that peak to raise the German war flag. It is strange that it is that single, militarily pointless, mission which is the chief memory of the advance of 17th Army into the Caucasus, rather than the rapid capture of the high passes and the likely loss to the Soviet Union of its major oil fields.

With the stage set and the terrain described let us now consider the battles, but let me state at the outset that this account is not a description of the whole campaign. The movements of divisions and corps are of less interest in mountain warfare than the action of small groups of men holding positions isolated from their main force, enduring terrible hardships in regions of thin air and perpetual ice. The interviews with many Gebirgsjäger friends who served in the operations in the Caucasus mountains have been grouped together to form a single narrative which will in some fashion describe the life and experiences, the fighting in which they participated, and the conditions which they endured, during the autumn and winter of 1942.

You can have no idea of how excited we were at the prospect of seeing once again a range of mountains. And what mountains they were. These were completely wild and rugged, unlike our ranges at home which have been tamed and have good roads, tidy walks and trails clearly marked. There was nothing like that in the Caucasus, the mountains were as wild as on the day of Creation. Great stone boulders some of them over 20 metres high had to be rock-climbed. The pass roads were unbelievably bad and just like the Romans before us we built, or rather, rebuilt the roads as we advanced. They were not in their original state capable of being used by any sort of vehicle but we had soon made some of them so by sheer hard, stone-breaking, tiring work.

There were very few people in the area. By comparison our loneliest Alpine valleys can be said to be overcrowded. The natives were either Cherkassians or Kharachians and were Arabic-type people. They were bitter enemies of the Communist government which they saw as atheistic and in conflict with Islam, for they were Muslim. They had had the most shocking experiences under the Soviet government with mass deportations and mass executions, some of which had taken place as recently as 1938. These natives volunteered to fight for us and remained loyal even when it was clear that we could no longer hold the Caucasus and would have to withdraw.

God alone knows what they lived on for they seemed to be herdsmen or hunters and there was little cultivation that I saw. Perhaps the women did the agricultural work in remote patches of ground. We seldom saw any women and almost none of marriageable age. The very few we did see were splendid looking and as fearless as the men. The Caucasus was the only area I remember where eagles are frequently seen and some villagers catch and train the birds for hunting. The men are splendid horsemen, and living so close to nature has given them a channel of communication with animals, for they control their horses with unusual skill. The natives were skilled mountaineers but lacked our specialist equipment and could not even attempt the rock-climbing that we did. Their houses were stone and clean, unlike the bug-ridden hovels of the other parts of southern Russia in which we had fought. But like the other places there was a primitiveness which we would have found unacceptable at home. For instance, across most streams the only bridge was a tree trunk. This may have been suitable in summer but in icy conditions such things were dangerous and could not be tolerated. One tree trunk bridge crossed a chasm hundreds of metres deep; no guard rails, nothing. At home the local council would have organised the building of a safe bridge.

In the afternoon of most days cloud built up and shrouded everything in thick mist. Imagine trying to find and use a foot bridge in total darkness. We first strung cartridge cases to indicate the location of a crossing place until the pioneers had time to build more secure and safer bridges. Some of the native constructions must have been decades old and replaced others which had rotted away and had crashed down into the valleys.

In the mountains the hours of daylight are shorter than on the plain. This is because the peaks cut out the light. The high peaks from which we could see the dawn come up about 04.30hrs, cast shadows which meant that the light was not seen in the valleys until an hour later. Similarly, by the time that the sun sank on the peaks it had already been pitch dark in the valleys for nearly an hour. For those of us on the peaks there was between ten and twelve hours of daylight, but those in the valleys had no more than six. You can appreciate that supply trains to forward positions could not even make the ascent in a single day, and that there were more men on portering than in combat. This is, of course, a fact of mountain warfare that the ratio of porters is 3:1 over riflemen, but in the Caucasus because of the terrain difficulties this ratio rose to 4:1 in autumn and 8:1 during the winter. This imbalance covered only basic things like food, ammunition and clothing. The numbers required to move a wounded man in the worst period of winter rose at one time to a 12:1 ratio.

On the open mountain tops on clear nights there was sufficient star light for some illumination but in the valleys or in places away from the crests it really was pitch dark, and to add to the difficulties there was often fog. If this persisted it was because there was no wind but when it did blow the wind force was so strong that it was difficult to stand erect. When winter came this wind really was the icy breath of death and drove before it great drifts of snow, great white walls marching across the open slopes.

The cold was so intense that I cannot even now believe its severity. I have known of teeth fillings contracting, coming loose and then falling out. My own brother died of the cold. As a sentry he was in a forward position and when his relief came, and they changed every twenty minutes, three times to the hour, they found him standing frozen. He had died from internal freezing and this lowering of the body's resistance must be due to the poor rations and the living conditions. There were no houses in the forward zone in which we could shelter and after September we were in snow and ice the whole time. The first snows had fallen as early as 3 September.

We lived in tents or igloos and wore every piece of clothing that could be fitted. Rations came up man portered from kitchens in the nearest possible valley. It was a difficult but not particularly dangerous climb. We received our rations after dark and used the tinkling cartridge case system to indicate our positions when there were too few men to act as guides. Luckily our opponents were not all that good soldiers although they did improve later both in tactical skill and in mountaineering ability.

The first Ivans we met, about the middle of August, were a mish-mash, but then these were probably the survivors of the divisions which had opposed us on our drive from the Mius river. In the mountains proper we encountered soldiers who said under interrogation that they were from mountain regiments, but these were not true Gebirgsjäger. A number of them were quite elderly, more than 35 years of age, far too old for mountain warfare. Nor were these men Cherkassians but had come from low down on the Caspian Sea. They may not have been as skilled in mountain techniques as we were but they were first-class shots and were marvellous at camouflage. Their patrols were very patient and would hide in the snow of fresh avalanches until one of our patrols came up to flag a new route around the obstruction. Then Ivan would open up and often he would use anti-tank rifles against the rock walls to create fresh avalanches and to smother our patrol.

There was then a build-up of enemy strength in place of the scattered detachments backed by a few so-called mountain regiments whose divisions were brought into line out of the Trans Caucasus. Corps Intelligence positively identified the 20th Mountain Rifle Division, the 265th Regiment, 174th, the 64th and 379th Rifle Regiments as well as independent artillery and howitzer regiments. Although the 20th was described as a mountain rifle division it had had no formal training for that role and seemed to differ from a standard Red Army rifle division only in the large number of supply trains of mules and horses with which it was equipped.

The "mountain" units were put into the line to hold us; we were still advancing at that time [the early weeks of September] and were only 30kms from the Black Sea. The Red Air Force, always

in evidence whatever the tactical situation, was used in large numbers and used to side slip across the mountain crests bombing and
machine gunning everything, even individual soldiers. They frequently waited for the Red Cross Fieseler Storch aircraft which
evacuated our wounded, but their attacks were often unsuccessful
as the Storch was so manoeuvrable and could fly into valleys
where their faster YAKs could not follow. When the Reds recaptured the Pechu valley they had, once again, a forward field aerodrome from which they could give even closer support to their infantry and could also air drop supplies. We felt the loss of the
Luftwaffe very much.

At the end of September the German offensive in the east Caucasus failed and the main effort swung to the west. Even there the
Soviet troop build-up of non-specialist soldiers was sufficient to
hold the trained Jäger and, after a short advance down the Black
Sea coastline, the German offensive halted. The initiative had
passed to the Red Army and after a build-up period the Soviet
High Command concentrated on driving 17th Army out of the
Caucasus in a series of offensives lasting from November to March
1943.

Throughout the weeks of campaigning we had been fighting
without relief or reinforcement and even an Italian Alpine Corps
which was to have portered for us was diverted from our front and
taken to Stalingrad. That town on the Volga was an ulcer which
drained away the strength of the army group fighting there and
that of our own army group as well. The whole concept of the
summer campaign was faulty, in any case. Two armies diverging
upon separate objectives until a gap of over 1500kms separated
them. In that gap the Red Army could and did mass and through
it he struck to take us both in flank. The summer campaign was a
recipe for disaster.

Another serious situation which weakened our drive was the
emergence of a strong Soviet partisan organisation which struck
against our long and difficult lines of communication. Our battalions were all understrength and the rear echelons were combed
and combed again to produce men for the firing line. We had none
to spare for counter-insurgency operations. Our worn out weapons
were not replaced and in fact divisional units like the reconnaissance and the replacement battalions had their heavy weapons,

mountain equipment and pack trains taken away so as to supply the men in the forward positions. We were still confident of reaching our objectives even though we were weak in numbers and a sort of stalemate had set in because we were too weak to advance. We had achieved so much in so short a time. By the end of August we had seized the southern passes and had gone on to capture the highest parts of the Caucasus range. Then our one railway line back to Rostov had failed and for weeks nothing at all came through. When the track was repaired it could still only bring forward about two-thirds of our essential supplies. We were expected to live off the land but there was nothing to buy and our bread ration at one time was reduced from 600g per day to 120g. Still we hung on.

The Russian soldiers, with a shorter supply route, were even worse off than us. The Red Command was more concerned to bring ammunition rather than rations up to the front line and their troops lived on a diet centred around biscuits in the autumn and porridge in the winter. They also had a sort of pre-cooked rice and sugar. That and a small packet of tobacco among four men completed their ration.

Prisoners told us that in their supply columns each man portered 10 to 12 kilos of supplies or ammunition, in addition to his own equipment. Each company had its own column which brought up only ammunition or supplies, never rations, and the foot march from the railhead to the front line lasted between three and four days. Pack animals were used to bring up the heavy equipment but the animal losses in winter were so great, with the beasts freezing to death on the open peaks, that their use was discontinued and Ivan, the Russian infantryman, struggled through the deep drifts bringing up the ammunition. When the weather was so bad that the trains failed and all the rations had been eaten Ivan's officers told him, "Take what you need in the way of food from the German invader" and then they would attack us to seize our small rations. As prisoners they were surprised at the quantity and variety of the food we received although our rations were by that time quite poor.

It is almost impossible to imagine warfare in the high mountains. The air is thin and every moment, every step, is tiring. The lungs are starved of oxygen and just to think is an effort. The at-

Jäger of 1st Gebirgs Division climbing the 4,000-metres-high Mount Elbrus, during the summer campaign in the Caucasus, 1942, when an assault group conquered the peak.

A photograph of the highest mounted gun in action during the Second World War. It was mounted on the Asau glacier in the Caucasus, during the summer campaign of 1942.

A machine gun post of the divisional High Alpine battalion during the assault on the Dombai Ulgen, during the summer campaign of 1942, when the Gebirgs divisions fought in the Caucasus.

On 24 August 1942 the German War flag and the divisional insignia of the 1st and 4th Gebirgs Divisions were raised on the summit of Mount Elbrus in the Caucasus, after a special group drawn from men of both divisions had conquered the peak, the highest mountain in Russia.

Men of the 13th SS Gebirgs Division "Handschar" on an anti-partisan
operation in Bosnia. These soldiers were drawn from the Muslim
population of the region and were bitterly opposed to, and by, the Christian
peoples of other nations which made up Yugoslavia.

As Muslims they wore the fez and not the Gebirgsmütze, were deeply
religious and had strict dietary taboos.

A gun team of the "Prinz Eugen" anti-tank artillery in action against the partisans during the 5th offensive. The gun is the standard 3.7cm weapon but with special lightweight wheels for ease of transport in the mountains.

After the withdrawal from the Caucasus the 1st and 4th Gebirgs Divisions fought in the swamps of the Kuban bridgehead. Here a patrol is seen working its way through the swamps of that region of the Soviet Union.

Late in 1944 the Finnish government sued for peace and the German armies fighting in Finland had to retreat into northern Norway. This photograph shows the type of country through which the retreat was made.

The Gebirgsjäger used each and every type of animal to bring their food and equipment forward. In temperate climes they used mules and horses. In the Caucasus and other desert regions of the Soviet Union they used camels. In the icy conditions of the far north reindeer were used to pull sledges. This train of sledges is seen passing through a Finnish village at night.

The bitterness of the war in the Soviet Union impressed itself upon every German soldier who fought there.

Because of the difficulties in bringing supplies forward in the heavily forested and mountainous area of the Caucasus, engineers of the Gebirgs Corps set up cable railways to porter supplies and ammunition to the highest peaks from the valleys.

tacks which we made against Ivan or which he made against us were not the mass assaults of battalions, regiments or divisions fighting for strategic objectives but small groups of ragged men moving slowly and carefully across frozen wastes to take out a single machine gun post.

Ragged? Yes we were, and lousy too. We were all unwashed, unshaven and there were frost sores on our faces and hands. Our uniforms, worn continuously for weeks on end, were in rags. Our boots were wearing out, everything was becoming worn out and useless. We must have stunk but were only conscious of smell when we took Ivan prisoner and the Ivans did stink. By the end of September our battalions had sunk to the strength of companies, no more than 50 men strong, and some of our heavy units could not be employed as there were no men to use them. The line was being held by small battle groups who held sectors, in most cases far too wide for them to cover adequately. Across the sectors our patrols would range, up and down the valleys which were on our part of the front and in the front line there would often be only two men and a light machine gun every 50 metres or so. That was all the strength we had. Before us lay Ivan and behind him lay Asia.

By the onset of winter, visibility was almost down to single metres for much of the day. The afternoon cloud masses of autumn no longer dispersed and we lived in an opaque, twilight world of continual snowstorms. Through these swirling clouds of snow we would go out to attack some small irritating Red outpost and we would traverse the snowy slope, sending out the LMG's on the flanks to give covering fire while the main group went in with hand grenades or entrenching tools. Combat on the peaks was nearly always a matter of close-quarter fighting. Almost anything explosive, like hand grenades or mortars, lost half their effectiveness in deep snow.

When Ivan attacked there was none of the "Ooraying" nonsense which we had encountered on the flat terrain. Here every breath was precious and there was no shouting, even of orders. Economy of speech and gesture was the best way. They had a battle drill, so did we. Orders were unnecessary. Anyway the objects of most assaults at platoon or company level were tactical, intended to dominate no-man's-land, not to capture more ground.

During the worst winter period the Soviets moved back into the comparative warmth of the woods on the southern side of the range. Their front line was then held by cadets from military academies but even they deserted to us. Poor devils, they were completely new to mountain warfare and especially to battles in the depth of winter. Their rations consisted of cubes of frozen dried bread and cubes of frozen, dehydrated salted meat. They had to suck these slowly so as to extract the maximum benefit. Their Komsomol party books were of little use to them up on the peaks and they died in scores from exposure and other evidences of bad leadership. In fact from lieutenant downwards the leadership standards in the Red Army were abysmal and NCOs, who are usually the back-bone of any military system, seemed to be completely useless, certainly in abnormal conditions.

The exception to the poor quality of our opponents were the men from one of the Red Army's high mountain battalions. One of these men deserted on his second night in the line. He couldn't stand the cold or the loneliness. According to our Intelligence Officer's interrogation report there were five battalions of these troops all in action in the west Caucasus. They wore no steel helmets and were equipped with a higher than average number of machine pistols, light machine guns and mortars. Other than that they had little in the way of specialist equipment although each had been trained for three weeks in the use of crampons, ice picks and rope work. Their rations were soup in the morning, a millet porage at midday and soup or porage in the evening. On active service 35g of sugar per man was issued daily together with 500g of biscuit and a fifth part of a tin of meat. The specially prepared, high Alpine diet of concentrated foods that we could prepare quickly and turn into hot nourishing dishes were completely unknown to them.

I do not know how their wounded were evacuated but on our side to be wounded badly enough to be evacuated was to enter a private hell of suffering. With light wounds one stayed in the line hoping that the injury would not turn septic and gangrenous. One went for a dressing and returned to the company position again. It was a matter of honour not to leave the line for superficial wounds. Those which were so bad that walking was impossible were an unimaginable Calvary. In addition to the shock of being

wounded and then the pain of injury itself there lay ahead often
three days of portering, of being carried on a stretcher by relays of
men. Eight porters were required: four to carry and four to relieve
when the first team was exhausted. A system of relay stations was
set up and the wounded man would be passed through these receiving fresh treatment at each place. In the freezing cold, usually
in snow storms, or on the lower slopes in pouring rain, the bearers
would inch their way down the sodden, greasy surfaces of the
mountains, thankful when a stretch of flat ground made the going
easier. At a main dressing station accommodation was in wet tents
or dug outs. In fine weather a Fieseler Storch would sometimes fly
out two wounded men with each air-lift, but in winter the onward
journey had to be made by ox-cart or on a panje waggon. Many
never reached that stage of evacuation. By the time that the
wounded man had arrived at a main dressing station his wound
would have complicated by cold, lack of correct treatment or simply because he had been dropped by his bearers when they came
under mortar fire or attack by snipers. Legs shattered by shellfire
would have become, in the period from front line to dressing station, so putrefied that amputation, usually by the light of a hissing
carbide flare, was the only way of saving the soldier's life. Germany in the first post-war months, before the bulk of men held as
prisoners of war returned, was a land of one-legged or one-armed
cripples.

The depths of winter increased the misery of the wounded. Cold
produced apathy which in turn lowered resistance and the will to
fight and survive. To combat the severe cold sledges were filled
with straw, hot stones were heaped around the wounded and ther-
mos flasks of hot tea helped to keep the wounded conscious of
their predicament so that they did not slide off into sleep and then
death. The distances between relay points were reduced in the
winter, wooden poles were used on stretchers in place of metal
ones; paper bandages which retained body heat longer were used
in place of linen, and regular, frequent inspections of the wounded
were made to ensure that there was no alarming deterioration in
their condition.

When 1st and 4th Gebirgs Divisions were moved to the west Caucasus a single Jäger regiment was left to cover the area, a sector

nearly 100kms in width. The 99th went about its task of defending the region and of preparing for the worst of the winter weather in a most determined fashion. Along the whole of its 80kms-long line of communication to the forward dump, ration and evacuation points were established. The greatest part of that route could only be covered by man portering but to cover the whole route 200 ox-carts, 900 porters and 2000 animals were employed. The absolute daily minimum of supplies was 30 tons, of which the greatest amount was in ammunition and at any time no less than a third of the carts, animals and men were on the road forward, one third were on the return trip and the remainder resting from the strain of moving along roads of mud into which the mules often sank up to their bellies.

The last major German offensive to force a breakthrough to Tuapse opened in the second half of November. Battle groups struck through the Red lines and seized tactically important heights. The Soviets seemed to be in confusion but according to Grechko this was a tactic which brought success. In the vast emptiness of the mountains the small groups of German Jäger were swallowed up. Those who penetrated the Soviet lines were allowed to advance and then behind them Russian troops re-occupied the former positions to cut off the follow-up troops from the men of the spearhead detachments. The farther the assault units advanced the more isolated they were and against the overwhelming Russian counter-attacks the point units had to run the gauntlet of Soviet mountain battalions and were nearly wiped out. Those who did, after incredible battles against the enemy and the weather, reach the German lines were totally exhausted and unfit for future combat for weeks ahead. The mountain Corps had shot its final bolt and with the failure of this offensive passed on to the defensive, withdrawing under pressure from the masses of Red Army units which had now been brought into the battle.

The deteriorating position of Paulus's 6th Army, and indeed of the whole German right wing, now placed both 17th Army and 1st Panzer Army in the gravest peril and during January 1943 the great withdrawal began, out of the high country of the Caucasus and into the fever-ridden swamps of the Kuban bridgehead. "The Caucasus Round Trip" had ended but before this chapter closes let us recall, once again, that assault upon the Elbrus carried out by selected teams taken from the most skilled mountaineers in the Gebirgs corps.

The real ascent to conquer the Elbrus peak began on 17 August and by last light of that day the group which would be making the assault had reached the point past which all portering would have to be carried out by the men themselves. Ahead lay a glacier and behind that vast sheet of perpetual ice lay the twin peaks of the mountain. Last light comes early in the mountains and although it was only 17.00hrs twilight had fallen when on the following day the men, each of them carrying between 35 and 45kgs of equipment, reached a hotel which they named the "Elbrus Hut". There the actual assault group and the portering groups rested and an attempt was made on 19 August to rush the peak. The attempt was driven back by shocking weather conditions. The Elbrus was not to be taken that easily.

The point group did cross the giant glacier, however, and began the final assault at midday on 20 August but was driven back and rested in the "Elbrus Hut" until the following morning. At dawn on 21 August the assault group set out. Thick fog forced the climbers to march on compass bearings and before the journey had been half completed bad weather set in. By now it was a case of win or turn back and the assault group forced their way forward in fog, with visibility of only a metre, and through a blinding snow storm. By 11.00hrs the summit had been reached, the national flag raised and the divisional insignia nailed into the flag staff. The Gebirgsjäger of the German Army stood on the highest peak of the Caucasus range.

The triumph was short-lived. When the Red Army offensive crossed the area and almost as a first priority an assault group from the Red Army scaled the Elbrus, found the remnants of the Gebirgsjäger enterprise, flung these away and raised above the point on which the Germans had flown their war flag, the banner of the Soviet Union.

C'est magnifique, mais ce n'est pas la guerre.

The Years 1943–1944

The year 1943 saw the confounding of German hopes. The great summer offensive to take out the vast Russian salient around Kursk failed to achieve the successes which Adolf Hitler had hoped for and, thereafter, except for victories of a purely local and tactical nature, the German Army in the East was forced to take a defensive posture.

In the rear areas of the German Army fighting in the Soviet Union and in the Balkans guerrilla movements had sprung up and were drawing away from the main battle line the ground forces which were needed to stem the Russian assaults. More and more often Gebirgsjäger formations were engaged in battles against the partisans: in France, Italy and, principally, in Yugoslavia.

To overcome the problem in the Balkans the SS High Command raised their own Gebirgs divisions of which the 7th, "Prinz Eugen", is the most famous. It is no part of this book to describe the bestialities which were carried out, by both sides, against the troops and civilians of the other, but guerrilla wars are known for their bitterness and destruction. Certainly the partisan raids and the anti-partisan operations were carried out in every country of occupied Europe with a fanatical ruthlessness.

The Gebirgs divisions of the German Army now stood on every battle front. The 1st was in the Balkans; 2nd, 6th and 7th were in Lapland; and the 3rd, 4th, and 5th on the Eastern Front. In Tunisia a newly raised Gebirgsjäger Regiment, the 756th, formed in Austria as the "Kriemhilde Regiment" and sent to North Africa, was engaged in battle with the British 1st Army. In the fighting around Long Stop Hill near Medjez el Bab its three battalions were all but destroyed in a series of attacks known as the Battle of the Peaks, and the survivors were taken prisoner when the campaign in Africa ended in May 1943.

1944 was a bitter year for Germany both politically and militarily: a foretaste of the greater bitterness that came in 1945 when the Third Reich, its cities destroyed by aerial bombardment and its armies cut to pieces by the victorious Allied armies, collapsed in ruins.

The collapse of Army Group South in 1943 had allowed the Red Army to gain jumping off points west of the Dnieper river and the failure of the German summer offensive of July passed the initiative firmly into the hands of the Red Army. The STAVKA did not maintain the pressure on the southern flank but moved it northwards. The siege of Leningrad was raised, Minsk the capital of Byelo Russia recaptured and the German battle line just west of Kiev pushed back to the pre-war frontier with Poland. Then the full might of the Red Army struck again in the south and in fast dramatic advances the Russians entered Bulgaria and Romania forcing those countries to desert Germany. Not only were they compelled to ally themselves to Russia but, as a token of good faith, had to find military contingents to fight against their former allies. The 1st and 4th Divisions together with other formations of Army Groups South were driven back into the Carpathians where for some time they were able to hold the storming Russian onslaught. The Soviet point of maximum pressure then passed northwards again, soon the Hungarian border had been crossed and the capital city of Budapest surrounded and then captured. In the far north Finland, too, had been compelled to sue for terms and the Gebirgs divisions on that front were soon moving out of Finnish territory and into northern Norway.

In Italy the 5th Gebirgs Division was involved in the bloody battles around Cassino and then, in the autumn, in the delaying action fought out in the Gothic Line. The Anglo-Saxons invaded western Europe and by the end of the year stood, at some places along the battle front, on German soil. The advance could not be halted for long, and even though a major German offensive was opened against the Americans in the Ardennes during December, this was only a temporary setback to the Allied march of conquest.

Finland 1944

By the end of 1944 the German Army was fighting a wholly defensive war. This statement demands the qualification that there were, of course, areas in which, and times at which, its units undertook successful but tactical counter-offensives. In the main, however, the German Army had been forced to accept the bitter truth that no longer had it the strength to carry out an offensive strategy and that henceforth, and until the end of the war, it would no longer be a force which carried out acts of military initiative but one which had to react to the moves of its opponents.

By the end of 1944, too, Germany's former allies had begun to desert her and to withdraw their soldiers from the battle line. Some nations did not merely capitulate to the Russians and remain, thereafter, passive but took up arms against and participated in active military operations against their former comrades with whom they had fought shoulder to shoulder. Others less militant demanded only that there should be an immediate evacuation of their land. One such nation was Finland which had left the war on 2 September 1944 and which had been one of Germany's staunchest allies.

With the loss of Finland and thus the whole of the far northern area running from Archangel to Leningrad, the German Army's flank in the Baltic countries was placed in jeopardy. Between Army Group North on the Baltic and 20th Gebirgs Army garrisoning Norway there now yawned a gap which could not be filled. The withdrawal of the German forces in Finland having been demanded and acceded to, meant, so far as those divisions and corps in central and southern Finland were concerned, that they would have to undertake a march of nearly 1000kms, because there were insufficient ships in German service to bring them home by sea. The long march would take the retreating formations out of central Finland and northwards to that point in Scandinavia where the frontiers of Finland, Sweden and Norway met. Once the troops had passed from Finland into Norway they would be held there to reinforce the garrison, a garrison whose commanders daily anticipated an invasion by an Anglo-American army.

Of all the troops on the establishment of the German Army in
Finland it is with the exploits of one division, 7th Gebirgs Division,
with which this short account will deal. The 7th, on active service
on the Eastern Front and, specifically, in Soviet Karelia, had to disengage itself from the Russian enemy then to march into Norway.
That it would be pursued by the Red Army was anticipated, but it
was further hoped that the Finns would remain at least passive, and
at best unwilling to harry their erstwhile comrades in arms. This
proved to be a vain hope and it is with the march of the 7th Gebirgs
Division to Rovaniemi, capital of Lapland, that this account deals.

Only an outline of the whole story is given but these details will
show the difficulties that the Gebirgsjäger troops underwent as they
were forced back to their homeland from which they had set out on
roads to conquest so many years before.

The order to evacuate Finland was issued to 18th Gebirgs Corps,
part of the Lapland Army, during the night of 11–12 September and
the 7th Division, forming part of that corps, left the positions which
it had been holding in Russian Karelia ready to undertake the long
foot marches that would be necessary if it was to evacuate Finnish
territory within the agreed time and thus to avoid the danger of falling into Soviet hands as prisoners of war. Day after day the regiments carried out the long and exhausting marches that would carry
them into Norway. The minimum distances covered during those
weeks was 30kms daily, but more often the rate was 50kms and
sometimes more. Often the marching columns were soaked by the
autumn rain so that, wet through, they would have to lie down for
the night in wet uniforms on sopping ground, hoping that the gale
force winds would not blow away their tiny two-man tents. When the
rain finally stopped falling out of the low flying, heavy grey clouds,
the soaked trees of the forests continued to drip for hours. Those
damned forests whose mysterious silence drove the soldiers into fits
of depression. The closeness of the trees limited all horizons and this,
to men who had been accustomed to view panoramas of mountains
of incredibly far distances, was the most miserable aspect of this war
in the arctic regions. These mountain men were fighting just above
sea level in stinking swamps. They enjoyed no vistas seen from high
peaks, just the small horizons and the aching loneliness of unending
forests where nothing grew but the trees and where the only wild life
with which they had any close contact was vermin.

We were all completely lousy all the time, except when we went home on leave, and there were field mice everywhere. Any dug out had a garrison of mice almost before the pine boards which lined the inside walls had been put in place. These little animals chattered, whistled and scampered about the whole time behind the wooden boards. Only in one sense were they useful. Either their hearing was extra sensitive or they had a sixth sense. Whatever the reason may have been it was a fact that before a Soviet bombardment or an air raid their noise would increase in volume and they would scurry about more than usual. They were a very reliable and efficient air raid warning.

The terrain of Finland is remarkable for the great number of lakes which are to be found throughout the length and breadth of the whole country. In those silent lakes and in the marshes there bred millions of mosquitoes, midges and other winged insects. These pests made the life of the soldier almost unbearable. Anti-mosquito nets were worn draped over the helmets or caps and were tucked into the neck of the shirt or jacket. But these were only effective if they were not disturbed. Any movement of the head brought the net out of the collar and exposed the wearer to swarms of buzzing, biting insects which were attracted by the salt sweat.

The nets were as useless as the anti-insect tar-oil that was issued and the only really effective repellent was smoke. Almost every soldier soon had his own home-made thurible. The most primitive of these smoke-pots were empty food tins while, at the other end of the scale, there were glistening shell cases from the infantry guns. The perforated container was unimportant. It was the content of the container which mattered and this was a filling of damp wood chips laid on glowing ashes. The greater the volume of smoke produced the more effective was the pot. A string or wire handle enabled the owner to be always accompanied by his own smoke cloud whose pungent smog may perhaps have kept the pests away but which certainly did make the eyes run and leave them red and inflamed.

Flies were, as everywhere, an everlasting plague and were neither driven off by smoke nor affected by height as mosquitoes were. These latter seemed unable to fly above the height of four metres and the tormented soldiers even climbed trees so as to avoid them. Flies seemed to breed by the million in Finland, probably because there were so few birds and thus no natural predators to keep the numbers in check. The usual fly-borne diseases were thus endemic in summer.

In *Kaputt,* a book written by Curzio Malaparte, he described the misery of life in the forests of Finland. The unending stretches of gloomy pines, the isolation, the feeling of imprisonment and the absence from the mountains engendered within the troops a neurosis which led to a higher than average rate of suicide, by shooting, hanging or drowning.

But now, in late 1944, the dripping trees, the grey skies, the vermin and the emptiness were all being left behind as the divisions marched northwards. On 24 September at Ylmaa, the 218th Gebirgsjäger Regiment of 7th Gebirgs Division halted to form the division's rearguard and to hold off the Red Army's attacks or to defeat the infiltration and encirclement of their units by men of the Finnish rifle battalions. Marching some distance behind the 7th came the 6th SS Gebirgs Division "Nord", with the task of forming the rearguard for the whole Lapland Army in its northward retreat.

Before it had prepared its defence thoroughly the 218th Regiment was fired upon as the Finns tried to obstruct the movement of the German Corps. The days were filled for the men of the 218th with marching, with digging positions then holding off the assaults by elite Finnish troops whose orders had been now changed and who had been directed to fight their former comrades in arms. Step by step the 218th withdrew through the bitter woods forcing back the enemy and holding him off until the main body of the division had begun its daily march. One terrible night, after hours of combat the orders came for the rearguard, the 1st Battalion of the 218th, to detach itself from the enemy and to withdraw. This instruction was soon countermanded. Information was received that forty badly wounded Gebirgsjäger had still not been evacuated because no transport had come up and none knew how long it might be before the ambulances did arrive. The rearguard was ordered to stand fast to protect the movement of the wounded who were lying weak and soaked through from the torrential rain which was falling over the battlefield. Soon the 1st Battalion had been surrounded but the order was still to hold and to maintain the positions allotted. A small number of ambulances came forward through the dark and rainy night, evacuating small numbers of men with each journey, until at last only fifteen remained. Still the line held and then late in the night the last vehicle

had gone bearing its freight of wounded men and the Jäger of
1st Battalion were allowed to withdraw, force-marching their way
through the Finnish encirclement to gain touch with the main of the
regiment. On 11 October there was another and more serious rearguard action to withstand Finnish pressure which was now being exerted against the whole of the German line of withdrawal. The battle,
so far as 7th Gebirgs Division was concerned, was fought around
Taipolo to the north of the important centre of Rovaniemi. It was a
struggle which was to last for days.

Major groupings of the division were surrounded in the fighting
which threatened to outflank the formations, but these battled their
way through the rings of encircling Finns, often engaging in hand to
hand combat and in desperate bayonet charges to break the enemy's
clutch. The Gebirgsjägers' final drive, mounted by 3rd Battalion of
218th Regiment, was fought under appalling conditions with the
Jäger having to wade waist-high through swamp and across flooded
streams to reach, engage and to destroy their enemy. The threat to
the division's flank had been dealt with and, through this last assault,
the Finns were shown that 7th Gebirgs Division was a unit whose morale was high and intact. Rovaniemi the capital city of Lapland was
held until the last soldiers of its own 18th Corps had crossed the
bridges and had marched out of town. Closing up towards Rovaniemi
came the SS Division and some time between the evacuation of the
town by the one Gebirgs unit and its occupation by the other mountain men an unexplained and sad event took place.

It must be understood that Rovaniemi had been the headquarters
of the German Army in Lapland and that it was the communications
centre of the whole region. With a population of 3000 Rovaniemi
was not much more than a very large village, but its size bore no
relation to its importance, its vital importance to the German troops
who were moving towards Norway. Columns of marching soldiers
were forbidden to pass through the centre of the town for otherwise
traffic jams would have been produced. Military policemen were on
duty to reinforce this ban. To clear a field of fire, should a strong
defence be necessary, it had been planned that some of the buildings
near the banks of the river would be blown up, but no further destruction was intended. During the night of 14 October, however,
fires broke out and two civilians, a man and a woman, were found by
the military in the town otherwise totally deserted by the civilian

population. So complete had been the evacuation that even the fire brigade and the police had left. Only German military rearguards were still in the place. Whether the captured civilians had in fact been the arsonists was not determined, but the wooden buildings constituting 98 per cent of Rovaniemi caught alight and created a blaze which had soon grown too great to be controlled by the troops still in the town. In attempts to isolate the blazes pioneer troops blew up houses to create firelanes but thereby only more damage was created. Then came a tragedy. It was found that a goods train which was standing in the station was loaded with explosives and shells. A locomotive was quickly obtained, steam was raised and by using an armoured fighting vehicle to add power the train was brought away from the flames. But a few hours later, and inexplicably, it was brought back again into the station where the highly dangerous cargo was soon alight and exploding. Shells whizzed through the air to explode on houses in the town; heavy detonations shook the whole area as mines and rocket charges blew up and burning fragments were flung far and wide to begin other fires.

There was nothing that the soldiers could do to save the town and this chain of accidents resulting in the destruction of Rovaniemi has passed into many accounts of the battle as an example of the atrocities against property caused by SS troops.

The explosion caused a number of casualties, and flying glass from blown out windows caused many severe eye injuries. The few dead of the rearguard killed in the town, together with 53 men of the Gebirgsjäger regiment who had been killed in action, were laid to rest in Finnish soil. Fifty-three dead in a casualty list of 217 men of the regiment lost as dead, wounded or missing.

Although long and arduous marches and terrible weather lay ahead of the 7th Gebirgs Division before at last it passed over into Norway, its aggressive action was directly responsible for the fact that 18th Gebirgs Corps was able to evacuate the Rovaniemi region without being further molested by the Finns.

The Year 1945

It was during 1945 that a tottering Germany crashed in defeat. In the first week of January the fighting in the Ardennes, which Hitler had anticipated would destroy the Anglo-American armies in north-west Europe, was dying away in the snows of Luxembourg. Then, on 13 January, the Russian winter offensive opened on the Central Front. With a superiority of at least 7:1 in their favour, the Red Army's 163 divisions of infantry, cavalry and tanks, numbering more than two million men and six thousand armoured fighting vehicles, struck across the Vistula and before the Soviets halted, as a result of outrunning their supply columns, they had charged across the pre-war German frontier and had established bridgeheads on the west bank of the Oder.

In the East the end was not far off. Nor was it in the West where a massive force of Allied divisions was fighting its way towards the Rhine across which it then passed in assault craft and by airborne descent. Down in the low mountainous country of Württemberg, from whose Kingdom a Jäger company had been raised to help form Germany's first Gebirgs units in 1915, the 2nd Gebirgs Division, lately arrived from Lapland via Denmark, was embattled against the US army. Hitler, fearing a British attack upon Norway, had refused to withdraw his first-class, up-to-strength division in garrison there and both the 6th and 7th Gebirgs Divisions ended the war without having been committed to action during 1945. In Italy the German collapse came in April and in the general debacle the 5th and 8th Gebirgs Divisions, the latter newly raised, were taken captive.

It was on the Eastern Front that the final great offensives took place. One of Hitler's plans to recapture Budapest bled to death in

February 1945, stuck in Hungarian mud. Immediately after the battle and without waiting to regroup the Red armies of the Russian left wing thrust into Austria and Czechoslovakia. On the establishment of the German armies holding those countries were the 1st, 3rd and 4th Gebirgs Divisions, soon to be joined by a 9th Division, one of two with the same number and both raised at the same time.

On 17 April the last great Russian offensive of the war in Europe opened along the whole line. At some places advances of 20kms per day were registered; at others the tenacity of the German defence limited these to less than a single kilometre, but the movement was always maintained and continued until, during the second week in May, the most destructive war in European history was brought to an end.

The final account in this book is the action of a Gebirgsjäger regiment, the 99th, in eastern Austria. The one regret that I had when that account was written was that lack of space stopped me from describing another and smaller Gebirgsjäger unit. This was battle group Ringel, a scratch group of convalescents, recruits and volunteers who, armed with three cannon taken from a Graz museum, not only drove the Russians back in eastern Steiermark from Feldbach to the Riegersburg, but held that line, a salient driven into the Soviet front, until after the armistice had been signed.

In those last weeks of battle along the Eastern Front there were many units which were rolled over in the Russian advances; some crushed under a frightful barrage of shells or pulped beneath the wide tracks of the T 34s. There must have been many companies caught in the great retreat whose men died, fighting back to back and to the last round. There must have been many such but they died anonymously, their battles unrecorded. A full account of the 99th's part in the last fight was written and it describes those days in great detail. The 99th Regiment is one of the few, the very few, units which, in the bewildering days of May 1945, maintained a record and it is upon that and the stories of friends both military and civilian that I have drawn for this closing episode.

Austria 1945

Above some battlefields hangs, like a thick and suffocating cloud, an awareness of the tragedies which occurred there and no visitor to say, for example, the Somme or to Waterloo can fail to sense in those places an atmosphere so strong as to be an almost tangible thing.

The battleground of which I now write is almost unknown to the ordinary British traveller and those who do not know the Austrian province of Styria must accept my word that it too is haunted. Not that it has either the brooding horror of Waterloo or the melancholy of the Somme. Rather it evinces a sense of outrage that modern war should have crossed its dreamily gentle forested hills and its imposing mountains.

It is an area that I knew as a soldier of the army of occupation and in the weeks of my first arriving in the province, during the late summer of 1945, the evidences of heavy fighting were present everywhere. Any drive in those first weeks, particularly in the more remote rural areas, passed burnt-out SPs and personnel carriers. The woods were still thickly sown with mines, the dead interred singly under makeshift crosses had not, at that time, been gathered into central cemeteries. Military detritus lay spread far and wide across the fertile countryside. There were few people to be met with. The young men who had survived the war were still in prisoner of war camps and the others, in their thousands, lay in graves from the Arctic circle to Africa. Civilians who had fled for fear of the fighting or of the avenging Red Army had still not returned. Only the very old and the very young were met in any number.

From conversations with those who had remained I gained a first outline of the fighting and then, in the passage of years, answers to questions put to those who had taken part in the fighting of the final weeks of the war clarified points hitherto obscure. Research then completed the picture—or nearly so—for there still remain shadows around some small point of battle, shadows which will never be illuminated now because the survivors either did not come back from prison camp or have died in the years which have elapsed since 1945. The main story is, however, in this chapter.

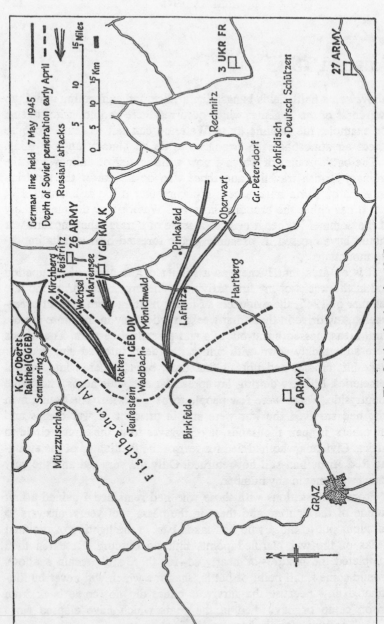

The fighting in Austria, 1945

It is now three and a half decades since the European war ended in May 1945. Thirty-five years of peace may have driven the memory of the suffering from the minds of those who live in the principal cities and the larger towns of the Styrian Bundesland, but in the small villages and on the isolated farms in the eastern marches of the province, late at night there is a sudden mysterious silence and the region seems to hold its breath as if waiting for some new thundering barrage, which will bring once again behind its red-hot destruction the tank waves and the hordes of khaki-clad men whose first clamours were for schnapps, women and watches.

The memory of the assault of the Red Army is still deep, but no less abiding is the memory of all the Gebirgsjäger who fought in the province and of whose several units I have chosen the story of but one regiment: the 99th of 1st Gebirgs Division. Not that the story of the other mountain divisions at that time is less interesting or re-counts less brave deeds. It is only that 99th fought in Styria which of all the land of Austria is dearest to me; a subjective choice certainly, but one which I hope will be forgiven.

During the third week of March 1945, those Austrians who still chose to remember it would have recalled the annexation of their country and reflected that only seven years earlier armoured fighting vehicles of a German occupying Army had rumbled across the frontier and had paraded in triumph, in front of Adolf Hitler, along the Ring Strasse in Vienna.

Now, in the spring of 1945, the tanks of another enemy, the Red Army, were menacing the "Alpine and Danubian Districts", the dull, provincial names which had been bestowed upon the former Empire of Austria by the National Socialist government. The Red Army was drawing near and the realisation was fearful. In February the newspapers had been full of an all-out offensive which would recapture Budapest and smash the Soviet forces in Hungary, but now even to the most casual reader of a newspaper, reduced by war to a single sheet of newsprint, it was clear that the great German drive had failed and that a massive Soviet counter-blow was about to strike Austria. Despite the warmth of those sunny days of March 1945, many Austrians shivered in fear at the prospect of their capital city and their country becoming a battlefield. Considering that the capital of the Third Reich was to the north in faraway Berlin and that the final battles of the war would, almost certainly be fought in Prussia, Brandenburg and Saxony, why was it they wondered that two giant Russian army groups, the 2nd and 3rd Ukrainian Fronts, were rolling, seemingly unstoppable, towards the frontier? How had it come about?

In his authoritative and well-documented book, *Krieg in Österreich 1945,* Dr Manfred Rauchensteiner gives his reasons for the massive effort by the Red Army's southern wing to capture Austria; an effort out of all proportion to what had become, militarily, a side show, a secondary operation. He suggests that despite post-war claims by Soviet historians in which the destruction of Army Group South is given as the principal objective, strong military action was undertaken to support a political decision.

In every war there are, behind the military activity, political motives and consequences and World War II was no exception. By the end of 1944 the defeat of Germany had become only a matter of time and the shape of the new Europe was being drawn. The intention of the Soviet regime was to ensure that around her there would be a cordon of countries over whom her influence would be unchallenged and she determined, therefore, to occupy a succession of States running from the Baltic to the Adriatic. To guard the western flank of her satellite Hungary and the south-western flank of another satellite, Czechoslovakia, and also to be the link between those two countries it was essential, so the Soviet leadership thought, to occupy certain areas of Austria. In the normal course of military operations, given the deteriorating condition of Germany, the Red Army's battle line in Austria might have been expected to roll forward, fighting certainly, but not being directly engaged in the decisive battles which were being fought out in eastern Germany. In their own good time the Russian forces, advancing westwards, would expect to occupy those countries which Stalin and his government had decided were vital to Russia. Thus it might have stayed, with 2nd and 3rd Ukrainian Fronts keeping their place on the left flank of the massive Soviet advance, but for a message which was passed to the Russian leaders by the American ambassador. He had been advised by Field-Marshal Alexander, the Allied commander-in-chief in Italy, that senior officers of the German armies facing him in Italy had made overtures to sue for peace. In accordance with Allied policy he had made this

fact known to the US ambassador in Moscow and had asked him to
advise the Soviet leadership of this development.

For the Russians this news brought a fear that, while their armies
were engaged in fighting on the Eastern Front, in Hungary and
Czechoslovakia, those of Britain and America, freed by an armistice
in Italy from the need to fight, would advance without opposition and
capture the principal cities of Austria. The Red Army would thus not
be in possession of those parts of Austrian territory which the Soviets
considered it essential for them to hold. This must never be allowed
to happen and Stalin demanded that the German overtures to Alexander be broken off. The Western allies acceded to his demands and
the armistice talks were not resumed until the end of April, by which
time the Red Army had taken Vienna and those regions of Austria
which it had always intended to occupy. Stalin had won the game
and the political fate of Europe was decided.

Since we are concerned chiefly with Styria, it would seem that the
Soviet government had no interest in that province and that the
fighting with which this part of the book will deal had as its principal
aim the tying down of the German forces there, so that they could
not be moved northwards to Vienna and to Bohemia where the main
Red Army thrusts were to be made.

That, however, is to anticipate events and we must return in time
to the situation at the end of February 1945 when the commanders
of 2nd and 3rd Ukrainian Fronts had received orders to prepare for
"Operation Vienna", the assault which would take out the Austrian
capital.

The word "Front" when used in connection with the Red Army
can be defined as a major grouping of Soviet military units, corre-
sponding approximately to a German army group and thus with no
fixed organisation, but with one that was enlarged or reduced to meet
the strategic requirements. Facing Austria, the 2nd Ukrainian Front
the more northerly of the two, was commanded by Marshal of the
Soviet Union Malinovsky while 3rd Ukrainian Front was led by Marshal of the Soviet Union Tolbhukin. It was against the corps and
divisions of 3rd Ukrainian Front that German Army South, with
whom we are dealing, had to fight. The order of battle for both sides
gives no real indication of the disparity in strength between them.
Losses incurred by the German forces could never be made good;
any vehicle put out of action was a total write-off. Units were dan-

gerously weak and became weaker as more and more men became casualties and no reinforcements came up. There was a desperate shortage of ammunition and so little fuel for the armoured fighting vehicles that such expedients as one tank towing another, or even two others, were used to conserve petrol.

The Red Army suffered no shortages. Its losses during the war had been enormous, but enormous too were the reservoirs of man power upon which it could draw. The factories of Russia, far removed from German bombing, could and did produce an almost unending stream of machines, weapons and equipment with which to supply the armies of the field. Neither shortage of men nor of weapons confronted the Soviet forces.

The Order of Battle of 3rd Ukrainian Front for the battles in Austria was:

6th Guards Tank Army with 5th Guards Tank Corps and 9th Guards Motorised Corps.

4th Guards Army with 20th Guards Infantry Corps, 21st Guards Infantry Corps, 31st Guards Infantry Corps and 1st Guards Mechanised Corps.

9th Guards Army with 37th Guards Infantry Corps, 38th Guards Infantry Corps and 39th Guards Infantry Corps.

26th Army with 135th Infantry Corps, 30th Infantry Corps and 104th Infantry Corps.

27th Army with 18th Tank Corps, 5th Guards Cavalry Corps: 35th Guards Infantry Corps, 33rd Infantry Corps and 37th Infantry Corps. 57th Army with 6th Guards Infantry Corps; 64th Infantry Corps and 133rd Infantry Corps.

1st Bulgarian Army with 3rd and 4th Bulgarian Infantry Corps.

Facing this impressive array of strength was Army Group South whose depleted formations from north to south were: 8th Army controlling the 43rd Infantry Corps, Feldherrnhalle Panzer Corps, 72nd Infantry and the 29th Infantry Corps. The right wing of 8th Army touched the left flank of 6th SS Panzer Army. The SS army had two corps on its establishment: 1st and 2nd SS Panzer. To the south of the SS stood 6th Army, a force with an unfortunate reputation, for the original had been destroyed at Stalingrad and its successor had been badly mauled in the long retreats between the summer of 1943 and February 1945. The 6th Army covered the eastern provinces of

Austria and extended southwards almost to the borders of Yugoslavia where it touched 2nd Panzer Army. The corps on the strength of
2nd Panzer Army were 68th Infantry, 22nd Gebirgs and 1st Cavalry.

The 6th Army is the one with which 99th Regiment of 1st Gebirgs
Division was to fight and, as it is with that regiment that this section
of the book deals, its order of battle, as at 1 April 1945, is given
here:

4th SS Panzer Corps had battle groups from three panzer divisions: 1st, 3rd and 5th SS Panzer, together with the SS Norge Battalion.

The 3rd Panzer Corps was the stronger of the two corps on the establishment of 6th Army—at least on paper—but most of its battle
groups were weak infantry formations. They were: Battle Group
Gottwald, Battle Group Siegers, Battle Group Schweitzer and one
made up from units of the rear area. The only full strength and
battle-ready unit in corps was the 1st Gebirgs Division. A Hungarian
fortress battalion, the SS Battalion Ney and two battalions of replacements for 1st and 3rd Panzer Divisions completed the corps
order of battle.

Weak though 6th Army may have been, and as 3rd Panzer Corps
also was, it was against them that the great weight of 3rd Ukrainian
Front was to be put in the weeks of battle which were to last until
the end of the war in Europe. By 1 May 3rd Panzer Corps was reduced to the remnants of 1st Gebirgs Division and a battle group
from 1st Panzer Division. Such was the scale of the fighting in eastern Austria.

Thus we have the forces arrayed and the political need outlined
which would cause a massive blow to be launched against Austria.
There remains to complete the picture only a description of the battlefield and the immediate background history of military events.

The province of Austria known as Styria (in German die Steiermark) is so extensively covered with pine forests that the name "the
green heart of Austria" has been given to it. The farmland is intensively cultivated and set among villages each with its onion-domed
church and small main square. From these villages run small roads,
chiefly through river valleys, towards market towns and from these

places larger roads then move in towards the provincial capital, Graz, or to the other large towns. Communication follows, chiefly, the lie of the land and the direction of the principal rivers. There are several important north–south highways connecting Graz and the capital city of Vienna.

In the extreme south, Styria borders on Yugoslavia. To the east of the province lies Hungary and to the north lie the Austrian provinces of Burgenland and Lower Austria. Much of the south-eastern corner bordering on Yugoslavia and Hungary is made up of very low, rolling hills heavily forested and cut with several river valleys. Once through this slight barrier to any attacker from the east, Graz lies in a shallow basin surrounded by a range of hills which extend westward and northward. The northern range increases in height as it moves northward until on the border of Steiermark with Lower Austria the high hills become mountains: the easternmost point of the Austrian Alps.

The area thus favours the defender over the attacker, always assuming that there are sufficient defenders to maintain an adequate front to block the obvious routes of attack which are along the valleys of the rivers. The battles in which the 99th Gebirgsjäger Regiment took part were, principally, to halt the advance of the Red Army along such approaches and to block the penetrations which it had made.

The immediate history of the war in Austria began in February when the two Front commanders, Malinovsky and Tolbhukin, were ordered to prepare "Operation Vienna". Given the political urgency which subsequently became the primary consideration they added to their already great strength in men the 9th Guards and 6th Guards Tank armies, first-class units made up of regiments which had distinguished themselves in battle. In the Red Army there were Guards units from divisional to army level. These elite formations had colours with distinctive markings and all ranks had the honour title "Guards" as a preface to their military rank; as for example "Guards Sergeant", "Guards Rifleman", etc. The rate of pay of Guards units was higher than that in standard units and, just as in Tsarist days, these formations were made up of picked men who were selected to set an example of military valour to the rest of the Army.

While the southern wing of the Russian line was being strengthened for "Operation Vienna", there was a short pause in active operations and pressure upon the German armies was temporarily eased. On their side of the line the Red Army was resolving the temporary problems of shortages which had arisen as a result of their advance outrunning the supplies services. Stocks of ammunition were replenished and the men retrained. When all this activity had been completed the left wing Fronts of the Red Army's battle line could resume their westward advance. During this time of temporary Soviet military inactivity there was a sudden flare-up from the German side when a major offensive was launched in Hungary.

Hitler, obsessed by the loss of Budapest and of the Hungarian oil fields, had decided to recapture both, had reinforced 6th SS Panzer Army and had given orders for the Magyar capital and for other objectives to be recaptured. Under the cover name "Spring Awakening", the offensive was launched but it was doomed to failure. The SS Panzer Army may well have been equipped on a scale that had not been seen for years in the German Army, its weapons may have been first class, its Command confident of success and its soldiers determined to bring about this victory. All these things may have been true but the Soviet High Command, informed by British Intelligence of the forthcoming attack, realised that this was a last-gasp attempt and did not allow the German offensive to upset the rhythm of their own build-up. Come what may, they knew that in a war of attrition they could not lose. Numbers were on their side.

One of the few non-SS units called upon to play a part in "Spring Awakening", was 1st Gebirgs Division which was posted to Hungary from Yugoslavia where it had been engaged on anti-partisan operations. There was a need for a strong, battle-hardened and reliable unit to protect the flank of the SS advance and the mountain division filled all those needs. The offensive opened on 6 March but despite initial successes it lost impetus and soon began to falter. The SS commanders and the planners at OKH had failed to take into account the factor of terrain which in that part of Hungary is marshy, together with the allied fact that heavy armoured fighting vehicles crossing and recrossing such soil soon turn it into a deep mud in which they are held fast. The armoured assaults bogged down. Infantry was needed to bring the advance forward again and 1st Gebirgs Division was put in. The first attack at Kaposvar brought the regiments forward through three successive lines of Russian defences and, by 16 March, Csömend had fallen to their storming advance. But the strain of the heavy fighting and the appalling conditions exhausted the Jäger. The division's advance in the Lake Balaton region faltered and then halted, stopped less by the opposition of the Russian forces, numerically superior and backed by massed artillery and armour, than by mud, a natural element which had confounded German plans since the opening of "Operation Barbarossa", the attack upon the Soviet Union in June 1941. Hitler's strategic intention to recapture Budapest and to advance towards Romania was a dream without hope of fulfilment.

While the Germans were thus being frustrated in their offensive, Russian preparations for "Operation Vienna" were at last completed and military activity, hitherto latent, grew in scale as new artillery groupings "shot themselves in" and fresh infantry formations carried out aggressive patrolling. All the signs of an imminent offensive were there and *Fremde Heere Ost,* the military department of OKW which dealt with foreign armies and particularly with the Red Army, projected that this would be aimed at splitting the German southern front, to take out Vienna and to encircle the forces in southern Hungary, in eastern Austria and in Yugoslavia.

On 21 March the Russian offensive against 6th Army opened with an assault by 5th Guards Cavalry Corps spearheading the general movement. This first attack was quickly followed by others and soon a penetration by 1st Guards Motorised Corps began to fragment the 6th Army's front. Other drives carried out against both flanks threatened the army with encirclement, and the scale of the grand assault developed so fast that by the evening of the first day German Intelligence had identified no fewer than forty-two Red Army infantry divisions and eight mechanised corps. The threat against the army's left wing proved to be the most serious of all the crises, for the Soviet assault had found the boundary between 6th Army and 6th SS Panzer Army and had burst the seam wide open, producing a gap which was soon exploited by the flexibly-minded Russian commanders. The strategic intention was clear. It was to throw a small pincer arm in the north around 6th Army in Burgenland while a longer northern pincer through the valleys of the Raab and Feistritz rivers to threaten Graz. Thus the passes would be gained for a drive into Lower Austria and access obtained to the valleys of the Mürz and the Mur. A southern pincer arm would strike between 6th Army and 2nd Panzer Army to reach the area of Leibnitz. Although the Red Army's intention, to cut off and to destroy individually the German 6th Army on Hungarian soil, did not succeed, many first-class units, particularly 44th "Hoch und Deutschmeister" Division, were smashed. It was, indeed, the destruction of this elite Austrian formation, and the urgent need to replace it with another first-class unit, that brought the 12,300 man strong 1st Gebirgs Division from the strength of the SS Panzer Army and on to that of 6th Army.

By the time that the mountain division received the posting order on 24 March, the front of 6th Army ran from Balatonfüred via Magyvazsony to Devecser and was being taken back towards Szombathely. Thus the army's left wing had been driven back farther than that of the right wing and the battle line was concave shaped, running on a line roughly north-west to south-east. The sector on which 1st Gebirgs Division was ordered to fight forced the division to face and to do battle in two directions: north and east.

The task for which it had been selected called for a reliable unit to stand fast and to carry out one of the most difficult tasks in military operations. The units all around it had been broken and were in retreat after the failure of "Spring Awakening" and the massive drive by the Red Army. The Jäger had to open their ranks to let its own Army through and to remain uninfluenced by their defeat. At the approach of the Soviets the regiments were to close ranks ready to receive the Red assaults and to repel them, thus forming a shield behind which the shattered formations could be reformed. The 1st Gebirgs Division was selected for this difficult duty but before it could take up the positions allotted to it, on either side of the great east-west highway from Szentgal to Janoshaza, the regiments first had to break off the battle with the tenacious enemy with whom they were still locked around Lake Balaton, and this proved no easy task.

It is, therefore, no surprise to know that the division arrived piecemeal into its new area, and as the individual detachments arrived they were quickly put into the line and ordered to dig in. The highway presented a depressing sight for along it moved westwards and towards safety vast columns of civilians, all filled with stories of Russian rape and pillage, as well as military units moving back to new positions. Every highway, road and path was filled with traffic. Infantry groups interspersed with civilian horse-drawn carts, ancient motor cars and modern heavy tanks all filled the roads and with the pace of their movement dictated by the Red Air Force. The aircraft swept low over the slow-moving columns bombing and machine gunning, and each attack brought casualties which blocked the roads and reduced the pace of the retreat still farther. Day after day this mass of misery passed through the positions held by the Jäger battalions until at last it slowed to a trickle and then halted altogether, leaving behind it and spread across the flat fields only the wrack of a destroyed and broken force. The 1st Gebirgs Division then stood alone against the Soviet regiments which came in with a rush to overwhelm the defence; only to be repelled. Time and time again the Russian attacks came in and under this succession of heavy blows the division was forced slowly back, but even in this retrograde movement it continued to attack when ordered. More and more units of the division were being used as alarm detachments to plug those gaps in their line through which the massed armour and infantry of 3rd Ukrainian Front was flooding. The division succeeded in holding fast and in preventing 6th Army's left flank from being turned, but this could be only a temporary halt to the south-westerly advance of 5th Guards Tank Corps, even though the cohesion of the Russian attacks was being destroyed by the almost trackless woods through which the armoured regiments were forcing their way.

Colonel General Wöhler, commanding Army Group South, a talented and experienced soldier began to move his armies back in good order and frustrated that part of the Soviet plan aimed at encircling them. Step by step he withdrew his battered forces made up, for the greater part, of battle-hardened veterans who were fighting now to defend their own hearths and homes and who knew the terrain. Those last two factors and the *Reichsschützstellung,* the hastily dug field fortifications which stretched from the Baltic to Croatia and towards which the army group was pulling back, were it was hoped sufficient to shield the endangered eastern provinces while a massive German counter-blow was prepared which when unleashed would fling back the Red incursors.

There was another and militarily more important necessity for Army Group South to hold fast or to maintain, at least, a cohesive and orderly front. The armies of Field Marshal Löhr, four hundred thousand strong and retreating from the Balkans, were passing through Yugoslavia en route to Austria. Pursuing them was a group of Russian and Bulgarian armies, while partisan divisions under Marshal Tito, sought to slow down the Germans so that they could be overtaken and destroyed before they reached Austria.

Army Group South was the German shield in Hungary which protected the withdrawal of Löhr and his men. If that shield was smashed then the right wing of the whole Eastern Front would be torn wide open by a Red thrust coming out of Hungary and which would unite with the other Soviet forces in Yugoslavia to encircle the German troops. This threat Army Group South struggled to avert but even with a strength of 100,000 fighting men it was a shadow of that impressive and virile force which had stormed the Ukraine in the first years of the war with Russia, which had driven its panzers to the banks of the Volga and whose Gebirgsjäger had scaled the peaks of the Caucasus. The armies on its establishment were armies in name only; the divisions and corps the weak remnants of years of battle; and its regiments, for the greater part, no more than understrength battalions.

The shattered divisions of Dietrich's 6th SS Panzer Army were named in a report by a High Command inspector which stated that 1st SS was "burnt out", the 12th SS was "severely weakened", 3rd SS was "made up of remnants", the 6th SS "was weakened" and the 2nd SS was of "only average strength". South of the SS army stood 6th Army of whose formations only 1st Gebirgs Division with a strength of just over 12,000 men was the strongest. Of that number only 4738 were combat troops and the division was evaluated at OKW as Grade 2. The weakest of 6th Army's divisions was 13th Panzer which had a fighting strength of only 1013 men, 36 tanks, 12 self-propelled guns on Panzer IV chassis and 4 anti-tank guns. The evaluation of 13th Panzer Division had sunk to Grade 4.

Against the weak and battered formations of 6th Army the massive Soviet blows fell in rapid succession fragmenting and encircling where it could, but always with the main objective of gaining ground and reaching as far westwards as it could advance. The speed of the Russian advance brought Soviet units in some places up to the frontier and to the *Reichsschützstellung* and often their speed had been so great that they had reached the eastern wall before the retreating German forces. In the 6th Army area Soviet armour crossed the Hungarian-Austrian border just after 27 March 1945. The Red Army was on Austrian soil. To repel them the last reserves of men, a local defence force of civilians, known as the Volkssturm, was called up. Some Volkssturm units had been in uniform since December anticipating this day, but their numbers were too few. Now that the enemy was at the gates every man was needed and those who had still been allowed to carry on working in factories or on the farm were taken from bench and field, hastily uniformed, armed with whatever weapons were available and put into the line. The showing of the units varied. Some fought to the death or were murdered after surrendering. Others who had been sent forward without weapons found on arrival on the battlefield that there were no arms with which to equip them and their units were thereupon disbanded. Some, contrasting the strength of the Red Army to themselves, made discretion the better part of valour and tidily stacked their unfired guns alongside garden fences before they removed themselves from the fighting zone. Others accepted that the war was lost and were concerned that their village should not become a battleground and that the Red Army should not be incensed by military opposition into carrying out reprisals on those civilians who had not fled but who had stayed on in the village. The enemy was in the homeland; the nightmare had become reality.

At long last Balck, commanding 6th Army, gave the order for 1st Gebirgs Division to withdraw from its positions along the Szentgal-Janoshaza highway and to pull back to the *Reichsschützstellung*. It is then, on Good Friday, 30 March, with the division still on Hungarian soil at Janoshaza, but preparing to head for Austria, that we prepare to take up the story of 99th Gebirgsjäger Regiment.

During the day conflicting accounts came in and rumours circulated and it is evidence of the confusion of those days, and under those conditions, that military units were sent to attack an enemy whose presence had been reported by hysterical civilians, but whose precise location and strength had not been determined. Thus it was on Easter Saturday when the regiment was ordered forward to undertake another fire brigade mission. The object of this operation was to seal off Soviet penetrations at Grosspetersdorf, a small town near Rechnitz on the frontier, which civilians had reported was in Russian hands. A motorised Jäger battle patrol swept forward but neither they, nor the regimental commander, Major Groth, who had by this time arrived, could find any evidence to suggest that the Red Army had penetrated that far. As the regimental commander was about to lead his patrol away the staff car of the rear area commander, General Krause, came into the main square. The general gave immediate orders for the regiment to advance and to sweep the enemy back to the frontier, by whatever means available.

In issuing these instructions he was relaying the command of his superior officer, General Ringel, who had ordered the recapture of Rechnitz whose garrison of three Styrian Volkssturm battalions had been overwhelmed by the assault of a Guards Infantry Division.

Major Groth was, understandably, reluctant to open an attack against an enemy securely entrenched on high ground and General Krause then ordered the attack to go in from a flank. For this Groth began to prepare, waiting only upon the arrival of his battalions which were coming up in a foot march. Even as the leading files of men arrived there came with them the divisional commander who halted the attack preparations and took 99th Regiment to its designated positions in the *Reichsschützstellung,* around the village of St Kathrein, on the western bank of the small river Pinka. Another part of the division went on to attack Schachendorf and reached the centre of the town before being ordered back to its position in the Reich's defence line.

There then followed, for the Jäger battalions, a tiring march and the units had hardly arrived and been allocated their company positions when the first of a series of Soviet assaults by units of 26th Red Army was launched against them. The Red infantry battalions, whose approach was covered by the woods and orchards in and around the village, charged forward. The Jäger settled down, once again, to continue the fighting that had been the lot of some since 1939. Slowly, almost languidly, the weapons were raised. Butts fitted into shoulders long since accustomed to their feel and to their kick. Cheeks were laid alongside the rifle's stock, eyes squinted through telescopic sights. Then the slaughter began. The first groups of Soviet soldiers began to fall. The Red Army did not advance in long lines as it had done in the first years of the war but in small knots of men behind their company officers. It was clear that the men of those first attacked detachments were new to battle for they bunched under fire and made their own killing that much easier. The survivors broke, withdrew and vanished into the depths of the woods. On the bright spring grass there was left only the dead and the dying. A second charge came an hour later, a third some hours after that and then for some hours there was a lull.

With a sudden roar, a thunderous drumming, the Soviet artillery opened up. The purpose of the infantry assaults had been to locate and to pin-point the Jäger positions. Flesh and blood had been expended to find the mountain troops. Now Stalin's God of War, the artillery, would destroy them. Massed batteries, ranging in calibre from the lightest to the heaviest, bombarded the slit trenches in which the German soldiers sat patiently, waiting for the storm to pass. Pass it did but behind it came no storming Red infantry, at least not at that time. Not until the late evening of Easter Sunday, 1 April, did the Red Army attacks begin again but not on the sector held by 99th Regiment but against the left flank neighbour. This was a Hungarian infantry formation whose units had begun, according to the war diary of Army Group South, to go over to the Soviets. The diary also reported that some Magyar detachments had made common cause with the enemy and had taken up arms against the Germans.

It was against such Hungarian units, wavering between carrying out their duty or going over to surrender, that the first assaults of the Red Army came in. The Magyars cracked at Deutsch-Schützen and the left wing of 99th Regiment was laid bare. Experience had shown that the best tactic under such circumstances was for an immediate counter-attack to be launched with any forces immediately available and before the enemy had had time to consolidate his gains. The troops to hand at Deutsch-Schützen were men from the divisional engineer battalion and from the flak detachments. This ad hoc battle group swept forward, drove back the Soviet penetrations, and sealed the gap by taking and holding that sector in the line where formerly the Hungarians had held post. The situation had been restored but it could be at best only a temporary thing, for the whole front was a patch work of fragments or detachments holding impossibly long sectors of the front. Most units did not know who was the neighbour on the flanks, whether he was battle-hardened, what were his capabilities and whether he was still in position or was preparing to move back without warning.

Soviet armour broke through this weak and un-coordinated front almost at will and then regiments of T 34 tanks, who found in the south the boundary between 6th Army and 2nd Panzer Army,

What the lorried columns were to standard divisions the mule trains were to the Gebirgs units. This picture shows a heavily loaded mule climbing a bleak and steep hillside in the Balkans.

Students at an Army mountain guide course in Bavaria, being briefed for a map reading exercise. It was the ability to maintain direction in the high peaks which was vital and this class is being taught that skill.

A gun of the Gebirgs artillery of 1st Gebirgs Division firing at maximum elevation during the fighting in the mountains of the Caucasus, summer 1942.

Senior officers of the 7th SS Gebirgs Division "Prinz Eugen" during anti-partisan operations in Yugoslavia, summer 1943. It can be seen that SS Gebirgs Divisions also wore the edelweiss insignia on the right arms and on the left side of the cap. The eagle insignia on the left arm indicated that the wearer was in the SS. The other Services wore the eagle on the breast.

A Sturmbannführer (Major) of the 7th SS Gebirgs Division "Prinz Eugen".
The four-star insignia denotes his rank. The diamond-shaped emblem is
the badge of the "Prinz Eugen" Division. The officer is shown wearing the
Knight's Cross of the Iron Cross round his throat and the winter 1941
Russian campaign ribbon (the Frozen Meat Order) tucked into his jacket.

General Eduard Dietl, the hero of Narvik. The Gebirgs General is seen here wearing the Knight's Cross of the Iron Cross around his neck. The ribbon of the Second Class Iron Cross and bar is worn on the second tunic button. On his left breast pocket Dietl wears the circular Wounded badge. Above that the Iron Cross First Class of the First World War is shown and above that the outstretched eagle indicating a bar to the Cross awarded for his actions in the Second World War.

General Feuerstein, founder and first General Officer commanding 2nd Gebirgs Division.

General Dietl (left), General Ritter von Hengl and General Schlemmer (right) commander of 2nd Gebirgs Division in 1941, during a battlefield conference during the fighting on the northern sector of the Russian front.

General Ludwig Kübler, founder and first commander of the Gebirgs Brigade, later the 1st Gebirgs Division.

General Julius Ringel, General Officer Commanding 5th Gebirgs Division during its successful battle in Crete. In the spring of 1945 Ringel led a Gebirgs battle group which fought in Styria and which recaptured the Riegersburg from the Red Army.

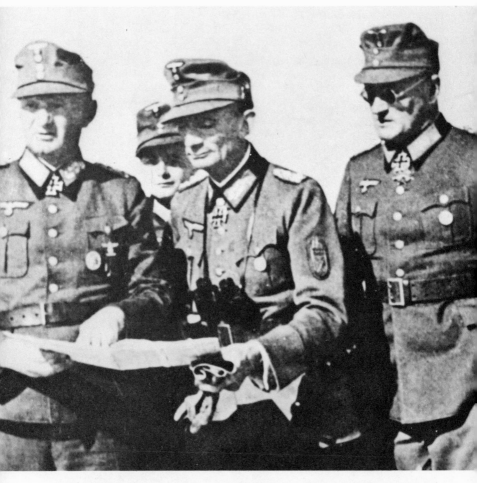

Three commanders of Gebirgs units. From left to right: General Ritter von Hengl who commanded 2nd Gebirgs Division (1942-1943), General Dietl and (right) General Schörner.

breached it and exploited the gains which had been made. There were now two wide gaps in the line. One on the left wing where 6th SS Panzer Army stood and the other on the right flank where the remnants of 2nd Panzer Army were battling. The 6th Army was isolated and almost outflanked as Soviet spearheads drove deep into Austria. It is, in fact, true to say that from the last week of March 1945 Army Group South had ceased to fight as a cohesive whole; it had fragmented into a number of armies each fighting its own bitter and individual battle without central direction.

The new Russian thrusts then took on a direction which OKW had not anticipated. The High Command had expected that these new penetrations would reinforce the northwards sweep towards Vienna and had, indeed, grouped the bulk of the German forces around the capital. Instead, the Soviet main thrust struck for the Semmering Pass heading west where it gained ground rapidly. Soviet historians describe how the intention was then to swing south to get behind 6th Army and 2nd Panzer Army and to link up with the Soviet forces coming out of Yugoslavia. The Russian intention was to encircle nearly a million German soldiers.

For the men of 99th Regiment fighting in Rechnitz whatever direction the Soviet main strategic thrust may have taken could be only of academic interest. More urgently, they had sufficient to concern them with the containing of the Soviet attacks. Snipers fired from house windows as Jäger patrols moved cautiously up the crooked streets of the old town. Under fire from a machine gun in a room the mountain men would duck into doorways and shout for the pioneers to bring up explosive charges. Shiny little rifle grenades would keep the Red machine gun team dominated while inside the houses the Jäger mouseholed from one room to another. A succession of explosions marked their passage as they broke through the inside walls towards the room in which the machine gun and its team was situated. At last the final wall was reached and blown down with a satchel of explosive. Then, as the stunned Soviet soldiers scrabbled about in the dust seeking to find their rifles, a rapid fire of bullets, the barking explosion of a stick grenade, or else an entrenching tool with its edge honed to a knife-blade sharpness, rising and falling with the awful dull sound of a body being beaten, would destroy the Russian machine gun nest.

In some houses the Red Army troops would swarm out to make

their own attacks and then there was hand to hand fighting on stairs. and landings of houses occupied by the Jäger; faces half concealed in the shadows or smothered with dust and sweat. The battle for Rechnitz, the little frontier town, was one that would be remembered by all those who survived it for the physical effort employed by both attackers and defenders. In Deutsch-Schützen the regiment's pioneer battalion was driven back, and all the time in and around the regimental sector shells rained down from regiments of Russian guns which suffered from no shortage of ammunition.

The Russian infantry attacks suddenly halted and for days only the barrage crashed down. Otherwise along the Pinka river, where the 99th held post, there was little ground activity and it seemed to many that the Soviets were passing their soldiers around this Gebirgsjäger obstruction to their general advance. As a result of this inactivity, for much of the following week various battalions of the regiment were taken from those static positions, formed into battle groups and put into fire brigade operations, being rushed from one crisis point to another. They were set against Russian infantry concentrations of 26th Army or tank columns of the armoured brigades which had broken through on sectors held by other and less reliable units. It was the last hope for Krause had no reserves which could be put into the fight. The battle groups of the 99th were his only firm weapons.

On 5 April the German front along the Pinka and around Rechnitz began to collapse as the troops who had replaced the Jäger failed under the weight of renewed and heavy thrusts by troops of 135 Corps. Once again the Soviet Command began flinging masses of men into its infantry attacks and where, in built-up areas, German garrison thwarted the Red advances artillery, massed in division or corps strength, would begin systematically to raze the buildings to the ground, seeking to destroy the small knots of defenders still inhibiting the forward movement.

Of much of the bitterness of the battles of those days against neighbouring units the 99th, temporarily no longer a fire brigade, was in ignorance. Their defence was so well constructed with interlocking fire zones and with all dead ground covered, their patrolling so aggressive and their morale so firm that the local Soviet leaders probed for, sought and found some less proficient battalions against whose front they could drive their furious assaults, hoping there to achieve that breakthrough which could never be achieved against the mountain men. One attack on 5 April drove back the German troops holding Oberwart and their retreat laid open the regiment's flank. Through the gap poured masses of Red infantry and tanks seeking to exploit the breach, to pass behind the Jäger battalions and to threaten them with encirclement.

Driving with the fierce exultation of victory the troops of Soviet 30th Corps smashed their way forward flooding across the fields like a brown river, spreading wide, overlapping into the woods and killing in their trenches the Jäger who sought to obstruct them. The forward platoons facing enemy hosts coming from the east then found themselves under fire from Russian troops coming at them from the west. At places the khaki tide suddenly seemed to halt, seemed to recede a little, but then gathered strength again and swept forward with greater impetus as the last Gebirgsjäger died in a storm of bullets or in a welter of stabbing bayonets. Some Red groups began to roll up the battalion line while others swept towards Kohfidisch where regimental headquarters was located. From positions in the houses of this little town, hardly more than a large village, Jäger opened fire upon Russian troops charging up dusty streets and through sun-flowered gardens. The masses of infantry that STAVKA had put into the battle for this small group of ochre-coloured houses were prodigious, and soon their numbers began to tell. They stormed into the houses, fired their machine pistols through the windows, flung hand grenades through open doors and then engaged the German soldiers in man to man combat.

Slowly the companies of the 99th began to fall back, slowly but then driven to a quicker pace by the insistent "Ooray", the Russian battle cry, and it seemed as if Kohfidisch would be lost to the enemy. Then as a Red battalion, seen only dimly through the dense cloud of golden dust which had been thrown up by the movement of battle, stormed towards the main square and to regimental headquarters which was situated there, a minor miracle occurred. Outside the HQ building now only a pistol shot away from the onrushing Soviet columns, a small convoy of troop transporters roared up to halt before the building and from the vehicles 120 fully armed replacements quickly debussed. There was little need for orders and under the command of veteran NCOs the new, keen reinforcements settled down to their first action.

The Russian infantry swept into the square and were met with a storm of fire. As they reeled under the shock the young Gebirgsjäger went into a bayonet charge, primitive but effective, and each Red group as it was flung back added to the chaos and gave impetus to the rearward movement. Soon the Soviet troops were in full retreat and as the soldiers, stumbling back in disarray, passed down the streets up which they had only recently and victoriously passed, small knots of Jäger, still holding out in the houses, rushed out to join in the pursuit. They had been so long on the defensive and now forming part of an attacking movement their natural feelings were liberated and they drove back the Russian forces with fierce élan.

Slowly the enemy began to recover. Groups began to halt and return fire. Soon the retreat had halted and then the fighting swayed to and fro during which there occurred another crisis which the hard-fighting mountain men had to master. A Hungarian artillery battalion on the regiment's flank began to crack and in order to restore the situation the Gebirgsjäger executed an early morning counter-attack which drove back the Soviet forces in and around the village of Wappendorf. Surprise was total. The Jäger were in among the drowsy Red Army men before these had had time to comprehend the danger that surrounded them. The killing was prodigious and when the battle was over hundreds of Russian dead were found and the booty included machine guns, mortars and anti-tank guns. It had been a successful assault but the victory was a hollow one for a Soviet tank and infantry penetration on another flank at Kotezicken enfiladed the German positions with machine gun and mortar fire. The danger of being cut off forced the mountain men to give up the ground that they had won and they carried out a fighting retreat to the heights which lie to the west and to the south-west of the town. These they held with such obvious vigour and determination that the Russian operations in that sector were halted.

The course of the fighting in that area of Austria in which we are interested, and during the weeks beginning with Sunday 8 April, is of Soviet probes succeeded by heavy attacks along a line from the Hochwechsel to Mönichwald. These were assaults both from the east and the north, of which the northern drive made the deepest and the most threatening penetrations.

Simultaneously with these Russian movements there were counter-attacks by units of 6th Army. The first of these began on 10 April and aimed to cut off and to encircle the Soviet troops attacking in the Waldbach area. The second German counter-offensive aimed at driving back the Russian penetrations coming in from the north. This German thrust was countered by the Soviet High Command in a series of small but furious assaults against Hartberg, all of which were contained. When the German offensive was concluded a firm and a strong defensive line in the Lafnitz river valley was formed and this was held to the end of the war. It is this fighting which will be covered in the later pages of this section.

Leaving for a moment the regimental sector and passing to the northern sector of 6th Army's battle line, there had been on both 6 and 7 April a number of significant moves. To the north of 99th Regiment's positions Soviet motorised and cavalry units had reached Wenigzell and the upper Lafnitz, which was to be in the weeks to come the last battlefield upon which the 1st Gebirgs Division was to fight during World War II. The units of 6th Army fought desperately to hold the entrances to the river valleys for if these fell then the danger existed of the army being outflanked. A decision was taken to withdraw from the valley of the Raab, even though such a move would mean giving up the *Reichsschützstellung*. A withdrawal would, however, mean a shorter front to defend. At army group level Hitler had replaced the former commander, General Wöhler, by General Rendulic, a specialist in tenacious defence and a local man. If any General in the German Army could hold Styria against the Russian drive then that man would be Rendulic.

On 6th Army's extreme left flank a danger began to form. As a result of moves by 26th Red Army, whose task it was to cover the left wing of a Guards Cavalry Corps, a number of Red infantry patrols had begun to infiltrate through thinly held sectors of the line, chiefly on the Hochwechsel and other high mountain peaks. Baulked in the southern sector of 6th Army's front STAVKA had decided to push through the thinly defended mountains and to cut not only the secondary north-south roads but to advance and gain the main highway Graz-Bruck an der Mur-Semmering-Wiener Neustadt-Vienna.

This striking for the high ground was a move which OKW had not foreseen and to block these threatening moves Army began to organise strong battle groups. The first task of these would be to hold the Russian incursions; then to push these back and, finally to hold the line of the Lafnitz. To build up the strength of the counter-attack group the 117th Jäger Division was brought out of Italy and 1st Gebirgs Division withdrawn from the Pinka river sector.

The 99th was eventually to be engaged but for the whole of 8 and 9 April it held its positions around Kotezicken against the full fury of Soviet infantry attacks and artillery barrages which were seeking to smash it. The whole 6th Army was embattled along a line from the Semmering to Radkersburg, but it was against the battalions of the 99th, holding a post of danger, that the most determined assaults were made. Fierce drives by the Red Army on Sunday 8 April led to unusually severe losses in both the artillery regiment and engineer battalion, and the Russian troops succeeded at some points along the regimental sector in forcing penetrations which could only be restored after the alarm companies had been put into several costly counter-attacks.

By Tuesday 10 April 6th Army High Command had assembled troops sufficient in number to undertake a massive counter-attack against the Soviet masses which had now reached the Mönichwald-Waldbach road. The intention of the counter-offensive was not merely to halt the Russian drive but to encircle a number of the divisions spearheading it. Through their familiarity with the terrain the attacking German troops brought the advance swiftly forward even though Soviet resistance was particularly determined. This counter-drive may well have taken STAVKA by surprise but neither it, nor the difficult country across which their troops were fighting, were allowed to interfere with the Russian intent to break through on the Pinka river front. These attempts continued. The heavily wooded Styrian countryside; the steep mountain slopes and the sudden sheer drops did force the Soviet commanders to restrict their assaults chiefly to the use of infantry, or else to artillery fire of such proportions that one barrage on 10 April was the subject of comment in the 99th Regiment's war diary. Armour in mass could not be employed.

Within a day the high hopes of 6th Army's Command had been dashed and the counter-offensive began to falter. It needed to be reinforced and the 99th was alerted. While one of its battalions was temporarily detached to serve with Battle Group Groth, the remaining two battalions were ordered to undertake a night march and to withdraw to prepared positions along the Lafnitz river valley where three Soviet Corps, 135th, 104th, and 35th, were attempting a breakthrough.

By last light on 12 April all the positions which had been allotted to the regiment were firmly in its hands.

By a strange turn of fate the regiment was now to be involved in battles along the only sector of Army Group South on which there was any military activity. On 13 April STAVKA had issued orders for 3rd Ukrainian Front to go over to the defensive but Tolbhukin decided to continue his offensive until the Fischbach Alps had been crossed. There were simultaneous drives by 11th Guards Cavalry Division and 30th Guards Infantry Division and these downthrusting spearheads of Soviet 30 Corps met the German counter-offensive which was striking north-east. The 6th Army soldiers flung back the Russian advance guard and then went on to smash the 68th Guards Infantry and the 135th Infantry Divisions. St Kathrein was attacked and recaptured from the Soviets by 117th Jäger Division and fierce fighting for the villages and hamlets marked the course of the day. At night the sky was lit by fires from the blazing houses as the Soviet barrage crashed down, attempting to halt the German drive.

The position in which 99th Regiment was placed was one of vital importance to the success of the battle and against its companies and battalions was flung a succession of heavy attacks. Under this pressure the Jäger line began to bend and then at some places broke so that the Russians penetrated the regimental front. Aware of the location of regimental headquarters the Soviet Command sent in a solid phalanx of armoured vehicles which had soon smashed through the sector held by one of the battalions. After the battle, and along the line which this had taken, the bodies of the fallen and the smashed hulks of wrecked tanks were evidence of how bitter had been the struggle. The path of the Red Army advance was marked by the dead; khaki and field grey alike, for it should not be thought that casualties to the regiment had been light. More than 180 officers and men from the 99th fell in action on Friday 13 April and it would be no exaggeration to say that on that day the Gebirgs Division fought for its life.

The most determined efforts had been required to defend regimental headquarters against the Red armoured drive. A scratch force of the survivors from overrun companies and from rear echelon men took the field, while to hold the wavering line firm and to stiffen the crumbling defence, the motor cycle company, its men armed with machine pistols, was rushed from one threatened sector to another. In close combat the Jäger from the rifle companies fought back the

Soviet armour and attacked the steel giants with explosive satchels, panzerfaust and magnetic charges. Throughout the long April day the 99th fought this unequal battle, which rose to a peak of ferocity in the four hours between last light and midnight, as the Russian leaders flung in attack hoping by persistence to wear down the men whom numbers alone could not defeat. For hours the pattern of attack, defence, counter-attack and renewed thrust went on but then as the night advanced the fury died down and by 02.00hrs of 14 April there was quiet.

The regiment, weakened and strained by the severity of the fighting, had been given an 18km sector of line to hold, which stretched from the Hackerberg to Muhlbreiten. This was considered to be so vital an area to the defence of Styria that the 99th was supported by a brigade of self-propelled guns, heavy anti-tank guns, and eventually a panzer detachment with seven vehicles. Despite this support the regiment was eventually forced to yield and moved back to the heights on the eastern bank of the Lafnitz.

The direction of the Soviet thrust then swung away from 99th area towards Birkfeld hoping to force a decision there. To ensure success in their efforts to force a crossing of the Fischbach Alps the Red Command poured in men regardless of casualties.

Their assaults came in a regular and rapid pattern but many were echeloned so that two consecutive attacks were not made against the same company or battalion but against its neighbour, thus giving opportunity to the first defenders to recuperate, to repair positions and to replenish supplies of ammunition. The German defenders, conscious of how vital was the part they were playing in the defence of their country, stood and faced the ordeal with resolute calm. There was so little German-held territory left that there was now no place to which the defenders could retreat. It was stand and die; or else surrender to an enemy who had shown himself to be an implacable foe.

The front now had to hold. Every day helped the major formations to move the heavy equipment and to switch forces to form a firm defensive front. And so the regiments held. Battered from bombardments, under almost constant pressure, exhausted from the strain of battle, hungry and cold though they were, they held. They did more than just hold. Not only did they fling back the violent Russian assaults, tumbling them into ruin but then set the seal upon their local victories with counter-attacks and aggressive patrolling which dominated the Reds completely.

To meet the Soviet thrust towards Birkfeld the Army High Command grouped men and put them into another counter-offensive in which the 99th was not at first involved and in this period of relative calm, for Russian pressure had eased, the battalions had time to reorganise and to strengthen their positions. There were minor irritations to overcome, of course, from the troops on their own side. One of these was a battalion of Volkssturm which, attached to the 2nd Battalion of the Gebirgsjäger, proved so much of a hindrance because of its untrained state and unreliable habits that the Jäger battalion officers seriously suggested that it be disbanded and the VS men sent home.

On the sensitive Upper Styrian front the German counter-offensive succeeded in throwing back the assaults of a Cossack cavalry corps which had made penetrations in the Sassnitz and the Feistritz valleys, but as if to contemptuously dismiss this counter-assault the Soviet Command maintained its own offensive and set against the 99th a great part of 5th Guards Cavalry Corps supported by the infantry of 26th Army.

It soon became clear that this was the opening of a fresh offensive aimed at forcing a breakthrough. From probing attacks by tanks against just No. 13 Company the assaults opened like a fan until both 1st and 2nd Battalions were heavily committed. The defence was firm, the counter-attacks vigorous and the Gebirgsjäger unceasing in their efforts to halt the Russian thrust. They were usually successful as trained troops must be against raw levies but there were Cossack patrols who used the huge and silent woods as a cover to infiltrate in classic Red Army style. By ones and twos the riders would walk march their horses along lonely rides in the dark green forests. Little grows under pines for these tall trees take from the poor, thin soil in which they stand all the nourishment for their own growth. On slippery carpets of pine needles the Cossacks and their horses passed from one tree's shadow to that of another. Where they came too close to German sentries the rider would take his horse down wind so that its heavy stale urine smell would remain undetected by the outposts.

Once past these sentinels Red cavalrymen would rendezvous at a point remote and hidden. Then would begin their work of creating panic and fear in the German Army's rear. Despatch riders would fail to arrive at their destination and telephone calls between German officers would be interrupted by a Slav voice speaking poor German but whose threatening message was plain enough. Little hamlets or isolated farms in the quiet green countryside would suddenly hear the clatter of hooves and the creak of leather. Then in through the door would burst Cossacks in their high-shouldered black cloaks, demanding with loud and guttural voices food, drink and women. Small children would gaze wide-eyed in astonishment as these giant men, and such they seemed to be, filled the rooms with their huge cloaks smelling of horses and leather, looting with a laugh or destroying for the joy of it. The children were always safe, even the girls up to about the age of 12, but woe to the women for these men spared none. Husbands who tried to prevent the multiple rape of the womenfolk—wives, mothers or even grandmothers—were often castrated before being sabred to death. The task of the Red cavalry was to spread terror and this they did so well that the treks of refugees who had come out of Hungary in advance of the Red Army, were soon joined by farmers and inhabitants of villages of eastern Austria. Great, slow-moving columns of the despairing and the displaced filled the roads, moved along bridle paths and tracks heading westward out of the clutches of those terrible fur-hatted men whose appetites were as insatiable as their methods were brutal. And these treks, inspired by rumours of rapine and pillage, so filled the roads that military convoys could not use them, except with difficulty so that supplies of food and ammunition for the front were delayed. A chronic shortage of shells, bullets, explosives and the implements of war began to affect every unit and batteries of German guns lay silent because they had no shells to fire.

The bitter fighting in upper Styria involving the 99th continued without let up, but behind the battle line the first preparations were being made in the event of another withdrawal. Roads in the valley of the Lafnitz were reconnoitred and the availability of paths noted on military maps. Meanwhile the fury of the Soviet attacks grew with each passing day. In groups, in companies, by battalion and by regiment the Red Army infantry charged time after time. As often as they attacked they were driven back. Sometimes under thundering barrages they would pour forward in masses; at other times small files of them would advance sheltering behind squadrons of tanks.

The Jäger with the Panzerfaust or teams armed with the Panzerschreck would fire their rocket weapons and black, greasy smoke columns would rise to show where a victory had been scored. The Red infantry huddling behind the stricken tank would seldom advance but would remain at the back of the vehicle until bursts of machine gun fire dispersed or destroyed them. The Russian troops showed a complete lack of tactical skill and it was clear to the mountain men that great numbers of their opponents were in action for the first time. These young Russian soldiers may have lacked the sheer ability of the Red Army regiments of 1941, '42 and '43, but they still retained the dogged will to succeed which had brought the men of the Soviet Army victoriously from Stalingrad to the heartlands of Europe.

They advanced without hesitation, time and time again and across a carpet of their own dead. The casualties they suffered were enormous, both in vehicles and in infantry.

These losses had their effect upon some as did the terrible weather in the mountains. Added to the iron cold was the important fact obtained from interrogation, that food supplies to the Russian regiments in the mountains often did not arrive because of the shortage of adequate roads in the area. The Red Army were exhausted, cold and hungry. Desertions to the Germans became a steady trickle. Little groups would suddenly appear through the mists waving the white leaflets which they thought were the passports to freedom. Some even volunteered to stay with the Gebirgsjäger and in fact the regiment's ration strength at the end of April included 1688 former Red Army men, many of whom had been with the regiment for years.

However determined the German resistance may have been the Soviet advance to the valley of the Feistritz could not be halted—it could only be reduced in tempo—and during the morning of Thursday 19 April, Russian soldiers scaled and captured the commanding heights just one kilometre to the north of Feistritz town. A counter-attack along the river valley carried out by the last vehicles of 1st Panzer Division supported by 117th Jäger Division proved to be a long, bloody and unsatisfactory affair in that the summit remained in Russian hands. At other places there were minor successes and batches of Soviet troops, cut off during these German counter-thrusts, were either captured or destroyed.

The High Command of 6th Army, deeply conscious of how vital

to their plans was the retention of the Feistritz valley, determined to push back the Russian incursions and to establish a new and firm defensive front along the river line. To succeed in this enterprise required troops of high quality and such men were to hand. The 99th Gebirgsjäger Regiment was selected because the battle area was one of high mountains, and was ordered to move from the sector which it held and to proceed with all despatch to the valley of the Feistritz river.

Sunday 22 April was a day which began quietly enough with none of the heavy and prolonged assaults which had marked the passage of the previous week. During this lull the Gebirgsjäger had a chance to repair the ravages of the bitter fighting which had been their lot. Companies were reorganised, the rear echelons combed for soldiers to man the firing line, positions strengthened and weapons repaired. In the afternoon, however, a sudden and fierce infantry attack preceded by a concentrated bombardment upon the positions held by 1st Battalion, cost it 31 casualties in dead and wounded.

During the hours of darkness the first Jäger units were relieved from their positions and as an example of how thin the German defensive line had now become was the fact that the battalion of 2nd Panzer Grenadier Regiment, which took over the positions of 2nd Battalion of the 99th, had only a small number of effectives being no more than 160 men strong with 7 machine guns and two mortars. The mountain unit was three times as strong as the unit sent to relieve it. To bolster the defence of these panzer grenadiers most of whom were without any sort of training in infantry warfare, several of the Gebirgsjäger companies remained in the line until Wednesday 25 April.

The new task awaiting the mountain men was to bring fresh impetus to the German offensive in upper Styria, which had been slowed by a combination of bad weather and tenacious Russian defence. Determination had brought the advance forward until it reached Wenigzell, half-destroyed by the barrages which had fallen upon it, but at that point the forward movement had come to a halt and needed the infusion of skilled and proficient mountain men to revive it. The first assault by 99th captured a Soviet ammunition dump and four tanks and villages near Hartberg were retaken from enemy garrisons, one of which fled in panic as the Jäger stormed into the town, for interrogation summaries indicated that the Red Command was unaware of the move to that sector of the 1st Gebirgs Division.

The embussed battalions arrived in their sectors, chiefly into an area under the control of 117 Jäger Division to which formation 99th was temporarily attached. The nature of the ground prevented the establishing of a continuous front and the 5kms gap which existed between 1st and 2nd Battalions was a source of anxiety even though it was constantly and vigorously patrolled.

We had some anxious moments in our patrols, particularly when our group was in the area of the Hochwechsel. The forests there are particularly dense and are almost what I imagine a jungle must be like, except that in those Styrian woods there was seldom a sound to be heard. A bird might chatter or a fox bark, but that was all for the closeness of the trees muffled almost all noise. Our patrols would move forward in skirmishing order with machine gunners on both flanks and heavily supported by Jäger armed with machine pistols. There was no fear of tanks so the awkward Panzerfaust or Panzerschreck were not carried. Most of us favoured grenades and entrenching tools for encounters with the enemy were usually the result of a meeting at close range. You must understand that the advance by units during the previous week had cut off whole bodies of Ivans and that these were hiding in the woods waiting for their own army to come up and relieve them. They carried out a sort of partisan warfare against us, keeping very quiet and concealing themselves cleverly both on the ground as well as in the trees. At very close range they would open fire and then it was a quick burst of fire or a rifle grenade in the trees to bring down their look-out man who was also a sniper. Many of them must have evaded us and just melted into the forest which covers such a large area of ground. God knows what they lived on being cut off from their own units, for there was almost nothing which grew in the woods that they could eat except berries or mushrooms and there were very few houses from which they could steal or requisition food.

Our patrols also kept the ground between the 1st and 32nd Battalions of the regiment. Our 3rd Battalion was on detached duty and did not rejoin us until the last week in April.

When 3rd Battalion did come up it formed on the left flank of 2nd Battalion and both were ordered to attack and capture the Hochwechsel while 1st Battalion, supported by No. 303 Brigade of self-propelled guns went in against Mönichwald. It will be remembered that the regiment was attached to 117th Jäger Division and that formation was fighting a confused and difficult battle. One of its regiments was embattled around the Hochwechsel while the greater part of its second regiment was cut off and surrounded in Mönichwald. It was to be the task of 1st Battalion of the 99th to smash the Russian encircling ring to bring out the trapped units, and to take over the positions within the encirclement.

The whole of 99th Regiment was now in that area of Styria and upon that battlefield where its men were to fight their last battle. None of those to whom I have talked realised quite how close was the end of the war in Europe.

There was little news except the OKW communiques, letters from home no longer came from those families who lived in the areas of Germany occupied or threatened by the rapid advance of the American Army in southern Germany. There was, of course, realisation that the Russians and the Allies were deep into Germany but still the hope, belief is a better word, that some miracle would occur which might yet bring victory. There was talk of wonder weapons, of a new alliance with the western Powers who would join with the Germans in the destruction of the Red enemy. But there was nothing concrete, only a nagging fear that those at home were not safe, that the war might be lost; but that every day gained by holding out helped to stave off the defeat which would mean the ruin of Germany. And so they stood their ground, the Gebirgsjäger, went into attack, conducted a stubborn defence, struggled and endured in the hope that their sacrifice might yet bring a victor's crown to reward them for the years of battle and suffering.

No sooner had the battalions of 99th arrived in their designated areas than they were told off for the attacks which would bring forward the German line and straighten it in the Mönichwald sector. The 3rd Battalion was the first to arrive and it was immediately put into an assault against Breitenstein which, if successful, would clear the Schrimpf valley. The companies swung forward moving along the sides of wooded hills and through dead ground until by late in the afternoon they had taken the village in an assault which drove the Red

Army infantry back to the valley of the Feistritz. The reconnaissance detachment then went on to carry the advance north-eastwards through the valley of the rivulet which leads towards the Hochwechsel. The next unit of 99th to arrive in the concentration area was the motor cycle platoon which was ordered to carry out a reconnaissance towards Waldbach in the valley of the upper Lafnitz. Reports came in that in Waldbach there was a detachment of ten Russian T 34 tanks and, with that flair for the dramatic which possessed many at that time, the commander of the motor cyclists decided to attack and to destroy them. A quick check found that there were no anti-tank grenades among any of his men and that their only weapons were their personal arms and grenades. The planned destruction of the Red tank detachment would have to wait until the 303 SP Brigade came up.

Then the 1st Battalion arrived and their having taken up all-round defensive positions allowed the motor cyclists to continue their reconnaissance towards Mönichwald and Point 1054. There seemed to be no enemy in the area and the cycle-mounted Jäger extended the area of their probing searching for a weak point in the Russian ring around Mönichwald. Moving cautiously by night through bushes and along side roads it was soon discovered that a narrow gap did indeed exist and slipping quietly through the Russian ring first contact was made with the encircled men of 117th Jäger Division. A wider gap needed to be made to bring out the units of 117th and Gebirgsjäger undertook the nerve-tearing task of silencing the Russian sentries. Quietly they moved, only metres at a time from the shadow of one tree or bush to another until they could first hear and then see the unfortunate sentinels whom they would have to silence for ever. If there was a group of sentries in a listening post then a sudden descent of mountain men would crash in among the Russians and the post would be taken out in a welter of blood and muffled screams. Through the gap which the Gebirgsjäger had carved, the trapped units of 117th Division were brought out platoon by platoon and replaced, platoon by platoon, by Gebirgsjäger.

The OKW communique for Friday 27 April 1945 read "The southern sector of the Eastern Front was dominated by our counteroffensive, during which the Reds were driven from an area south of Mürzzuschlag to the Lafnitz sector". The bald words of the official report gave no hint of the battle which was fought to achieve the capture of Mönichwald and the capture of the summit of the Wechsel massif.

The attack by 99th Regiment had been a night attack to capture the peak and it fell to an assault group from 2nd Battalion, whose furious assault not only seized the height but surprised the soldiers of the Red garrison shivering miserably on the summit and captured them. The Wechselberg is a vast area of ground and there were now so few Gebirgsjäger left. The question was raised at battalion HQ and with regiment whether it was worth attempting to hold the peak with the weak garrison which 2nd Battalion could afford. As it was, platoons from the regimental headquarters group had had to be brought forward to thicken the line, and men from the motor cycle and from the pioneer platoons were spread around the peak and in the ground immediately below this.

While 2nd had been thrusting for the summit the 3rd Battalion had been given the task of clearing up enemy pockets of resistance in the upper Schrimpf valley with orders that, once this essential task had been completed, to return with best possible speed to thicken the defensive line on the summit of the Wechsel. One company, the 2nd, arrived on the peak in time to participate in bearing off a Soviet counter-attack while a reconnaissance group led by the regimental commander penetrated into the village of Feistritz. The sector held by 99th Gebirgsjäger Regiment could now be considered firm and preparations were made to prepare defences strong enough to meet the severe counter-attacks which were certain to come in and also to consolidate the regiment's hold on the area.

To carry out the latter part of this standard procedure 3rd Battalion pushed itself past the left wing of 2nd Battalion and, near Rettenegg, the Inselberg was captured against the most desperate Soviet resistance. The entry for 28 April in the regimental account of the battle records that penetrations of the Soviet front were made as far as the Kanisberger Schwaig on the Niederwechsel, and to the Lorenzkogel east of the Waldbach valley, and that in the latter area the dense and extensive woods were found to be occupied by Red Army units making obvious preparations for imminent assault upon the Jäger positions.

The size and weight of the imminent Soviet offensive to recapture the ground which had been lost forced a retraction of outpost lines on the Hochwechsel and the isolated groups were pulled back to main defensive positions. A storm was about to break over the 99th as the Soviet Command determined to break through and to force a passage for its armies. There was an urgency in the Russian moves for during 28 April overtures had been made by Colonel General von Vietinghoff, the German Commander in Chief in Italy, to conclude an armistice with the Allied armies. The German front along the Apennines had collapsed and the army group had lost much of its heavy equipment in its retreat across the Po. On the Adriatic side of Italy the British 8th Army, fanning out on the far side of the great river barrier had swung towards Venice, Trieste and the Istrian peninsula, while on the Tyrhennian side the Americans advanced towards Milan and the cities of the industrial north. Stalin's fear that an armistice might allow the western Allies into Austria while the Red Army was still engaged in battle seemed about to be realised. The troops of Tolbhukin's front were ordered to attack without let up until the obstruction represented by the 99th Regiment had been overcome, and a rapid advance south-westwards could cut off 6th Army and 2nd Panzer Army before linking up with the Red Armies in Yugoslavia. The attacks were ordered to succeed cost what they might and evidence of interpretation of Tolbhukin's orders is shown in the fact that, during the drive towards Vienna when a similiar urgency was required, his driving pace had lost his 6th Guards Army 267 tanks against a dying enemy.

On the summit of the Hochwechsel and the other peaks of Upper Styria it was to be no question of armoured fighting vehicles but of men, of the eternal infantrymen who win the battles by physically driving the enemy from the ground which he occupies. In the days to come the gateways to the capital of Styria and to the southern marches were to be assaulted with a fanaticism that surpassed the heroic, and were to be defended by men who, like the men of Thermopylae, were determined that the enemy, intending to ravage their homeland, would never pass except over their dead bodies. None, perhaps, of the Gebirgsjäger saw the coming battle in quite so historic or dramatic terms. To them it was merely another series of heavy Russian assaults that they were to undergo. There would be no armour and the only real problems were the rock splinters, flung up by the explosions from the Russian shells, which acted as a sort of natural shrapnel, and whether there would be enough ammunition to enable them to strike back adequately against all the attacks that were going to come in against them.

The first heavy assaults came in during the afternoon of 28 April against 1st and 2nd Battalions. These were clearly diversionary thrusts to hold the German reserves while the main effort went in against Point 154. The Gebirgsjäger holding that point were subjected to a barrage of such ferocity that many of other companies who witnessed it doubted, at the time, whether any would survive. They were soon to have their doubts removed for even as the first lines of Soviet infantry moved slowly towards the summit one machine gun, then a second and finally from a number of places on that shell-torn slope, Jäger, recovering from the shock of the barrage, sighted along barrels of machine guns and began to repay the Russian soldiers for the misery that they had had to endure in the bombardment. Flung back after the first assault the survivors of the Russian line were caught up in the second wave that then began its own attempt to reach the summit, and those who had survived the Gebirgsjäger fire were brought forward again. The result was the same. At regular and timed intervals the brown-coated Russian infantry would storm out of the shelter of the trees and charge uphill towards the Jäger who now, with nerves restored, shot them down and created a shambles out of the brave attempts.

Then the attacks opened up along the whole of the regimental front during which the bravery of the Russian soldiers brought them up to the main German defensive line, so that in some sectors it was hand to hand and man to man to decide the outcome of the day. Day ends quickly in the mountains and the last rays of the late afternoon sun slanted across the meadows of short Alpine grass and into the eyes of the Russians making yet another assault. Nor was this the last for even after dark their breathless "Oorays" echoed around the peaks as they stumbled, as tired now as the Gebirgsjäger against whom they were pitting their courage and determination. The fighting lasted well into the night and when it was early morning it began again. Dense masses of Russian troops rushed towards and captured the summit of the Hochwechsel flinging down the Gebirgsjäger who had defended it. Seeing the course of the battle from 3rd Battalion headquarters, only a few hundred metres below the scene of the fighting, the battalion's commander ordered forward the alarm companies and these swung into a fast-moving drive straight for the summit, destroying the Soviets who had had insufficient time to consolidate their hold on this vital position. A second Red infantry assault captured the peak and again they were driven back from it. The Soviet commanders were determined, regardless of loss, to seize it and sent in one assault after another, causing serious and heavy losses to the 11th and 13th Companies of Gebirgsjäger who were defending the summit.

Such was the pressure and so frequent the assaults that although the summit eventually did remain in German hands, at least for the remainder of 29 April, the battle line had to be taken back to Point 1455 and 1456. The regiment was fighting an isolated battle, for there was no contact with the left flank neighbour.

Such casualties were suffered during the fighting of this terrible Sunday that an alarm call went out for fresh units to thicken the line and, to this post of honour at which only the bravest were fighting, the Army Command sent a fortress battalion made up of men too old or too infirm to serve as line infantry. The 1st Battalion of 99th was pulled out of the front during the night and its place was taken by a battalion of the 98th the sister Gebirgsjäger regiment. The 1st Battalion was then inserted into the gap between the regiment's 2nd Battalion and the fortress unit.

During the night which led up to 30 April the Soviets brought up some SP artillery pieces to assist the tired Red infantry, and these guns came in against the positions held by the 98th Regiment's battalion but were driven off. At dawn the Russian infantry attacks were renewed and this time against 2nd Battalion which had first to endure a fierce bombardment. One of the battalion calculated that four thousand rounds fell in the battalion area during the single barrage. But the Soviet infantry made no penetrations and were driven back time after time with heavy losses. The losses were not all one sided, however, and as a result of the fighting of the past days the companies garrisoning the peak of the Hochwechsel had been almost totally destroyed. Those who remained were a shattered and despairing remnant.

But the front held and the second Soviet attempt to break through to Graz had been thwarted by the mountain men.

The last week of World War II in Europe began on Tuesday 6 May and throughout that day German radio stations announced the death in Berlin of Adolf Hitler. Along all the embattled fronts German armies fought back in the rapidly diminishing area of territory which they still held, only in the Protectorate of Bohemia and in Austria were there still extensive tracts as yet not overrun by the Allied armies.

May Day it was expected would bring with it a massive assault by the Red Army and this proved, indeed, to be the case. The barrage of shells and bombs which fell upon positions held by 99th Gebirgs Regiment was one which was recorded in the war diary as being of unparalleled ferocity, being far greater than that of the previous day due to the massing on the regiment's front of a Soviet corps artillery group. For hour after hour the sound of gunfire echoed among the wooded Styrian hills and the red glare of the discharge of regiments of Katyushas was reflected on the low-flying rain clouds.

From first light to dusk the pounding continued against the thin Jäger lines in and around Mönichwald; this was clearly an attempt to smash once and for all the front of the defiant Gebirgsjäger and to pass through the gap the infantry divisions of 33rd Rifle Corps. Troops from those units stormed through the dark woods towards the 99th's positions. At times they came on even before their own barrage had stopped, taking casualties in an effort to close with the men of the 1st and 2nd Battalions and to destroy them. The Jäger had, however, chosen their positions well; some of them were grouped along a small stream which flowed from the summit of the Hochkogel to join the Lafnitz river near Mönichwald.

Silent under the great pines which cover the slopes the little knots of mountain men waited and waited until, slipping through the trees, the first sections of Red Army men came into sight. These moved quickly behind the barrage passing along the side of the slope and when they reached the small but swift-flowing tributary and had still not been fired at they slowed the pace of the advance, each seeking to cross the water without wetting his feet. As they stood there the Red Army men presented a perfect target.

The bullets pouring from the muzzles of the MG 42s and the machine pistols killed them and soon on the banks of this little mountain stream there lay only the dead. The barrage which had brought them forward marched on, unsupported by the infantry, planting giant black craters in the short Alpine grass and tearing off the tops of the green and stately pines.

Time after time throughout the late May day the Russian infantry came on and were beaten back. Sweating with the strain of the climb, despite the bitter cold temperatures, they struggled up and down the slopes in their approach marches and were committed almost without pause or rest to the attack. Their assaults died under the fire of machine guns and machine pistols whose cloth-tearing sound reverberated among the dark, pine-treed hills. No German shell killed any of them. The guns without ammunition could make no reply and they stood, facing east, but impotent to help the hard-pressed Jäger.

Some regimental mortars still had a few rounds but these were held until real crises came, for isolated Soviet infantry attacks, even of large proportions, were not emergencies but everyday occurrences.

As the last of the Russian attacks was driven off and darkness fell, the Gebirgsjäger sat in their positions hungry, cold and confused. Chaos on the roads behind the front, roads congested with civilian refugee columns and those of military vehicles stopped the ammunition and ration trucks from reaching "A" and "B" echelons. The wildest and most improbable rumours circulated. The Führer's death would mean a new government and this would align itself with the Americans. Then, side by side, the US and the German Armies would fight their way eastward to destroy the Soviet Army. Only a few days to wait and then out of the west would come the American infantry, young, keen and well equipped. The word spread: "Hold on for a few more days and everything will be all right again".

There were some, however, who viewed the immediate prospects with a more sober eye and who convinced themselves that to fall in the last days of a dying war and for no great tactical purpose would be a senseless and a ridiculous sacrifice. One such group of men were the remnants of No. 3 Company. Exhausted by the fighting, frozen in their snowy trenches, dispirited and worried about their families who were now in parts of Germany being fought across by the Allied armies, their high hearts drooped and they deserted their positions during the night of 1 and 2 May. Those who went over to the Russians were treated no less harshly than any prisoners taken after a fight which had caused the attackers grievous losses. Human nature being as it is there were blows and beatings, but also food and warmth and, most important of all, the fact of survival.

The first five minutes of surrender are the most difficult ones. One surrenders one's wristwatch to the first insistent *Oori*, their pronunciation of our noun *Uhr* (watch). For many of us these wristwatches had been first Communion gifts and their loss was bitterly felt. Married men had their wedding rings stolen. Pocket torches, combs and even spanners from the machine gun cleaning kit, all would vanish into the capacious pockets of the Russian uniform. Now was the testing time. Were they satisfied with their looting, were they in a hurry to push on or did a few of them feel like a walk downhill to company headquarters and then back uphill again to rejoin the fighting line?

If they couldn't or wouldn't spare the time, then we were dead. Our captors, however, confident in the belief that with four words: *Frau komm, schnapps* and *Oori,* they had mastered the basic essentials of the German language brought us along with repeated shouts of *"Davai, davai"* [come on] until we reached a headquarters from which we were moved down the line with the blows becoming more frequent and heavier the farther our distance from the front. The rear echelon heroes who, if they were anything like our Army troops, had never heard the sound of bullets, were the most brutal. They needed, perhaps, to convince themselves that they were striking a blow for Mother Russia.

Those who deserted the line and headed for home had a longer and more dangerous gauntlet to run. Flying patrols of the SS, empowered to try drum-head courts martial gave short shrift to any that they caught away from their units without authority. Sentences were swiftly carried out and the trees along the roads of eastern Styria bore a fearful fruit in that frightening spring: the bodies of German soldiers hanging, usually with a placard that was inscribed with the crime for which they had been tried, sentenced and executed by the flying tribunals.

Back in No. 3 Company's positions NCOs and officers loyal to their soldierly oath tried to hold the line with those who were still left, concerned that if the Russian infantry attacks of May Day were to be repeated in number and weight then the regiment's front would crumble and the massive force of the Red Army would sweep into the Steiermark.

Unknown to any but the most senior commanders were the plans that were being laid to facilitate a fighting withdrawal through Austria. No heavily manned Alpine redoubt existed—the myth of a last

Nazi stronghold—at least not in fact but only in a few fevered minds on the German side and apprehensive ones on the Allied. There was no series of mountain fortresses but the advance of the Red Army could be delayed and his giant strength reduced at every mountain barrier. To bring this about the rear lines had to be kept open to move back the heavy weapons, new positions had to be dug, new troop dispositions made to face the Allies, advancing not only from the east and the south-east out of Yugoslavia, but also out of Italy.

An armistice in Italy, signed on 2 May, would, it was believed by the German High Command, release a flood of Anglo-American divisions to pour through the passes into Austria and across the lines of communication of the formations fighting in eastern Steiermark, so speed was essential. The order was given to the commanders of those units in Styria: "Hold fast". The unspoken, unknown qualification was that they had to hold until the rear had been organised and roads for the retreat marked out and charted, for it was the intention of 6th Army commander to pass the 4th SS Panzer Corps into Carinthia, which the British would occupy, the 3rd Panzer Corps into the US zone of occupation at Liezen, and the 117th Jäger together with 1st Gebirgs Division also to the Americans in Upper Austria.

The Jäger in the trenches knew nothing of this vast planning. The only concern to 3rd Battalion was the crumbling resistance of 119th Fortress Battalion, whose low moral fibre had been reduced to vanishing point by the absence of food or shelter; the usual active service conditions of infantry warfare and for which the battalion had not been trained. For the 2nd Battalion 99th the day passed quietly except for an attack upon a saddle in the valley of the Froschnitz, which Rauchensteiner in his book condemns as having been made for no apparent reason other than to still a vague rumour regarding Russian lorried movement in a south-westerly direction.

During the early morning of Thursday 3 May the first of a fresh wave of heavy and presistent Russian infantry attacks was launched. The Red Army troops came on in greater number than on May Day and one Jäger Company lost 60 men killed and missing. It was upon the 3rd Battalion that the most severe assaults came in and there were now so few troops left to man the positions that the waves of Russian infantry eventually overran its forward positions. The Jäger who had been firing at the Soviet troops at long distance with machine guns, then engaged them at medium range with machine pistols

and were finally locked in close combat, man to man, body against
body, heaving and straining with the effort of trying to kill in a
press of bodies. Russian and German soldiers close-twined, rolled
over low precipices. Rocks held tightly in bleeding fists crashed down
to crack open the enemy's skull through his thick lambswool cap.
Jäger hunting knives rose and fell and breath came in short gasps as
each man struggled to destroy his opponent.

Suddenly the Russians broke and ran leaving behind their dead
and wounded as well as prisoners who, like the deserters of No. 3
Company, had had enough. Where the Soviets broke, alarm companies alerted and ready for their task swung forward to the attack,
moving with the seemingly slow but ground-covering lope of the
trained mountaineer. Fire and movement; outflank and encircle; grenade and bullet brought these storm troop detachments crashing
through the groups of Russians who still had not emerged from the
strain of immediate past combat and had not consolidated on the
ground that they had won so dearly. The tactic of immediate
counter-attack had proved its worth time and time again and every
front and here, in Steiermark, every hour gained helped to hold the
Eastern Wall.

Each attack was held, although some must bear the qualifying
word "eventually", and each piece of ground lost to the Reds was
recaptured, so that by last light the line, though battered, still held.
The visit which General Wittmann, the divisional commander, made
to the regiment during the day may have strengthened the resolve of
the mountain men, for they still formed a shield behind which organisation to meet the final struggle was taking place.

Desperately the regiment sought men for the firing line and the
rear echelon units were combed and combed again. The most ill-
assorted groups of reinforcements came up to join the battalions. One
was a group of 40 Army officials, pen pushers and officer storesmen,
who had been found surplus to establishment at some rear echelon
and who had been sent to the Styrian hills to play their part in holding back the Red Army. These reinforcements to the Jäger line, civilians in uniform, were sent back without being posted to a battalion.
Conditions were hard enough but the presence of untrained and unfit
troops was an encumbrance.

The armistice in Italy had, by 6 May, long since come into effect
and the end of the war in Europe waited on the threshold of the next

day. The Commander-in-Chief of Army Group South, Rendulic, gave orders to his troops in the West to cease hostilities against the American forces on 7 May, but gave no such order to the troops manning the Eastern Front. Rendulic feared that the issuing of such an instruction would open the floodgates to a Soviet advance into the southern provinces of Austria sweeping all before it and producing a military catastrophe.

In Reims, where the armistice ending the war in the West was to be signed, Jodl, one of the German signatories, made it clear that those German armies still battling in the East, particularly those of Field Marshal Löhr in Yugoslavia, of Rendulic in Styria and Schörner in Czechoslovakia, would not lay down their arms until their men had fought their way through to Germany or to German territory. Rendulic himself ordered his four armies to maintain their positions until the evening of 7 May. At last light on that day they could begin their wave westward.

Unofficially, two days remained after the time of the formal "cease fire"; two days during which the great mass of the armies were to seek to cross the Enns river leaving the rearguard to make, at the last moment, its storm dash for the river which formed the demarcation line between the Americans and the Russians. After 9 May all military movement had to halt and it was the enemy against whom one had fought the last battle to whom one surrendered. To reach and cross the Enns before 9 May was the difference between Lucky Strike cigarettes and three US meals a day and lead, iron, coal and salt mines of Siberia.

Of the grave testing time which lay only hours away the men of the 99th Gebirgsjäger Regiment knew nothing officially, although there were signs enough. The transport was withdrawn to rear echelon; always the first move presaging a retreat and as always there were rumours. So far as the regimental commander was concerned he was to hold his positions along the line of the Lafnitz and this he was determined to do even though there were increasing indications that morale in his Command was crumbling. The number grew of those who in the darkest part of those cold May nights left their trenches and slipped away. One group, fired upon as it was thought to be a Russian patrol, turned out to be sub-units of the divisional artillery withdrawing without orders.

It was fortunately for the regiment a period of quiet. Ivan was for the moment content to send only patrols forward probing for weak spots in the Jäger line.

Monday 7 May saw the official end to the war in Europe and all along the battle line in Austria units began, or prepared to begin, the move towards the Enns. In an effort to thin the numbers of men trekking westward Rendulic ordered the release from the Service of Austrian soldiers and of those Russian prisoners of war who had been elected to serve with German units, the so called Hiwis. Many of the former Red Army men refused to leave their units and stayed until the end. Others who did leave then moved on to the main roads westward adding to the numbers that Army Group Commander had tried to reduce.

Some units achieved the move to the river Enns boundary with little or no difficulty. The 2nd Panzer Army, for example, reached the river and passed over by 8 May, as did the still aggressive units of 6th SS Panzer Army. The 6th Army was unlucky. Behind it lay a mountainous region lacking sufficient east/west roads and such roads as existed were congested with civilian treks and by military vehicles. Many of these had been so long in service and were so deficient in power that they were, in many instances, unable to climb the steep mountain gradients, remaining halted and obstructing the traffic flow until impatient and frightened hands pitched them bodily from the roads. The days were sunny, the skies cloudless and full of Russian fighters and bombers who swept down low over the retreating columns playing their part in slowing down the rate of retreat.

The orders to withdraw were completely misunderstood at 6th Army or, perhaps, had been badly worded. Whatever the reason the 6th Army did not move back towards the Enns as a compact body. When the army group order came the instructions from army to the corps and divisions under its control were issued piecemeal and with such intervals of time between them that many units had still not received them twenty-four hours after the first instruction had been given. Some did not receive any withdrawal orders at all. According to Lanz, writing in his book on the First Gebirgs Division, no such order was received by that formation and when clarification was sought from corps it was found that the staff had already broken up and dispersed. In the absence of firm orders, and aware that some strong and capable unit would have to guard the withdrawal of the rest of 6th Army, the 1st Gebirgs Division stood fast, intending to move back by bounds and selecting an area known as Auf der Schanz upon which to form a new defensive line which 99th Regiment would hold.

The commander of the 99th went to divisional headquarters and was there told not only of the signing of the unconditional surrender but also of the difficult lot which had fallen to the division and to his regiment. He knew that most of his men would stand fast upon his order. They were still engaged in fighting back the new wave of infantry attacks which regiments of the Red Army had been launching since dawn of 8 May. Time after time the barrage had come down. Time after time behind it stormed the lines of brown-overcoated Red Army infantry, and time after time these had been driven back. If any Jäger felt that it was senseless to die on the last day of the war none showed it. Coolly they aimed, sighted and fired as they had done through all the years that they had fought together. Poland, Norway, Russia, the Caucasus, the Balkans. The war had been a series of names where they had marched and fought, frozen in the bitter cold or scorched in the summer's glaring heat; struggling up vertical rock faces or wading through stinking swamps; aiming, firing, killing or being killed.

The enemy was still trying to smash through and as the fresh groups of Red Army men came on toward the Jäger positions the mountain men with a hundred-fold experience of combat selected the officers, the commissars and the NCOs and shot these down knowing that the loss of the leaders would cause the remainder to waver and halt, uncertain and hesitant like calves in an abbatoir. But it was not always thus. One violent assault carried out during the morning of 8 May struck across the positions held by one company of Jäger killing them all, and roared on until it had almost reached regimental headquarters.

There it was finally held by a scratch force until the alarm companies came forward, beating down the Red Army attackers and driving them back. The line still held and at 21.00hrs the noise of battle died away. The fighting, difficult enough, had been made more so by Battle Group Raithel, which had held post on the Semmering and which had withdrawn in accordance with its orders. But this move, made without warning the regiment, had laid open the flank of the 99th creating a gap through which the first Red Army groups were moving.

The order for the regiment was to disengage and to foot march to a point south-west of the Teufelsstein, Auf der Schanz. Small groups of men began to thin the line, each led by a guide who brought the handfuls of soldiers on to dark roads where they met other sections. Back in the line the trenches were deserted save here and there where a skeleton force kept watch and ward over the withdrawal by their comrades. Then at 23.00hrs the last men facing east, towards those dark hills on which the Soviet enemy lay, climbed out of their trenches and slipped away into the concealing darkness. Only hours remained. These men had held the line to the last, their firm discipline and great tactical ability had enabled them to hold firm in conditions that tested the strongest nerves.

The regiment set off en route for the Teufelsstein with 3rd Battalion forming the rearguard and under orders to hold off, by force of arms if necessary, any Soviet attempt to interfere with the regiment's withdrawal. The columns moved on foot through the night, all motor transport had been sent back to the rear and the foot troops were to move to Strobl a concentration point where they would embus for the road journey to the Enns river and safety. Dropping down to Waldbach and along the road back to Falkenstein in the Feistritz valley, the journey then continued along the valley of another mountain stream followed by an upward climb until the Teufelsstein was passed at the 1499 metre line, before dropping abruptly some 300 metres to the Schanz.

The north-south road to Gloggnitz was blocked. The north-west road to Krieglach was blocked and the Schanz road to Kindergdörfl was stuffed full of traffic. The intention to reach the Enns river thus became an ambition which had no hope of realisation for lorries, carts and military vehicles of every sort were halted in a traffic jam and among this congested mass was the regimental transport, its anti-tank guns and heavy weapons. All were lost in the confusion. The Gebirgsjäger threaded their way through the almost solid mass of traffic, but soon cohesion between the groups was lost; the regiment was disintegrating.

In a desperate effort to reach the concentration point, Auf der Schanz, where he expected to form a new defence line, the regimental commander set out on a long and circuitous drive. Slowly battling his way along crowded woodland paths he began to approach the

Schanz from the west and about 04.00hrs met, en route, his 2nd Battalion whose commander passed to him an order from division. This stated in bald and stark terms the fact of which he was now aware for the first time, that any man who had not crossed the Enns by 09.00hrs would be considered as a prisoner of war of the Red Army. The only hope for his men would have been the local railway line which ran along the valley of the river Mürz but even had a train been ready and even if it had a clear run the train could never have reached in time the Enns bridge, some 110kms distant. So far as the 99th Regiment's commander was concerned this order condemned his men to imprisonment in the Soviet Union. His efforts to clarify the situation with divisional headquarters were in vain, nor was he able to rejoin his men because of the press of traffic on the roads.

At 09.00hrs, the time by which all military movement was to cease, the Gebirgsjäger battalions, now reassembled and concentrated under their commander, were still marching along river valleys en route to the Schanz, when ahead of them and out of the woods on either side of the narrow country road there appeared the low, distinctive and unmistakable shapes of T 34 tanks. The battalions were surrounded. Still determined to evade capture they dispersed and broke up into small groups. Many men, using their last reserves of energy, went through the waters of the Mürz river or climbed into the snows of the Mürztal Alps striking westwards in ones and twos to hide themselves in the mountain fastnesses until they could move openly and without fear of apprehension by the Red Army when they had reached the haven of the west bank of the Enns.

Thus in confusion and uncertainty ended the war of the 99th Jäger Regiment of 1st Gebirgs Division. The Gebirgsjäger had been selected in February to support an all-out offensive and in the months succeeding the optimism of that grand assault had held the Eastern wall to allow others to escape. Carrying out one such endeavour they had sacrificed themselves and all for nothing, for Löhr's Army Group of 150,000 men was surrounded and passed into that captivity by the Yugoslavs from which the 1st Gebirgs Division had hoped to rescue it. And yet was it for nothing?

The Gebirgsjäger had demonstrated, particularly in the last months and weeks, all the military qualities and that virtue which

Christianity teaches us shows the greatest love: that of laying down one's own life for a friend. If this is true then the sacrifice of the Gebirgsjäger of 99th Regiment in Steiermark in the closing stages of World War II cannot have been in vain.

Epilogue

In May 1945 the war in Europe came to an end. During the last months of battle, as the Allied hosts fought their way in from the south, west and the east, compressing the shattered remnants of the German Army into what remained of the Third Reich, the Gebirgs divisions were active on each side of the fighting fronts.

The 1st Gebirgs Division, an account of whose 99th Regiment is given in the preceding chapter, was on the Eastern Front together with the 3rd, 4th and 9th Divisions. On the southern front were the 5th and 8th Gebirgs Divisions, while in Lapland, and thus effectively out of the final battles, were both the 6th and 7th Divisions. The 2nd fought on the Western Front against the US Army in southern Germany, and in Yugoslavia there were the remnants of the SS Gebirgs formations.

A friend whose war experiences went back to before World War I was sent to Norway as a Field officer, to arrange the surrender of part of the German forces there. On the docks at Narvik he saw the men of 20th Gebirgs Army arrive to embark to go home to a shattered and occupied Germany. The embarkation of the other military, naval and Luftwaffe units had been unremarkable, the lines of grey-looking men shuffling along, despair on every face. But then there came a distinct and thrilling change from the monotony of an army in defeat. The men of the Gebirgs divisions swung, singing, down the road to the jetty and Major Harvey was moved by unexpected and deep feelings. Passing before him he saw not the soldiers of a defeated and alien enemy force but the type of man who had formed the ranks of the infantry regiments of the British Expeditionary Force in 1914 and whom he had led in the desperate battles around

Ypres and on the Somme. Young, confident, superbly fit, trained and self-possessed these men of the enemy's Army swung past Jim Harvey as he stood there choked with the emotion of memories of soldiers whose officer he had been. The assessment of those men of one Army by a professional soldier of another was that these were soldiers whom he would have been proud to lead into battle for these, he knew, were comrades in arms, reliable and dependable.

Those virtues which Jim Harvey recognised were also appreciated by the General Staffs of the armies of Germany and of Austria. Within a few years of the ending of World War II frontier detachments had been formed and those units whose province lay in the mountains formed Gebirgsjäger frontier companies. With time and the reformation of a German Army to serve within NATO, came an expansion of those companies into regiments so that now in the service of the Federal Republic there is a Gebirgsjäger arm of service with a tradition created out of the battles of two great wars. Austria as a neutral may have no alliances and her Army is smaller than that of western Germany, but in her order of battle are the Gebirgsjäger, descendants of the men who under Andreas Hofer held the Tirol against Napoleon and under Hötzendorff became the Edelweiss Corps, the crack formation of the old Imperial and Royal Army.

Tactics may change. Helicopters can now bring the Jäger, their supplies and even their rocket-propelled artillery from valley to mountain peak in minutes, and save the strain of climbing for hours or even days. But for those situations in which, because of weather conditions, the choppers cannot fly and the call is for the high ground to be taken, then it will be Jäger infantryman, tough, tireless and confident who, overcoming all the difficulties of climate and terrain, will fight his way forward to the objective and be found waiting to receive his enemies with accurate fire from well-chosen positions. The Gebirgsjäger, like the mountain flower which he wears in his cap, will be found flourishing and resilient on the loneliest and most inaccessible peak.

Organisation

The Order of Battle of the Gebirgsjäger Formations of the German Army

Higher Gebirgs Commands of the Army

1st Gebirgs Division

The 1st Gebirgs Division was formed in Garmisch Partenkirchen around the nucleus of a Gebirgs Brigade and the regiments were located in Bavaria when mobilisation was ordered on 26 August 1939.

The 98th Regiment had all its three battalions in Mittenwald but 99th Regiment had only one battalion ready for active service and this single battalion was stationed in Füsson. The 100th Regiment was up to its establishment of three battalions and these were located in and around Bad Reichenhall, while the four battalions of the 79th Gebirgs Artillery Regiment were in and around Garmisch Partenkirchen. As the establishment of a Gebirgs division was two Jäger battalions the 100th Regiment was surplus to establishment and was posted, together with an artillery battalion, to 5th Gebirgs Division.

The composition of 1st Gebirgs Division remained unaltered until 1943 when 54th Gebirgsjäger Battalion was taken on strength and 1st Battalion of 98th Regiment posted to 3rd Hochgebirgs Battalion. Although there was no alteration in establishment from 1943 to the end of the war there was a change of titling when, on 12 March 1945, the division was renamed as 1st Volks Gebirgs Division. The addition of the term "Volks" (Peoples) was a propaganda attempt by the leaders of National Socialist Germany to identify certain elite units more closely with the masses and less with the Army hierarchy.

1st Gebirgs Division fought in southern Poland during the autumn of 1939, in the campaign against the Western Powers in the summer of 1940, and, when the armistice was signed, was trained for the amphibious operation "Sealion", the proposed invasion of Great Britain. When "Sealion" was cancelled units of the division were then posted to Besançon for proposed assault upon Gibraltar.

During the campaign in the Balkans in the spring of 1941 the division served with 2nd Army and took an active part in the fighting in Yugoslavia. When war came against the Soviet Union the 1st Gebirgs Division served on the establishment of Army Group South and was one of the units of that army group which fought its way down into the Caucasus during the summer offensive of 1942. Upon the evacuation of that area at the end of March 1943 it was posted to the Balkans. It then served in Epirus, Corfu, Serbia and Bosnia before being pushed north-eastwards to Hungary where it took part in 6th SS Panzer Army's attack around the Platensee in March 1945.

The division then fought a delaying action withdrawing into central Styria where in the last days of the war some of its units were sacrificed to cover the retreat of German 6th Army.

2nd Gebirgs Division

The 2nd Gebirgs Division was formed on 1st April 1938 in Innsbruck from the former 6th Division of the army of the Federal Republic of Austria.

In 1939 when mobilisation was ordered it had the following establishment: 136 Gebirgsjäger Regiment with three battalions of its own and a supernumerary battalion, the 2nd belonging to 140th Regiment. The second Jäger regiment was 137th Regiment with three battalions all stationed at Lienz. The 11th Gebirgs Artillery Regiment was stationed at Hall and the 1st Battalion of that artillery regiment was, in fact, the 1st Battalion of the 113th Gebirgs Artillery Regiment.

In April 1940 the 2nd Battalion of 136th Regiment was ordered to be posted away and the supernumerary battalion of 140th Regiment was then taken on strength.

The 2nd Gebirgs Division served in Poland during the campaign of 1939 and then in Norway during 1940. As part of Gebirgs Corps "Norway", 20th Gebirgs Army, it served in Lapland. Late in 1944 the 2nd Division was sent to Denmark for re-organisation and during February 1945 took part in the fighting in Württemberg, southern Germany where it surrendered to the American forces at the end of the war.

3rd Gebirgs Division

This Division was formed on 1 April 1939, in Graz, from the former 5th and 7th Divisions of the army of the Federal Republic of Austria.

The order of battle was 138th Regiment, whose three battalions were garrisoned in Leoben, 139th Regiment with three battalions in and around Klagenfurt, and 112th Gebirgs Artillery Regiment whose three battalions were in Graz.

The war service of 3rd Gebirgs Division began in Poland and in 1940 the division fought in Norway and stayed in garrison there until December 1941, when it was posted to Finland. From a group of rear echelon men and those Left out of Battle when the division went to fight in Norway, a cadre was raised around which 141st Gebirgsjäger Regiment was formed in May 1940 and posted to the newly raised 6th Gebirgs Division.

In September 1942 when 3rd Division left Finland the 139th Regiment did not accompany it but together with 1st Battalion of the division's artillery regiment stayed on to become 139th Brigade, serving as Army troops. The main of the division then moved to the Leningrad sector of the Eastern Front until December 1942, when it was transferred to Army Group Centre and fought on the Don front.

In the last months of World War II it fought in Hungary and Slovakia as well as in Upper Silesia where it passed into Soviet captivity.

4th Gebirgs Division

It had been intended that a 4th Gebirgs Division would be raised early in 1940 and the two Jäger regiments, the 142nd and 143rd, together with an artillery battalion were formed. The successful outcome of the campaign in the West made this addition to the Gebirgsjäger establishment redundant at that time and the units were disbanded.

On 23 October 1940 a new order was issued and the new division began to take shape around the nucleus of an independent divisional headquarters. Two regiments, the 13th and 91st, were obtained from 25th and 27th Infantry Divisions respectively. Those two divisions were among the group selected for conversion to panzer grenadier or to panzer status and each, therefore, had an infantry regiment sur-plus to establishment. Those divisions also supplied artillery detach-ments to form 94th Gebirgs Artillery Regiments of the 4th Gebirgs Division.

After service in Yugoslavia the division was sent to the Eastern Front on which it served for the whole of the war, chiefly with Army Group South.

5th Gebirgs Division

The cadre around which 5th Gebirgs Division was formed in the autumn of 1940 was 100th Gebirgsjäger Regiment, which had once formed the third Jäger regiment of 1st Gebirgs Division. Upon mo-bilisation in the August of 1939, the 100th Regiment, together with an artillery battalion, was posted away and eventually became one of the two Jäger regiments of 5th Division. The second regiment was obtained from an infantry division undergoing conversion to panzer grenadier status.

The establishment was, therefore, 85th and 100th Gebirgsjäger Regiments as well as 95th Gebirgs Artillery Regiment which had been built around artillery battalions supplied by 1st Gebirgs Divi-sion and 10th Infantry Division.

After fighting in Greece and in Crete the 5th stayed on in Crete as part of the occupation force before being posted, during October 1941, to the Eastern Front where it served with Army Group North. It fought on the Leningrad sector until November 1943 when it was despatched to Italy, in which theatre of operations it served until the end of the war, distinguishing itself particularly in the fighting around Cassino and in the Gothic Line battles.

6th Gebirgs Division

The 6th Gebirgs Division was formed at Heuberg on 1 June 1940. Its infantry composition was the 141st and 143rd Gebirgsjäger Regiments. The former had been constructed around a cadre of men left out of battle and belonging to 139th Gebirgsjäger Regiment. The 143rd Regiment had been intended for 4th Gebirgs Division but the 6th had achieved its growth at a much faster rate than either 4th or 5th Gebirgs Divisions and so the 143rd Regiment was posted to 6th, so as to complete its establishment.

The artillery regiment was formed out of 118th Gebirgs Artillery Regiment as well as 113th Regiment from 29th Division, the 1st Battalion of 752nd Artillery Regiment and 3rd Battalion of 112th Regiment belonging to 3rd Gebirgs Division.

The 6th Gebirgs Division served in the occupation of France and Poland before going on to fight in Greece in 1941. In the autumn of 1941 it was sent to the Eastern Front and specifically to Finland. It then moved into Lapland and then on to the Murmansk Front. As part of the order of battle of 20th Gebirgs Army it served for the remainder of the war in Norway and passed into British captivity in that country.

7th Gebirgs Division

On 15 November 1941 the 99th Light Division was converted to a mountain troop role and came on to the Gebirgs establishment as 7th Division. The infantry regiments Nos. 206 and 218, as well as the 82nd Artillery Regiment retained their numbers in the new division but were retitled Gebirgsjäger.

The 99th Replacement and Holding Battalion for the division was renamed as a ski battalion during September 1943, whereupon a new replacement battalion was formed.

The 7th Gebirgs Division served on the establishment of 20th Gebirgs Army in Lapland from April 1942 and upon the evacuation of that region moved to northern Norway where, at the end of the war, it passed into British captivity.

8th Gebirgs Division

During March 1944 it was proposed to raise an 8th Gebirgs Division around a cadre made up from 139th Gebirgsjäger Regiment. It was not until February 1945, however, that the division was completely formed by the renumbering of Reserve Division No. 157 to become the 8th Gebirgs Division.

The regiments constituting the division retained their numbers, 296 and 297 respectively. The artillery component was made up from 1057th Regiment.

For the short time that this division was on active service it fought on the Italian front and was captured by American forces at the end of hostilities.

9th Gebirgs Division

It was, perhaps, the confusion which prevailed in the German High Command as the war entered upon its last stages that led it to order the raising of two Gebirgs divisions each with the number 9.

The first of these was 9th Gebirgs Division "Nord", which was formed out of the divisional group Kräutler in Norway; while the second of the two divisions, the 9th Gebirgs Division "Ost", was constructed around the battle group "Semmering".

It would seem, however, that the "Nord" Division continued to be known and marked in operations maps as divisional group "Kräutler" and never as 9th Gebirgs Division.

The "Ost" Division was built around men taken from an NCO's training school—the Gebirgs Artillery School in Dachstein—an SS replacement Gebirgsjäger battalion in Leoben and ground crew from the Boelcke fighter squadron. These miscellaneous units were stationed in the eastern provinces of Austria in and around the Semmering pass. As with the "Nord" Division the new name and number does not seem to have gained currency, but this is perhaps because the title was not bestowed until twelve days before hostilities ceased. On most operations maps the battle group "Semmering" was marked as battle group "Raithel" and is shown as having been part of 3rd Panzer Corps of 6th Army.

20th Gebirgs Army

The 20th Gebirgs Army, formed on 15 January 1942, was first named "Lapland" Army and was made up of various groupings and formations stationed in Norway. It was not until 22 June 1942, that the name and number of 20th Gebirgs Army was bestowed. From 18 December 1944, command of all troops stationed in Norway was vested in it.

In February 1942 when it was still known as "Lapland" Army, the order of battle was:

Gebirgs Corps "Norway"	:	2nd and 6th Gebirgs Divisions
XXXVI Corps	:	163rd and 169th Infantry Divisions
III (Finnish) Corps	:	SS Gebirgs Division "Nord", 3rd Finnish Division
Army Reserve	:	7th Gebirgs Division

During May 1942 the 7th Gebirgs Division was taken from the Reserve and was replaced by 163rd Division. There were other regroupings throughout the army's life and at one time 7th Gebirgs Division formed part of III (Finnish) Corps. By August 1942 there were no troops at all in the Reserve and the III (Finnish) Corps had been struck off strength.

In April 1945 the Army's Order of Battle was:

XXXVI Corps	:	Panzer Brigade "Norway", MG Ski Brigade "Finland"
LXX Corps	:	613rd, 274th and 280th Infantry Divisions
XXXIII Corps	:	295th, 702nd Infantry and 14th Luftwaffe Division
LXXI Corps	:	230th, 210th and Fortress Brigade "Lofoten", 139th Brigade, 140th Brigade and 503rd Brigade
Army Detachment "Narvik" Also known as XIX Corps	:	193rd Brigade, 270th Infantry Division, 6th Gebirgs Division, the cycle reconnaissance battalion "Norway"
Reserve	:	7th Gebirgs Division

The operations which the army undertook include the advance to Petsamo and to Liza. Elements of the Gebirgs Army garrisoned those areas until the evacuation of northern Finland was undertaken during September 1944. As a result of the armistice between Finland and the Soviet Union the Gebirgs Army had to fight against both Finns and Russians during the retreat into Norway. The army then spent its time as part of the forces of occupation before taking over the duty of commanding the whole occupying force until the end of World War II.

15th (XV) Gebirgs Corps

Raised on 12 August 1943 in the Balkans and placed at the disposal of Supreme Headquarters German Troops in Croatia. The 15th Gebirgs Corps served in the Balkan theatre of operations throughout the war under the command of 2nd Panzer Army and of the Army Groups "F" and "E".

18th (XVIII) Gebirgs Corps

This corps was formed in Salzburg on 1 April 1938 as XVIII Corps and was made up of Austrian units taken over after the annexation of the Federal Republic of Austria. During December 1941 the corps title changed to include the description "Gebirgs" and the formation was placed at the disposal of the Supreme Military Commander in Serbia.

The 18th Gebirgs Corps served in Croatia, Serbia, Romania, Bulgaria and Greece before being withdrawn from the Balkans to come under the control of Army High Command (OKH). It served in this capacity until May 1942. Much of its military life was spent in Lapland and northern Norway but in January 1945 the corps was despatched to the Eastern Front and fought in West Prussia.

19th (XIX) Gebirgs Corps

Raised on 1 July 1940 in Norway from two main groupings, 21st (XXI) Group and 3rd Gebirgs Division. The formation was first known as Gebirgs Corps "Norway", but was renamed during November 1942. There was another change of name two years later when it became known as Army Detachment "Narvik".

The 19th Gebirgs Corps spent the whole of its service in northern Norway and in Lapland.

21st (XXI) Gebirgs Corps

Formed during August 1943 in the Balkans and placed at the disposal of the General Officer Commanding in Serbia. The 21st Corps served in Croatia, Serbia and in Albania as part of Army Group "F" and later "E" until the end of the war.

The principal operations in which this corps took part were against the partisan forces of Marshal Tito.

22nd (XXII) Gebirgs Corps

The 22nd Gebirgs Corps was raised on 20 August 1943, in Salonika, and was placed under the command of Army Group "E". It remained in Greece until posted to Hungary in April 1944. Then it returned to Greece and to Army Group "E". In December the corps was ordered, once again, to Hungary where it served with 2nd Panzer Army, a unit of Army Group South.

The name of the army group then changed to that of "Army Group South-East" when the whole of it withdrew out of Hungary and fought in Steiermark, the eastern province of Austria. It was in that Duchy that most of 22nd Gebirgs Corps laid down its arms; the remainder withdrew into Carinthia and surrendered there.

36th (XXXVI) Gebirgs Corps

The 36th Corps was formed on 19th October 1939 from troops serving with No. 14 Frontier Control Area Command in Breslau. The first name given to the formation was Corps Command for Special Purposes. On 18 November 1941 it was renamed as a Gebirgs corps.

After the campaign in Poland the corps served with the occupying forces and then took part in the fighting in the West, serving under the command of both Army Groups "B" and "C".

During September 1940 it was posted to Norway and later formed part of 20th Gebirgs Army stationed in that country and under whose command it stayed until the end of the war.

49th (XXXXIX) Gebirgs Corps

This corps was formed on 20 June 1940, but was stood down within a month. It was not formed again until October 1940.

From the early months of 1941 until the outbreak of war with the Soviet Union the 49th Corps served in France, preparing itself for an attack upon the Rock of Gibraltar. With the cancellation of that operation it was posted to Yugoslavia and then to Slovakia. On the Eastern Front, in the war against the Soviet Union, 49th Corps played an important part in the encirclement battles around Uman in the autumn of 1941.

During 1942 it took part in the advance to the Caucasus, penetrated to Kuban and then fought in the Crimea as part of Army Group "A". During this operation the corps was destroyed but a new one was immediately rebuilt around the cadre which remained.

Following upon the German retreat from southern Russia the 49th Corps moved back into Romania where it fought in the Carpathian mountains as part of 1st Panzer Army. It then withdrew into Moravia and was captured by the Red Army at the cessation of hostilities.

51st (LI) Gebirgs Corps

The 51st Gebirgs Corps was raised on 12 September 1943, in Austria, to replace the original infantry corps with that number and which had been destroyed in the battle for Stalingrad.

The corps served in Italy and fought in the battles connected with the town and the mountain abbey of Cassino.

The Hochgebirgsjäger Battalions

No. 1 This battalion of high Alpine specialists was raised on 20 July 1942 from No. 1. Training Battalion for Alpine Troops, situated in Berchtesgaden. The battalion establishment was five companies.

  The unit was disbanded during the winter of 1942/43 and the men posted to other battalions of 1st Gebirgs Division.

No. 2 The 2nd Hochgebirgsjäger Battalion was formed from 2nd Training Battalion for Alpine Troops, situated in Innsbruck.

  Formed on 20 July 1942 it was converted into 54th Gebirgsjäger Battalion on 12 February 1943.

No. 3 This battalion was raised on 20 November 1943 from men drawn from 98th Gebirgsjäger Regiment which was serving, at that time, in Dalmatia. The battalion was posted to Italy where in December 1944 it became 3rd Battalion of 296th Gebirgsjäger Regiment.

No. 4 This battalion was formed on 20 November 1943 from men drawn from units fighting in Dalmatia and was sent to the Italian theatre of operations.

Higher Gebirgs Commands of the SS

6th SS Gebirgs Division "Nord"

The 6th SS Gebirgs Division "Nord" grew out of an SS battle group "Nord" raised during March 1941, and which by June 1942 became a division. There were other titles and changes of name until the final description 6th SS Gebirgs Division "Nord".

The original battle group had been formed out of the 6th and 7th SS Standarten of the "Totenkopf" formations for service in Lapland and was made up of four battalions of Jäger, three mountain artillery battalions and elements from a Gebirgs pioneer battalion.

The division was posted to Finland during February 1942, where it served for most of its active service life. It returned to Germany via Norway in time for it to take part in the Ardennes offensive of December 1944. With the failure of that operation the division retreated into Germany through Thüringen and Bavaria where it passed into American captivity at the end of the war.

7th SS Freiwilligen Gebirgs Division "Prinz Eugen"

The "Prinz Eugen" Gebirgs Division was formed on 1 March 1942, with racial Germans (*Volksdeutsche*) forming the greatest number of men. The formation and concentration of the division was long and complicated chiefly because of the grave weapon shortage which existed. There was a wide variety of weapons on issue with the division. When arming had been completed the 7th SS Division was put into action on anti-partisan operations firstly in Serbia and then in Montenegro.

In September 1943, when Italy left the war, the division disarmed the Italian forces in its area and then resumed its anti-guerrilla campaign. One of the more spectacular of its operations was the participation in an attack to capture Marshal Tito, which was undertaken in conjunction with an SS paratroop battalion. In the ensuing battle the 1st Yugoslav Partisan Division was destroyed.

In October 1944 "Prinz Eugen" fought against the Soviet forces and a Bulgarian army which were moving into Yugoslavia and, during January 1945, the division began to withdraw from that country. At Cilli the last remnants of the division were captured by the partisan forces.

13th Waffen Grenadier Division of the SS "Handschar" Croatian No. 1

During February 1943 the Reichsführer SS, Heinrich Himmler, ordered the raising of a Croat division drawn from Muslim volunteers.

Despite the fact that large numbers of men came forward, there were difficulties connected with the raising of the division in its own area and concentration was finally completed in the south of France.

In February 1944 the division returned to Yugoslavia where it took part in anti-partisan operations chiefly in northern Bosnia. When the German forces began to evacuate Yugoslavia most of its Muslim soldiers were released from service. These losses reduced the 13th Division to the strength of only a battle group and this then went into action in southern Hungary. From thence it withdrew into Lower Styria, where it passed into British captivity.

21st Waffen Grenadier Division of the SS "Skanderbeg" Albanian No. 1

This division was raised at Himmler's order on 17 April 1944, in Koddevo, northern Albania. The task of forming the unit was more than usually difficult due firstly to an insufficiency of German officers. Then to the unreliability of the Albanian rank and file and finally to the lack of modern arms.

When concentration had been completed the detachments were sent out on anti-partisan operations. During these encounters many men of the division deserted to the guerrilla forces. As a result of this, and due to other circumstances, the division was reorganised and reduced in numbers. During 1944, reinforcements, totalling 3800 all ranks, came on to strength. The greatest number of these were German sailors serving in the Aegean who no longer had ships which they could man.

When the German forces retreated from Albania all the locally raised personnel were released and the division was then disbanded. The German members of the division were then posted to the "Prinz Eugen" Division.

23rd Waffen Gebirgs Division of the SS "Kama" Croatian No. 2

The 23rd Division was raised on 17 June 1944, in southern Hungary, around cadres of Germans and Muslims taken chiefly from 13th "Handschar" Division. The morale of the native soldiers was very poor and as a result of a great number of desertions the division had to be reorganised.

When this had been completed the bulk of the Muslims were sent to 13th Division "Handschar" and thus, within four months of its being formed, the 23rd Waffen Gebirgs Division "Kama" was disbanded.

24th Waffen Gebirgs (Karstjäger) Division of the SS

This division evolved from a single company which had been formed on 10 July 1942 for service in the Karst, the bare, high mountain areas of the Istrian peninsula. Within four months of its being raised the formation had grown to battalion strength and by 18 July 1944 the order came for it to be expanded to a full division.

The original company, with a strength of two platoons, had been raised in Dachau and was being formed as a battalion in the southern Austrian province of Carinthia when it was called upon to help disarm the Italian troops when Italy left the war.

The battalion then saw action in northern Italy on anti-partisan operations and, when the time came for expansion to divisional status, *Volksdeutsche,* Tyroleans and local inhabitants were all recruited. Numbers were, however, too few and the intention to form a Karstjäger division was not realised.

Gebirgs Division of the SS "Andreas Hofer"

A proposal to raise a Gebirgs division, and to name it after the famous Tyrolean hero Andreas Hofer, was made by General of the Waffen SS von Oberkamp to the Gauleiter of Tyrol on 22 February 1944.

Hitler refused to sanction the proposal on the grounds that the Tyrol could not raise sufficient men and the scheme was dropped.

5th SS Gebirgs Corps

This SS mountain corps was raised in Prague during July 1943 and the senior command posts were taken by officers of 7th SS Gebirgs Division "Prinz Eugen".

The corps was first put into action in Mostar during October 1943 and served continuously in the Balkans until the last months of the war when it was posted to the Eastern Front to serve with 9th Army in Army Group Vistula.

9th Waffen Gebirgs Corps of the SS (Croatian)

The Croatian Gebirgs Corps which contained the 13th Gebirgs Division "Handschar" and 23rd Division "Kama", was formed during the summer of 1944. Towards the end of September 1944 the 9th Corps came under the control of 2nd Panzer Army which was serving with the Supreme Commander South East Forces.

There were several changes in the establishment of the corps and at one time it had on strength 8th SS and 22nd SS Divisions.

Waffen Gebirgs Brigade of the SS Tartar No. 1

This unit was raised on 8 July 1944 from Mohammedan Tartars who had volunteered for and served with German police units in the Crimea. The unit officers were German. When the order came to withdraw from the Crimea these Tartar volunteers went with the German forces and formed the nucleus around which a regiment was raised. The proposed expansion to brigade strength was delayed, due to difficulties connected with the recruitment of sufficient men and the difficulties of procuring arms. It was, therefore, not until September 1944 that this began in earnest, but did not succeed.

Recruiting was then stopped and the brigade was disbanded on 31 December 1944. The men were posted to the East Turkoman formations of the Waffen SS.

The organisation of 1st Gebirgs Division

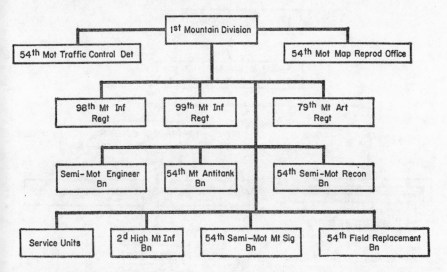

The organisation of a Gebirgsjäger Regiment

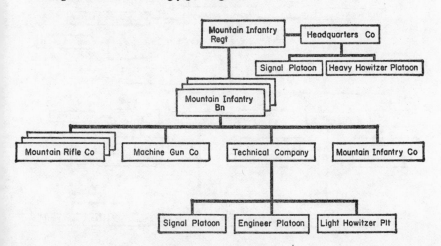

The organisation of a Hochgebirgs Battalion

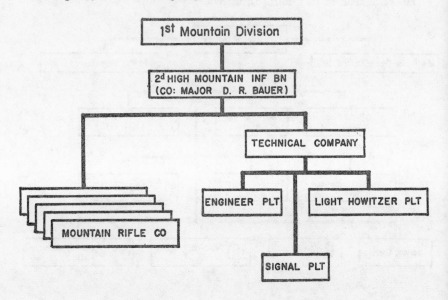

1st Mountain Division

2d HIGH MOUNTAIN INF BN
(CO: MAJOR D. R. BAUER)

TECHNICAL COMPANY

MOUNTAIN RIFLE CO

ENGINEER PLT

LIGHT HOWITZER PLT

SIGNAL PLT

The organisation of a typical Mountain Artillery Regiment

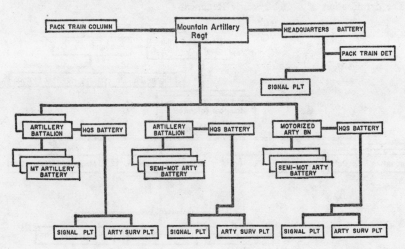

PACK TRAIN COLUMN

Mountain Artillery Regt

HEADQUARTERS BATTERY

PACK TRAIN DET

SIGNAL PLT

ARTILLERY BATTALION — HQS BATTERY

ARTILLERY BATTALION — HQS BATTERY

MOTORIZED ARTY BN — HQS BATTERY

MT ARTILLERY BATTERY

SEMI-MOT ARTY BATTERY

SEMI-MOT ARTY BATTERY

SIGNAL PLT | ARTY SURV PLT

SIGNAL PLT | ARTY SURV PLT

SIGNAL PLT | ARTY SURV PLT

The Organisation, Tactics and Equipment Used in Fighting at High Altitudes

The names of certain units, "Hochgebirgs" and "Karstjäger", which have been met in the text must be explained. In former pages mention has been made that after the campaign in France during 1940, certain former infantry divisions were converted to become panzer or panzer grenadier and that their surplus regiments were reformed as Gebirgsjäger and posted to Gebirgs divisions. Thus it can be seen that the former insistence upon specially selected mountain men was no longer being maintained, for it was considered at *Oberkommando der Wehrmacht* (Armed Forces High Command) that with sufficient training ordinary line infantry could function as ordinary mountain troops.

There were, however, specialist categories of mountain men whose skills could not be learnt as a drill but were achieved through a combination of birth in an Alpine area and years of living among and climbing the high mountain peaks. These men formed the Hochgebirgs companies and battalions and most of them were also qualified mountain guides. It was the task of these individual soldiers to blaze trails and they were usually formed into a Hochgebirgs detachment for that purpose. On other occasions their companies would lead assaults, particularly in the higher Alpine altitudes.

Such detachments, when serving in the barren, empty and rocky wastes of the Alpine regions of north-eastern Italy and north-western Yugoslavia, were known as Karstjäger, from the name by which that region was known.

The organisation and war establishments of German units in common with those of all armies, had a *"soll"* and an *"ist"* establishments. The *"soll"* was the laid down establishment of a unit and represented its full strength, while the *"ist"* was its actual strength. It will further be appreciated that, in the course of five years of warfare, manpower and firepower establishments changed and that when, for example, the MG 42 came into general use the firepower of a very small number of these weapons equalled that of a whole machine gun company on the 1939 establishment. Thus late in the war fewer men and fewer weapons were required to produce the same volume of fire as had been achieved by masses of men and weapons. The introduction into service of the rocket propelled antitank weapons, the Panzerfaust and the Panzerschreck, gave to individual men or a team of two the tank-destroying capability formerly possessed only by a complete anti-tank team. These increases in firepower made up in some part for the terrible losses in manpower which the German Army had suffered. Thus the strength of units, both in respect of men and weapons, did not remain constant during World War II.

To simplify matters unit strengths which are given below are the *"soll"* or the laid down establishments and are based on 1943 tables. From the accounts in earlier chapters of this book it will have become clear that the actual strength of a unit engaged in combat was often only a fraction of its total strength.

It must also be appreciated that when fighting in ordinary terrain Gebirgsjäger were considered as standard infantry and that, in such circumstances, the division was the standard tactical unit. The situation when the division was engaged in combat in Alpine altitudes was that a centralised command could not function and that the largest unit command was generally the battalion. It is, therefore, with the Gebirgsjäger battalion that we begin this description of establishments.

A standard battalion had a strength of 877 officers and men who were organised into three Jäger companies, a machine gun, an antitank and a heavy weapons company. Each Jäger company had a strength of 147 men and was equipped with twelve light machine guns and three light and two 8cm mortars as well as one anti-tank rifle. The machine gun company, with a strength of 208 men, had twelve heavy machine guns and four 12cm mortars, while the heavy weapons company with 201 men was equipped with four light machine guns and two 7.5cm infantry howitzers. The anti-tank company had four guns and two rifles.

Three Gebirgsjäger battalions and a headquarters group made up a regiment, which had a strength of 3064 all ranks. Regimental headquarters was composed of a signals platoon and a heavy mountain howitzer battery.

Two Jäger regiments and an artillery regiment, together with the usual services, made up a Gebirgs division. This formation had a strength of 13,056 officers and men. Included within the establishment were 2330 men of the artillery regiment equipped with twenty-four guns of 7.5cm calibre and twelve 7.5cm mountain howitzers, twelve 15cm howitzers and twelve 10.5cm howitzers. These weapons were divided among the four battalions which comprised an artillery regiment in a Gebirgs division.

A signals battalion, a semi-motorised reconnaissance battalion, a motorised anti-tank gun battalion, and a battalion of semi-motorised engineers were the principal ancillary units and the train, which completed the divisional establishment, included pack animals organised usually at battalion level but which, under difficult conditions of terrain, could be formed so as to supply individual companies. Most Gebirgs divisions had a Hochgebirgs battalion of five companies and a support company with a platoon of engineers, one of signals and one of light howitzers.

The distribution of weapons among the units of the division show that a Jäger regiment had 117 heavy machine guns and 172 light machine guns on establishment. There were twelve anti-tank guns of 3.7cm calibre together with thirty-six anti-tank rifles, twenty-seven mortars of 5cm calibre and eighteen of 8cm. Six howitzers of 7.5cm calibre completed the regimental arsenal. At divisional level the anti-tank gun establishment included twenty-five weapons of 5cm calibre.

In vehicles and animals a division had 447 motor cycles, 858 lorries of several sizes, 714 horse-drawn carts and 3506 horses or mules. These were organised into trains each made up of two hundred beasts. During the Russian campaign and particularly in the periods of mud and snow the number of horse-drawn vehicles was increased by the acquisition of panje carts, light wooden vehicles drawn by Russian breeds of horses which were better able to withstand the bitter winter conditions than were the standard European breeds.

When fighting in the mountains special rock-climbing equipment was issued to Jäger regiments and, indeed, every unit on the divi-

sional establishment had an Alpine scale of equipment which enabled
it to function as well in the mountains as on less inhospitable terrain.
Thus the medical teams were issued with special stretchers on which
wounded could be lowered down vertical rock faces, the mountain
artillery pieces could be broken down into mule loads and brought
forward on pack animals. The engineer battalion was equipped with
power saws and drills. Even the signals detachments had equipment
which could be adapted for pack transport.

It does not need to be stressed that such pieces of equipment had
to be lighter but more robust than those on general issue, although
they were all based on standard patterns. Metal pressing techniques
replaced the machined parts of many weapons, making for lightness
and cheapness. These factors were reflected in some of the weapons
brought into service in the last year of the war.

Tactics in Mountain Warfare as Set Out in Military Handbooks

During the war and as a result of lessons learned from active service
experiences a large number of pamphlets was produced dealing with
the subject of campaigning in mountainous areas. The training man-
uals covered every arm of service and its equipment and proved so
comprehensive that they have since formed the bases of official handbooks used by the NATO forces. The salient points dealing with
weapons, tactics, food, clothing and safety are outlined below.

The most important tenet, the thread which ran through each
booklet, and which was repeated over and over again, was the absolute need for the most careful preparation before undertaking any
Alpine operation, irrespective of how short its duration. As a corol-
lary, movement in the mountains, it was stressed, proceeded slowly
and required more time than warfare in normal terrain, thus the need
for the most meticulous planning was vital.

Not only was there the question of greater time to be taken into
account in mountain operations but, because such regions lacked an
adequate road network, the disposition of troops covered a much
wider area. It was, therefore, essential that such dispositions were cor-

rectly accomplished before a mission began, for once movement was under way then alterations in a lateral direction could not be successfully carried out. It was less a question of the flexibility of movement by Jäger companies than those of the supply columns and pack trains.

Great responsibility was placed upon quite junior officers and it was found that the long, intensive training which most of these had had in peace-time had prepared them to accept the burden of making long-range decisions. It was also found to be essential for all artillery and engineer units to be subordinated to the Jäger commander on the ground if a speedy and successful operation was to be completed. The motorisation, either fully or in part, of many of a division's subunits, enabled these to be deployed very quickly and the full exploitation of their capabilities led frequently to rapid success. This flexibility produced by wheeled or tracked vehicles was often sufficient to allow fewer numbers of Jäger to be committed to an attack than had previously been thought possible.

Two vehicles which found approval by almost every Gebirgs unit operating in high Alpine regions were the tracked motor cycle, its manoeuvrability was very marked even in very close country, and the Volkswagen light car. Any type of local animal which could serve as a beast of burden or to pull a cart was put into service with the most surprising results. In Lapland, for example, reindeer were widely used while in the Caucasus both 1st and 4th Gebirgs Divisions used Bactrian camels. In the Caucasus, too, small mountain donkeys of frugal eating habits and capable of carrying a load of up to 40kgs, proved to be a very efficient supplement to the mule trains.

Although wireless sets were carried down to company level the greatest reliance was placed upon communications by flags using the navy system. Two signallers, visible to each other, could send a message across a five-mile distance. Radio sets generally required aerials of greater than usual length to obtain good reception and additional height was often gained by fixing the aerial to the top of a tree. The peculiar atmospheric and climatic conditions met with in high Alpine altitudes often blanketed out reception or transmission, and the radius of activity was often so limited that wireless relay stations had to be set up to pass messages. It would seem that no attempt at setting up heliographs was ever undertaken by any Gebirgs unit.

So far as personal equipment was concerned it was shown that

short skis were indispensable for rapid movement across country and
that snow goggles were essential above an altitude of 2000 metres.
Crampons were essential for crossing glaciers or other large areas of
perpetual ice and special coloured ropes or cloths were used to mark
chosen routes. Rope railings were used to mark ice bridges across
crevasses in glaciers and these bridges, it was suggested in the pamphlets, should be checked daily. By night, in fog, or in some other
circumstance of poor visibility, the rope bridges were fitted with
simple noise-making devices, such as empty cartridge cases, whose
sound located the glacial bridge.

At troop level emphasis was upon that feature which had inspired
the authors of the first mountain training books: that the Gebirgsjäger had to be of exceptional mental and physical calibre,
properly trained and with a greater degree of stamina than usual because of the abnormal problems of living at high altitudes. Nevertheless, it was soon found that most men between eighteen and
thirty-five, were capable of meeting the rigorous requirements so long
as they were physically fit, were adequately fed and had been slowly
acclimatised to the thin air. Frostbite was avoidable and, wounds
or accidents apart, most cases of sickness were of diarrhoea brought
on by drinking water produced from melted snow or ice.

Food had to be high in calorific content but low in bulk. It also
had to be capable of being eaten either raw or of being cooked
quickly, as cooking at high altitudes requires more time and thus
more fuel than that at lower levels. It was found that air-dried meats,
canned food, dehydrated vegetables and biscuit were the best provi-
sions, although for operations of short durations chocolate, grape
sugar or dried fruit were the more practical foodstuffs. Concentrated
fodder for the animals in the form of cattle cake was used for short
periods and proved to be a successful substitute for hay and grain.

All Gebirgsjäger were familiar with the sudden and dramatic
moods of weather in the high mountains and, therefore, also aware
of the need to be able very quickly to construct shelters out of any
available material. Caves in the snow or ice were the easiest refuges.
The standard shelter half weighed down with stones proved, in the
short term, to be most effective. Finnish plywood shelters, capable of
being broken down and carried on pack animals, were mentioned in
many booklets as being particularly wind proof. Where high winds
made the construction of a shelter impossible then wind-breaker walls

of stone were erected in the lee of which the Gebirgsjäger sheltered. In such conditions double sleeping bags were used for it was found that these were particularly effective against the continual icy winds whose cold killed the unwary.

Captured Russian, down filled, quilted sleeping bags issued to Siberian troops and others in extreme conditions of climate, were greatly prized for they were lighter and warmer but less bulky than the issue blanket which each Jäger carried on mountain operations.

In the primitive shelters high on the mountain ranges light was vital and candles proved to be the most effective source of illumination at individual level. Company headquarters were usually lit by paraffin lamp in preference to electric light for it was easier to obtain paraffin than electric light bulbs.

The problems of avalanches and how to avoid these catastrophes occupied the authors of many of the handbooks. Careful map-reading allied to up-to-date forecasts of the weather were stressed for these could help troops to avoid the dangerous area or allow them to cross it with minimal danger. The selected trail having been chosen and avalanche equipment issued, the column would move off at proper intervals, at least 30 metres distance between soldiers, the whole column slaloming by bounds. This involved one group of soldiers making a bound and halting when safe ground had been reached. The next group would then make its crossing. It was laid down that the trail should zig-zag gently along the slope or ridge, for a descent or ascent was not to be carried out vertically or steeply because of the danger of dislodging snow.

Instructions on the action to be carried out by parties overtaken by avalanches, or by their rescuers, were detailed and lengthy as were the instructions issued for the evacuation of casualties. Little was left to chance in these handbooks which were intended to equip the Gebirgsjäger with all the information necessary to improve his chances of survival in the inhospitable terrain in which he fought. The weapons used at high altitudes were less extensively dealt with for these were standard issue, excepting of course the pack artillery.

When attempts were made to use standard artillery in the mountains these were generally unsuccessful, because these guns could not be broken down into convenient loads, and the weight of the individual pieces was generally greater than the carrying capacity of the animal.

German mortar bombs were ineffective in the loose snow of the higher altitudes and recourse was made to Russian weapons, particularly a wheeled mortar whose capabilities were superior to those of the German. The greater visibility afforded by the clear mountain air allowed the enemy to be seen more frequently than was usual in conventional terrain, and he could be fired upon at greater distances. For obvious reasons, not least the need to conserve ammunition, fire economy was vital and each bullet was expected to find a billet. To this end there were a greater number of sniper-telescope-fitted rifles available to troops in mountain fighting. Hand grenades were particularly effective in what close-quarter fighting took place but mines, the hidden scourge of every infantryman, were impractical in snow and ice and could only be used with effect in a few snow-free weeks of the year and then on the principal roads, chiefly in valleys and passes, which were being used as highways for a fast flow of traffic.

When dealing with tactics at Alpine altitudes, the correct use of ground was stressed both for the Jäger and for their supporting artillery. It was frequently mentioned that most high mountain operations were carried out over larger areas of ground and by smaller bodies of men than would be the case in standard terrain. Thus the fighting was very much a soldiers' battle, with responsibility placed upon Jäger, gunner and engineer officers of quite junior rank.

It says much for these men, and the training which they had been given, that the Gebirgs regiments achieved quite early in the war the reputation of being an elite force, the skill, determination and self-reliance of whose men could be depended upon, whether in attack or in defence.

Mountain Artillery

Parallel with the need for mountain infantry in the latter decades of the 19th century there grew up the necessity for artillery to support the Jäger regiments in action.

These weapons had to be mobile: capable of being transported as a whole through the mountains or else of being broken down and brought forward to the firing points by pack mule or by man-porterage. In addition they had to be compact in design, robust in construction and capable of firing at extreme angles of elevation and depression. So specialised did the construction of mountain artillery become that it formed a completely separate part of the gun designer's ability.

The artillery arm of the former Austro-Hungarian Army had been equipped with a Skoda-built weapon, the 7.5cm M 15, whose successful design kept it in production throughout World War I and in the armouries of most European military forces, and of Germany's specifically, until 1933 when new designs were sought by the German Army. A number of attempts failed at first to improve upon the M 15, but one very successful development by the Rheinmetall Company was the 7.5cm Gebirgsgeschütz 36 which remained in service until late in 1944.

To complement the GebG 36, a mountain howitzer was needed and the contract for a 10.5cm piece was won by an Austrian company. One unusual feature of the design of the Gerät 77, as it was known, was that when broken down loads were not carried by pack animals but were towed by small, tracked vehicles. This pattern of howitzer went into production during 1940, by which time the German Army's weapons department was casting about for an updated version of the GebG 36. These efforts were stillborn as were other projects, notably a 15cm Gebirgshaubitze, and with those uncompleted designs the development of purely German mountain artillery in World War II came to an end.

The German Army, however, drew upon the arsenals of those countries which it had occupied or conquered, beginning with the weapons which had been in service with the Austrian Bundesheer and, later, those which had been on issue to the Army of the Republic of Czechoslovakia. Various campaigns, notably those against France and Yugoslavia, produced other, and in some cases, more modern weapons. The war with the Soviet Union added a mountain gun of 1936 pattern, the 7.62cm, originally a Skoda weapon but one which had been manufactured under licence by the Russians. Large numbers of theses guns, captured by the Germans during the early years of the war against the Soviet Union, were put into service with mountain troops of the German Army.

From the frantic efforts of German artillery inspectorates it would seem that the German mountain troop organisation could not lay its hand upon sufficient mountain guns and impressed into service a wide variety of weapons some of which pre-dated World War I.

A list of the principal guns and howitzers, showing their chief characteristics, is set out below.

7.5cm Gebirgskanone (mountain gun) 15

This was the chief mountain artillery piece of World War I. Issued initially to the mountain troops of the Imperial Austro-Hungarian Army it then passed into service with the German and Bulgarian armies during that war. In the post-war years it was used by the military forces of the Succession States as well as by those of Italy and Turkey. It remained in service until the end of World War II.

length of piece	115cms
weight in action	613kgs
traverse	7°
elevation	minus 10 to plus 50°
muzzle velocity	349metres/second
shell weight	6.35kgs
rate of fire	6 to 8rpm
maximum range	8¼kms

7.5cm leichtes Gebirgsinfanteriegeschütz (light mountain gun) 18

This was the basic infantry gun of 1918 pattern modified for use in a mountain role. Although designed as a stop-gap weapon and introduced in 1937, large numbers of the 18 Model, both infantry gun and mountain gun, remained in service until the end of World War II.

length of piece	88.5cms
weight in action	440kgs
traverse	35°
elevation	minus 10 to plus 75°
muzzle velocity	221metres/second
shell weight	5¾kgs
rate of fire	8 to 12rpm
maximum range	3½kms

The original infantry gun, upon whose pattern this mountain gun was based, was developed during 1927 and issued in 1932 and was one of the most widely used weapons of its type in the German service.

7.5cm Gebirgskanone 28

This modernised version of the M 15 had the usual capability of being able to take a 9cm in place of the 7.5cm barrel. The characteristics of the GebK 28 were the same as for the GebK 15.

7.5cm Gebirgschütz (mountain infantry gun) 36

This weapon was first introduced into service during 1938 and remained in production throughout World War II.

length of piece	145cms
weight in action	750kgs
traverse	40°
elevation	minus 2 to plus 70°
muzzle velocity	475metres/second
shell weight	5¾kgs
rate of fire	6rpm
maximum range	9¼kms

10cm Gebirgshaubitze (mountain howitzer) 16

This gun and those which followed it were among the most widely used weapons of World War II and were in service not only with the German Army but also with the Italians. Designed and built by Skoda it was very heavy and large for mountain operations and could not be easily broken down into portable loads. Numbers of this howitzer were taken over by the Germans after their annexation of Austria.

length of piece	193cms
weight in action	1235kgs
traverse	5°
elevation	minus 8 to plus 70°
muzzle velocity	406metres/second
shell weight	13¾kgs
rate of fire	6 to 8rpm
maximum range	9¼kms

10cm Gebirgshaubitze 16

The successor to and a more modern version of the former 16.

length of piece	240cms
weight in action	1350kgs
traverse	5°
elevation	minus 7 to plus 70°
muzzle velocity	395metres/second
shell weight	16kgs
maximum range	9¾kms

10.5cm Gebirgshaubitze 40 (also known as Gerät 77)

The development of this mountain howitzer began in 1938 and the first deliveries to the troops in the field were made during 1942. This is the weapon which was broken down not into man- or animal-portered parts but into four units which were then towed by half-track vehicles.

length of piece	315cms
weight in action	1656kgs
traverse	50°
elevation	minus 5 to plus 70°
muzzle velocity	370metres/second
shell weight	14¾kgs
maximum range	12½kms

Foreign Mountain Guns in Service with the German Army

6.5cm Gebirgskanone 221 (f)

This gun was in the service of the French Army immediately before the outbreak of World War II where it was used mainly in infantry support. It had an abnormally high rate of fire: 18rpm.

7.5cm Gebirgskanone 238 (f)

Produced by Schneider and Co. and by Le Creusot during 1928 this weapon was designed as a replacement for the 1919 model of mountain gun.

7.5cm Gebirgshaubitze 254 (i)

This very popular howitzer was an Italian piece, a howitzer on a split carriage. It came into service with the Italian Army during 1934.

7.62cm Gebirgskanone 307 (r)

This Skoda-designed gun was taken on to Russian establishment and manufactured under licence. A very popular gun with German mountain troops, it could be broken down into 10-pack transport loads.

length of piece	163cms
weight in action	785kgs
traverse	10°

elevation   minus 8 to plus 70°
muzzle velocity   495metres/second
shell weight   6¾kgs
maximum range   10kms

10cm Gebirgshaubitze 16 (t)

Despite its weight and its bulk this piece was very popular with mountain gunners. To transport it the howitzer could be broken down into three loads. Originally with the Czech Army.

length of piece   193cms
weight in action   1235kgs
maximum range   9¼kms

10.5cm leichte Gebirgshaubitze (light mountain howitzer) 322 (f)

French mountain gun manufactured by Schneider and Co. and Le Creusot. An immediate post-World War I weapon.

10.7cm Gebirgsgranatwerfer (mountain mortar) (r)

This enlarged version of the standard Russian mortar was modified for use in mountain warfare and proved very practical. The tubular steel limber on which the piece was carried could be broken down into pack loads in difficult country.

length of piece   157cms
weight in action   160kgs
traverse   6 to 15°
elevation   minus 45 to plus 80°
muzzle velocity   302metres/second
weight of bomb   8kgs
maximum range   6kms

The Uniform and Specialist Equipment of Gebirgsjäger Units

The Gebirgsjäger uniform was distinctive and introduced several items of clothing which then went on to a general issue. One of these was the peaked, close fitting ski-ing cap known as the Gebirgsmütze, variations of which were eventually worn by most units of the German Army.

The details on uniforms and insignia which are to be found in the following pages have been taken from the definitive work on the subject written by Brian L. Davis, to whom I am indebted for permission to quote. The book *German Army Uniforms and Insignia 1933–1945** is indispensable to any researcher into the study of military costuming of the Third Reich.

The Bergmütze or mountain cap was worn by all ranks of mountain ski and Jäger units. It was worn in preference to almost all other forms of headdress and was worn as a form of pride. It had a short field-grey cloth peak and was based on the design of the Austrian Army's service cap.

An order dated 3 October 1942 permitted ordinary officers to wear silver aluminium piping around the crown of the Bergmütze and general officers to display gold-coloured piping.

For camouflage purposes in snowy conditions the Bergmütze was often worn with a pure white woollen cover.

The lace-up boots worn by mountain troops were designed for hard wear in poor conditions, gave support to the ankle and were heavily studded not only on the sole but also on the heel and around the whole of the welt.

* Arms and Armour Press, London, 1971.

With these boots white waterproof spats were worn, and another unusual item of leg covering were puttees in field-grey cloth fastened by a small buckle. These and similar items were used more and more frequently as the war progressed but heavy woollen socks worn outside the trousers, which had been a feature of Gebirgsjäger uniform in peace-time, were eventually discontinued.

The field service uniform worn by mountain troops had a standard service jacket but had differences in the design of the trousers. One pattern was a loose legged "knickerbocker" with which were worn the high woollen socks mentioned above. A second pattern was ski trousers tapered to fit inside the climbing boots. With these trousers it was usual to wear short socks rolled down to cover the top of the boot.

One special piece of clothing worn by Gebirgsjäger was the sage-green windjacket made from heavy duty, close-woven calico material. It was double breasted with adjustable cuffs and four pockets: two in the skirt of the jacket and two side pocket openings positioned at an angle on either side of the chest. These pockets were fitted with button-down flaps.

The sage-green windjacket was a loose fitting garment which reached to the wearer's thighs and was intended to be worn over the basic field equipment. The issue of this piece of clothing was restricted to about 10 per cent of any Alpine unit and was eventually replaced by an anorak which was on general issue to all arms of service. One pattern of anorak, which had been on issue to Gebirgsjäger as early as 1939, was a reversible, camouflage garment coloured white on one side and sage-green, later camouflage patterned, on the other. The reversible anorak had a drawstring at the waist and one around the hood. The cuffs were elasticised and the garment was fitted with two breast pockets both on the white and on the green side.

There were other types of winter clothing introduced into the German Army as well as specially designed winter camouflage clothing, but as these were on general issue they will not be described here.

Badges and Insignia

There were certain pieces of military insignia worn on the German Army uniform which not only represented a qualification but distinguished the wearer as possessing a special skill directly related to the type of military unit in which he was serving. These badges, therefore, tended to be regarded with more esteem by the recipient than was the case with the trade badges and specialist insignia.

For the purposes of this book we need mention only the Gebirgsjäger edelweiss arm badge in cloth, the edelweiss metal cap badge and the Bergführer breast badge.

The Gebirgsjäger arm badge was introduced on 2 May 1939. It was to be worn on the right upper arm 16cm from the shoulder seam on the field blouse on the uniform tunic and on the greatcoat by all qualified members of army mountain troop units. The badge consisted of an embroidered edelweiss flower with white petals and yellow stamens and with a pale green stem and leaves. Surrounding the flower was a twisted mountaineering rope in matt-grey thread with a silver-white piton (spike and ring). The entire design was worked on a dark green oval background. Two forms of this badge exist: the superior quality silk machine-woven type and the felt, embroidered version.

The edelweiss metal cap badge was also introduced on 2 May 1939 and was issued in two styles which were to be worn on both the Bergmütze, the soft long-peaked, close fitting ski-ing cap, and the Schirmmütze or standard peaked cap. That on the Bergmütze consisted of a white metal edelweiss flower with stem and leaves showing yellow metal stamens. This type of badge was worn on the left side of the cap with the stem of the flower set at an angle of 45° to the lower edge of the cap, and positioned with the tip of the stem 2.5cm above the lower edge of the cap and 2cm back from the end of cap peak.

The emblem used on the Schirmmütze was without stem and the petals of the flowers were in white metal with the stamens in gilt-coloured metal. This badge was worn positioned on the front of the cap between the national emblem and the oakleaf cluster.

The Bergführer breast badge, a small metal and enamelled pin-backed badge worn on the left breast pocket of the tunic, was a coveted award as well as being a mark of proficiency, worn only by those Gebirgsjäger who acted as mountain guides and who had had one year's qualifying experience.

It had a silver (with gilt centred) metal edelweiss flower without stem, set in a small, white-enamelled oval rim bearing the word Heeresbergführer, in Gothic lettering on the lower portion of the rim.

This badge was introduced for wear by an order dated 10 August 1936.

Specialist Equipment

In this section of the book which deals with arms and equipment only those weapons or items issued to Gebirgsjäger units will be described.

The earliest type of radio set used by mountain troops was the pack set, the Tornister Funkgerät. To transport this 35kg radio required a three-man team, two of whom actually carried the set. The first man portered the transmitting/receiving unit and the second man carried the battery packs. The third man was the operator. This simple piece of equipment had a limited range of 4kms voice and 16kms morse. It was used principally at company level. Standard signal equipment was used for main communications adapted for pack transport.

The bulkiness and weight of wireless equipment were often such an impediment that it was not carried and reliance was placed on flag signalling as the means of communication. However, late in the war, new and light materials together with developments in radio techniques enabled a less weighty signals pack to be introduced and two patterns of these, the Feldfunk Sprecher B and C, could be carried and operated by one man.

Dogs were frequently used to carry messages and were also used to carry ammunition belts, food and medical packs; St Bernards were used in mountain rescue medical teams.

Military action at high altitudes brought with it not only battle casualties but also victims of accidents met with in such terrain. The medical teams which accompanied Gebirgsjäger units had, therefore, to be proficient to deal with snow blindness, fractures, frostbite, rope burns and other injuries peculiar to such units. To help them evacuate the sick and wounded certain techniques using climbing ropes were employed. These were used, of course, only in the most difficult terrain. Standard Alpine evacuation of the wounded did however include a ski stretcher which could be broken down for man porterage and a unicycle stretcher, the design of which included folding legs so that it could be used, in emergency, as an operating table. This piece of equipment could also be broken down into portering loads.

There was also a specially designed "operating tent" made of lightweight material, inside whose 5-metre length emergency operating treatment of the wounded could be carried out. This tent together with the special medical equipment and supply chest were carried by a pack animal.

Mules and horses formed the main part of the Gebirgs unit's transport system and there were more than 3500 beasts on establishment with each division. The pack animals not only brought forward food and clothing but also portered mountain artillery guns and their ammunition, as well as other heavy pieces of equipment or weapons parts. There were, of course, a number of trucks and other motor vehicles on each divisional establishment and among the wheeled conveyances were motor cycles used by the battalion which was on the order of battle of each Gebirgs division.

The Senior Commanders of Army Gebirgs Formations

Boehme, General of Mountain Troops F.

Boehme was born on 15 April 1885 at Zeltweg in Austria and entered the Army as a cadet on 1 October 1900. Four years later he was an ensign and in 1905 was gazetted a lieutenant in the 95th Infantry Regiment. He fought throughout the Great War and served in the Bundesheer after the dissolution of the Austro-Hungarian Empire.

Transferred into the Wehrmacht he was given command of 30th Division, then 18th Gebirgs Corps and subsequently commanded 2nd Panzer Army. Boehme was promoted to command the German forces in Norway before taking up post as General Officer commanding 20th Gebirgs Army. He committed suicide on 29 May 1947.

His decorations include the Knight's Cross to the Iron Cross and the German Cross in Gold.

Degen, Lieutenant General Hans

Born in Rosenheim, Bavaria, on 18 December 1899, Degen entered the Army as an ensign on 18 September 1916 and joined 2nd Jäger Battalion with which unit he served during World War I. Remaining in the Reichsheer by 1938 he was GSO 1 of 2nd Gebirgs Division. He was transferred to 1st Gebirgs Division at the outbreak of war, again working in the post of GSO 1. He was then promoted to become Chief of the General Staff of 6th Corps and of 19th Gebirgs Corps before being given command of 2nd Gebirgs Division. While in that post he was badly wounded.

His decorations include the German Cross in Gold and the Knight's Cross to the Iron Cross.

Dietl, Colonel General Eduard

Born on 21 July 1890 in Aibling, Dietl entered the Army on 1 October 1909 as an ensign and was gazetted into 5th Bavarian Infantry Regiment in 1911. After service throughout the Great War he remained in the Reichsheer and as a major-general commanded 3rd Gebirgs Division on 1 May 1938.

He went on to command Gebirgs Corps "Norway" on 14 June 1940 and then led 20th Gebirgs Army. He was killed in an air crash in Austria during 1944.

His decorations include the Knight's Cross to the Iron Cross with Oak Leaves and Swords.

Englseer, General of Mountain Troops Karl

Born on 5 July 1890 in Bad Ischl, Englseer entered the Army as an ensign on 18 August 1908. On 1 May 1911 he was gazetted a second lieutenant in 87th Regiment and served throughout World War I. He remained in the Austrian Bundesheer.

After the annexation of the republic by Germany he was transferred to the Wehrmacht and on 25 October 1940 was promoted to command 4th Gebirgs Division. In 1942 he led 714th Division and the 18th Gebirgs Corps. He was killed in an aeroplane accident in 1944.

Englseer's decorations include the Knight's Cross to the Iron Cross.

Feuerstein, General of Mountain Troops Valentin

Valentin Feuerstein was born in Bregenz, Austria, on 18 January 1885 and served in the Imperial Army's 2nd Regiment of Kaiserjäger. The date of his gazetting was 18 August 1906.

He fought throughout World War I and remained in the Army of the Austrian Republic until the annexation to Germany in 1938. He then, together with the other Austrian Service officers, was transferred into the German Army.

He was successively General Officer Commanding 29th Division,

62nd Corps, 70th Corps and 51st Gebirgs Corps before being made General Inspector of the Tyrolean Standschützen (Riflemen's Clubs Association) and Commandant of the Alpine Front.

His medals include the Knight's Cross to the Iron Cross.

Hengl, General of Mountain Troops Georg, Ritter von

Son of a Bavarian aristocrat, Georg von Hengl entered the Army as an ensign at the age of 16 years and was commissioned into the Bavarian 11th Infantry Regiment. He then was posted to 2nd Jäger Battalion in 1915 and served throughout the Great War. In 1919 he left the Army and entered the Police Force.

Recalled to military service he was given command of 3rd Battalion of 99th Gebirgsjäger Regiment on 6 October 1936, and led that battalion in the first campaigns of World War II.

He went on to command 137th Gebirgsjäger Regiment, 2nd Gebirgs Division, 19th Gebirgs Corps and 59th Corps.

Among the decorations he received during his service were the Bavarian Max Josef Order and the Knight's Cross to the Iron Cross.

Jodl, General of Mountain Troops Ferdinand

Born in Landau on 29 November 1896, Jodl entered the Army on 15 August 1914 as an ensign. He was then commissioned into the Bavarian 4th Field Artillery Regiment and served throughout World War I.

After the armistice he remained in the Reichsheer and at the outbreak of World War II was Chief of Staff of 12th Corps. He was promoted to Chief of the General Staff of that formation, then of 49th Gebirgs Corps, Chief of the General Staff of 20th Gebirgs Army and then to command 19th Gebirgs Corps. Jodl then controlled the German forces in northern Norway which were grouped under the name "Army Detachment Narvik".

His decorations include the Knight's Cross to the Iron Cross.

Konrad, General of Mountain Troops Rudolf

Konrad was born in Kulmbach on 7 March 1891 and entered the Army as an ensign on 10 July 1910. He was then commissioned as a second lieutenant in the Bavarian 1st Field Artillery Regiment on 28

October 1912. He saw service in World War I and remained in the Reichsheer, the Army of the German Republic.

On 15 October 1935 he was given command of 100th Gebirgsjäger Regiment and then took up a Staff position as GSO 1 to the 2nd Group HQ. Konrad was then successively Chief of General Staff of 18 Corps and of 2nd Army, until given a field command, that of 7th Gebirgs Division, 39th Gebirgs Corps and 68th Corps.

His decorations include the German Cross in Gold and the Knight's Cross to the Iron Cross.

Kreysing, General of Mountain Troops Hans

Born on 17 August 1890 in Göttingen, Hans Kreysing entered the Army as an ensign on 22 October 1909 and was later gazetted to 10th Jäger Battalion. After war service he remained in the Reichsheer and at the outbreak of World War II was commanding 16th Infantry Regiment. He went on to command 3rd Gebirgs Division, then 18th Corps and finally 8th Army.

His decorations include the Knight's Cross to the Iron Cross with Oak Leaves and Swords.

Kübler, Lieutenant General Josef

Born in Munich on 6 April 1896, Josef Kübler entered the Bavarian Army as an ensign in 15th Infantry Regiment during 1915. After service in the Great War he remained in the Reichsheer and was an instructor at the War Academy.

He served as GSO 1 with VI Corps, in the same post with 12th Army and was finally Chief of the General Staff of 49th Gebirgs Corps. He then took over a field command and led 718th (later 118th) Jäger Division before going on to command 1st Gebirgs Division.

Josef Kübler was accused, tried and convicted of war crimes by the Yugoslav government. He was shot in February 1947.

Kübler, General of Mountain Troops Ludwig

Ludwig Kübler was born on 2 September 1889 at Unterdill in Oberbayern and entered the Army as an ensign on 20 July 1908.

He was gazetted as a second lieutenant into the Bavarian 15th Infantry Regiment on 23 October 1910.

His service in World War I was followed by that in the Reichsheer. By 1935 he had been promoted to command 98th Gebirgsjäger Regiment, then the Gebirgsjäger Brigade and by 1938 the 1st Gebirgs Division. On 25 October 1940 he took over command of 49th Gebirgs Corps and a year later was Commander in Chief of 4th Army. Accused of war crimes he was tried, condemned and executed by the Yugoslavians in 1947.

He was awarded the Knight's Cross to the Iron Cross.

Lanz, General of Mountain Troops Hubert

Born on 22 May 1896 in Eutringen, Lanz entered the Army as an ensign on 20 June 1914 and was gazetted as a second lieutenant in the 125th Infantry Regiment on 4 February 1915. Service in the Great War was followed by that in the Reichsheer and by 1938 commanding 100th Gebirgsjäger Regiment.

Among the posts he subsequently held were Chief of the General Staff of 18th Corps, General Officer Commanding 1st Gebirgs Division, and of Army Group Lanz until 1941 when he was given command of 22nd Gebirgs Corps.

Among the decorations which he was awarded was the Knight's Cross to the Iron Cross.

Ringel, General of Mountain Troops Julius

Julius Ringel was one of the really celebrated Gebirgs troop commanders of World War II.

He was born in Völkermarkt, Austria, on 16 November 1889 and entered the Imperial Army as an ensign on 18 August 1909. In November 1910 he was commissioned as a second lieutenant in 4th Landwehr Infantry Regiment, one of the Imperial Army's two specialist mountain infantry regiments. He served throughout World War I and remained in the Bundeswehr at the end of hostilities.

When Austria was annexed by Germany in 1938 he was transferred to the Wehrmacht and became GSO 1 in 268th Division before going on to command the 266th Infantry Regiment. He was given command of 3rd Gebirgs Division. The raising of 5th Gebirgs Division then gave him the command for which he had been originally selected, and he led that formation in Greece and in Crete with such success that he was given 69th Gebirgs Corps. Towards the end of World War II he formed and led a scratch detachment of diverse detachments of troops known as Ringel's Corps. This group of convalescents, sick and replacement troops, inspired by their commander, fought back the advance by the Red Army in southern Austria to such effect that the line of their front remained unchanged from the end of February 1945 to the date of the cease fire.

For his many services Ringel was awarded the Knight's Cross to the Iron Cross with Oak Leaves.

Le Suire, General of Mountain Troops Karl

Karl Le Suire was born on 8 November 1898 at Unterwössen, and entered the Army as an ensign on 1 December 1916. He was commissioned into the Bavarian Army's 1st Infantry Regiment and served throughout the remainder of the Great War. He continued in military service in the Reichsheer.

On 1 December 1938 he was given a post in the General Staff of Mobile Troops and was then successively GSO 1 of 30th Division and Chief of the General Staff of Gebirgs Corps "Norway" before being given command of a unit in the field. This was 99th Gebirgsjäger Regiment and he went on to command 46th Division, 117th Jäger Division and 49th Gebirgs Corps in which post he died during the fighting in Stalingrad.

Schlemmer, Lieutenant General Ernst

Ernst Schlemmer was born on 8 July 1889 in Wöllstein and became an ensign during 1909. In October 1911 he was gazetted as a second lieutenant to the 18th Bavarian Infantry Regiment.

At the end of World War I he entered the Bavarian Provincial Police Force with which he served until recalled to the Army. His first command was of 137th Gebirgsjäger Regiment and he was then posted to the Replacement Regiment of 136th Regiment before being given 2nd Gebirgs Division.

He served as liaison officer with the Italian Alpini Corps between August 1942 and February 1943, and then took over command of 188th Division, 418th Division and "Schlemmer Battle Group". Towards the end of the war he was commanding officer of Milan Army Detachment.

He was awarded the German Cross in Gold.

Schlemmer, General of Mountain Troops Hans

Born in Nesselwang on 18 January 1893, Hans Schlemmer entered the Bavarian Army as an ensign in 2nd Pioneer Battalion in 1913. By December 1914 he had been gazetted as a second lieutenant to 5th Bavarian Field Artillery Regiment and after serving throughout World War I stayed on in the post-war Reichsheer.

During World War II he commanded 3rd Battalion of 11th Gebirgs Artillery Regiment, he led 7th Artillery Regiment before becoming General Officer Commanding 84th Corps.

His decorations include the German Cross in Gold and the Knight's Cross to the Iron Cross with Oak Leaves.

Schörner, Colonel General Ferdinand

Born in Munich on 12 June 1892 Ferdinand Schörner entered the Army as a one-year volunteer with the Bavarian Leib (Bodyguard) Regiment during October 1911 and by November 1914 had been gazetted as a second lieutenant in the Reserve.

After war service he continued his military career in the Reichsheer and after commanding 98th Gebirgsjäger Regiment went on to lead 6th Gebirgs Division, 19th Gebirgs Corps and 40th Gebirgs Corps. His next promotion was to command 17th Army from which post he went to become Commander in Chief of Army Group South in March 1944, then of Army Group North and finally of Army Group Centre in January 1945.

His captivity in the Soviet Union lasted for ten years and he was not released until 1955.

His decorations include the Pour le Mérite, and the Knight's Cross to the Iron Cross with Oak Leaves, Swords and Diamonds.

Stettner, Lieutenant General Walter, Ritter von

Walter, Ritter von Stettner, was born on 19 March 1895 in Munich and following family practice entered military service as a cadet. By 17 August 1914 he was an ensign. He was gazetted into the

Bavarian Leib Regiment and was with this unit throughout World War I. After serving as commanding officer of 1st Battalion of 98th Gebirgsjäger Regiment, he went on to command the 99th Gebirgsjäger Regiment and then 1st Gebirgs Division.

He was killed in action in the fighting in Belgrade on 18 October 1944.

His decorations include the Knight's Cross to the Iron Cross.

Utz, Lieutenant General Willibald

Willibald Utz was born on 20 January 1893 in Fürth. At the age of 20 years he entered the Army as an ensign and by September 1914 had been commissioned and gazetted into the Bavarian Army's 13th Artillery Regiment. After the armistice he continued to serve in the Reichsheer and at the outbreak of World War II was commanding 100th Gebirgsjäger Regiment. He was then promoted to lead 100th Jäger Division and finally 2nd Gebirgs Division.

He was awarded the Knight's Cross to the Iron Cross.

Vogel, General of Mountain Troops Emil

Vogel was born in Zwickau on 20 July 1894. He was entered as an ensign on 3 August 1914 and subsequently gazetted into the 2nd Bavarian Pioneer Battalion with which he served during World War I.

He went on to various posts with the Reichsheer and then with the Wehrmacht. On 1 September 1939, the outbreak of World War II, he was GSO 1 to 7th Corps and Chief of the General Staff to 20th Corps. He was then given command of 101st Jäger Division and during August 1944 was promoted to lead 36th Gebirgs Corps.

His decorations include the German Cross in Gold and the Knight's Cross to the Iron Cross with Oak Leaves.

Wittmann, Lieutenant General August

Born in Munich on 20 July 1895, August Wittmann entered the Army as a volunteer in 1st Bavarian Field Artillery Regiment only two weeks after the outbreak of World War I.

By 1917 he had reached the rank of second lieutenant and was released from the Army in December 1918, a month after the armistice. He then joined the Bavarian Police Force and served with it until October 1935 when he rejoined the Army and was given command of 2nd Battalion of the 111th Gebirgs Artillery Regiment. He then went on to command 256th Artillery Regiment. Wittmann was then promoted to command 390th Infantry Division and successively 3rd Gebirgs Division with which unit he finished the war.

His decorations include the German Cross in Gold and the Knight's Cross to the Iron Cross.

Bibliography

Brackmann (Editor) *Unser Kampf in Polen*, Brockmann, Munich 1959

Buchner A. *Gebirgsjäger an allen Fronten*, Sporholtz Verlag 1955

Cooper M. *The German Army: 1933–45*, Macdonald & Jane's 1978

Dept. of the Army *The German Campaign in the Balkans*, Dept. of US Army 1953

Erickson J. *The Road to Stalingrad*, Weidenfeld & Nicolson 1975

Grechko A. *Bitva za Kabkaz*, Moscow 1971

Jacobsen & Rohwer *Der zweite Weltkrieg in Chronik und Dokumenten*, Wehr und Wissen 1961

Kameradkreis des Panzer Korps 'GD' *Panzer Korps 'Grossdeutschland'* (3 volumes), Traditionsverlag

Karpf Heinz *Bedrohte Heimat*, Graz 1956

Keilig W. *Das Heer: 1939–1945*, Henning Verlag, Bad Nauheim 1956

Muhleisen H. *Kreta 1941*, Rombach Verlag 1968

OKW *Front am Polarkreis*, Lempert, Berlin 1947

OKW *Kriegstagebuch des OKW* Bernard & Graefe 1961–1963

Rauchensteiner M. *Krieg in Österreich*, Stocker, Graz 1976

Spencer J. *Battle for Crete*, Heinemann 1962

Stewart I. G. *Struggle for Crete*, Oxford University Press 1966

(Unpublished works)

1st Gebirgs Division
   Kampfbericht (Frankreich)
3rd Gebirgs Division
   Kriegstagebuch 6.4.40–10.6.40

4th Gebirgs Division
    Kriegstagebuch 1.6.1941–15.7.1941
    Kriegstagebuch 16.8.1942–12.11.1942
    Kampfbericht 23.7.1941–10.8.1941
    Kampfbericht (Kaukasus)
5th Gebirgs Division
    Kampfbericht (Griechenland)
    Gefechtberichte 1.6.1941–7.3.1942
49th (Gebirgs) Corps
    Kriegstagebuch
20 (Gebirgs) Armee
    Truppengliederung März 1945
Regiment 85
    Zusammenfassung der Gefechtsberichte der Bataillone der Gebirgsjäger Regiment 85, über die Abwehrschlacht bei Voronezh 22 Juli–8 August 1943.
Kampfgruppe Lapp
    Gefechtsberichte der Kampfgruppe Lapp im Brückenkopf von Sseneserso 29.6.1944–11.7.1944.

Index

Afrika Korps, 33
Alexander, Field-Marshal, 158–9
Alexander the Great,
  losses crossing Taurus, xvi
Alexandria, 34
Ardennes,
  German offensive in, 146, 153
Australians,
  on Crete, 37
Austria,
  call-up of Gebirgsjäger by Germans, 3–6
  Edelweiss Corps, 202
  fighting in 1945, 155–200
  Gebirgsjäger divisions in German army, 3
  Gebirgsjägers in army today, 202
  mountain warfare in Italy, WWI, xviii
  refugees, 1945, 180

Balck, Gen., 168
Balkans,
  anti-German partisans, 145
  German campaign in, 1941 ("Operation Marita"), 21–32

Belgium,
  occupied by Germans, 13
Blaskowitz, Gen., 8
Boehme, Gen. F., 241
Braun, Major, 39
Brazlav, USSR,
  German advance on, 91, 92, 93–4
Budapest,
  captured by Russians, 146
  German attempt to recover ("Spring Awakening"), 153–4, 163, 165
Bug river, 89, 93, 94
Bulgaria,
  signs pact with Germany, 1941, 23
  taken over by Red Army, 146
  troops: 1st Bulgarian Army, 160; 3rd Infantry Corps, 160; 4th Infantry Corps, 160

Canea, Crete, 36, 39, 51, 53, 62, 64, 65, 67, 73, 82
  airfield, 36
  assaulted, 42
  captured by Germans, 70–1

Caucasus,
climate, 131, 132, 135
cold of, 135
geography, 131
German invasion of, 1942, 128–43; ratio of porters to riflemen, 135; evacuating wounded, 137, 140–1; failure of offensive, 137, 142; Soviet partisans, 137; problem of supply, 137–8; German withdrawal, 142
people of, 134
primitive conditions, 134
roads, 132–3, 134
size of front, 129
Churchill, Winston, 62
Cooper, Matthew,
The German Army 1933–1945, 8
Cossacks, 105–6, 179
atrocities by, 180
Crete, 21, 22
airstrips, 36
British garrison, 37
geography, 36
German assault ("Operation Mercury"), 32–82; heavy casualties among paratroops, 40; air invasion begins, 40–2; failure of sea-borne invasion, 42–8; partisan action, 54; British evacuation, 80; British prisoners, 81
German "Battle Group Canea", 39
German "Battle Group Maleme", 39
planning invasion, 34–6, 37–40
Cunningham, Adm., 43–4
Czechoslovakia,
occupied by Germany, 6

Degen, Lt-Gen. Hans, 241–2
Denmark,
German occupation of, 13
Dietl, Lt-Gen. Eduard, 7–8, 242
actions at Narvik, 13, 16, 18, 19, 20
Dietrich, Gen., 167
Don, river, 130
Dover, 13
Dunkirk, 13

Englseer, Gen. Karl, 114, 133, 242
acquires information on Caucasus, 131
Elbrus, Mt, 131
climbed by Germans, 130, 133, 143
climbed by Russians, 143
Enver Pasha, xvii

Feldbach, Austria, 4, 154
Feuerstein, Gen. Valentin, 8, 242–3
Finland,
myriads of flies, 149–50
sues for peace, 146, 147–8
France,
anti-German partisans, 145
Chasseurs Alpins, xvi, 18
defeated in 1940, 13
Foreign Legion, 18
Franco, General, 22
Freyberg, Gen., VC, 37, 62

Gaissin, USSR, 91
Germans advance on, 92, 94
taken by Germans, 95
Galatas, Crete, 56, 67
battle for, 57–62

Gebirgsjäger formations (numerically from Army down to Battalion)
20th Gebirgs Army, 201
    order of battle, 210–11
5th SS Gebirgs Corps,
    order of battle, 217
9th Waffen Gebirgs Corps of the SS (Croatian)
    order of battle, 218
15th (XV) Gebirgs Corps,
    order of battle, 211
18th (XVIII) Gebirgs Corps, 6, 8, 23, 27, 31
    in Finland, 148, 151, 152
    order of battle, 212
19th (XIX) Gebirgs Corps,
    order of battle, 212
21st (XXI) Gebirgs Corps,
    order of battle, 212
22nd (XXII) Gebirgs Corps, 161
    order of battle, 212–13
36th (XXXVI) Gebirgs Corps,
    order of battle, 213
49th (XLIX) Gebirgs Corps, 23, 85, 88, 89, 92, 95, 102
    history: thrusts salient into Russian front, 98; captures Uman, 106; final battles round Uman, 116–25; losses at Uman, 126; advances into Caucasus, 1942, 130–1
    order of battle, 213
    suffers Russian rain, 94–5, 96
51st (LI) Gebirgs Corps,
    order of battle, 214
1st Division, xx, 6, 7, 21, 23, 85, 88, 91, 128, 145, 154, 157, 161, 165, 175, 183, 225
    Battle Group Kress, 90, 102

Battle Group Lang, 90, 93, 95, 99, 102, 104, 107–8, 121
    history: advance and attack on Lemberg, 8–12; fighting in France, 1940, 13; trains for "Operation Sealion", 13; guards Bug bridgeheads, 1941, 90; on road to Uman, 91; presses retreating Russians, 93, 99–100; captures Brazlav, 94; moves on Gaissin, 95; actions round Uman, 97, 98, 102–8 passim, 114, 121, 124; in Caucasus, 141; driven back to Carpathians, 146; in attack on Budapest, 163; withdraws into Austria, 168; final battlefield, 175; end of war for, 196, 201
    men of climb Mt Elbrus, 133
    order of battle, 205–6
    strength in 1945, 167
2nd Division, xx, 7, 8, 21, 128, 145, 153, 201
    order of battle, 206
3rd Division, xx, 7, 8, 21, 128, 145, 154, 201
    fighting round Narvik, 13, 15, 18–20
    order of battle, 207
4th Division, 21, 23, 85, 88, 128, 131, 145, 154, 201, 225
    history: in action in Yugoslavia, 26; pursues Russians, 1941, 90–5 passim; holds circle round Uman, 101, 105, 115–16, 117; assault at Uman, 117–18, 120,

122, 124; in Caucasus, 141;
driven back to Carpathians,
146
order of battle, 207–8
5th Division, 21, 23, 26, 32, 34,
35, 128, 145, 201
"Advance Guard Group Wittmann", 36, 73–80
history: in action in Greece,
27–32; sails for Crete,
42–8; deaths sailing to
Crete, 48; air-lifted to Maleme, 48–51; in action in
Crete, 52–82; losses in
Crete, 81–2; in action in
Italy, 146; captured in
Italy, 1945, 153
"Krakau Group", 36, 55, 62,
76
order of battle, 208
role in Crete, 42–3
6th Division, 21, 23, 26, 31,
128, 145, 153, 201
order of battle, 208–9
6th SS Division "Nord",
order of battle, 214–15
7th Division, 21, 128, 145, 153,
201
fights way from Finland to
Norway, 148–52
order of battle, 209
7th SS Freiwilligen Division
"Prinz Eugen", 145
order of battle, 215
8th Division, 201
captured in Italy, 1945, 153
order of battle, 209
9th Division, 154, 201
order of battle, 210
13th Waffen Grenadier Division
of the SS "Handschar"
Croatian No. 1,

order of battle, 215–16
21st Waffen Grenadier Division
of the SS "Skanderbeg" Albanian No. 1,
order of battle, 216
23rd Waffen Division of the SS
"Kama" Croatian No. 2,
order of battle, 216–17
24th Waffen (Karstjäger) Division of the SS,
order of battle, 217
117th Jäger Division, 176, 177,
181, 184, 185
Division of the SS "Andreas
Hofer", 217
Waffen Gebirgs Brigade of the
SS Tartar No. 1, 218
13th Regiment, 115–19 passim,
123–4
85th Regiment, 32, 80
on Crete: arrives, 51; in action, 52–3; outflanks British, 62–70; takes Stylos,
71–2
91st Regiment, 114, 115–24 passim
98th Regiment, xx, 90, 189
99th Regiment, xx, 90, 94, 118,
179, 180, 195, 201
in Caucasus, 141–2; in Hungary and Austria, 1945,
168–71; battle for Reich-
nitz, 171–2; fighting and retreating, 173–5; assaulted
by Red Army, 176–7, 178;
final attack, 182–6;
counter-attacked, 188–90,
193; desertions from, 192;
attempts to escape Russian
captivity at end of war,
197–9

100th Regiment, xx, 56, 62, 64, 67, 80
  on Crete: en route, 42, 44; arrival, 51; in action, 52–5, 57–62, 71
136th Regiment, xx
137th Regiment, xx
138th Regiment, xx
139th Regiment, xx
  in action at Narvik, 15, 18–20
141st Regiment, 67
  attacks Canea, Crete, 70–1
218th Regiment, 150, 151
756th "Kriemhilde Regiment", destroyed in Tunisia, 145
Hochgebirgsjäger battalions, 214
Gebirgsjägers,
  Alpine rations, 140
  badges and insignia, 237–8
  genesis of, xv–xxi
  in present NATO forces, 202
  organisation in WWII, 221–4
  specialist equipment, 238–9
  uniform, 235–6
German army,
  marching ability, 86, 87
  parlous state, early 1942, 127
  partial motorisation, 86
German military formations (numerically from Army down to Group),
  1st Panzer Army, 142
  2nd Army, 23
  2nd Panzer Army, 161, 164, 171, 187
    escapes Russian captivity at end of war, 196
  3rd Army, 8
  4th Army, 8
  6th Army, 88, 89, 129, 142, 161, 164–8 *passim*, 171, 187

    counter-attacks in Austria, 174, 176, 181–6
    ends war in Russian hands, 196
  6th SS Panzer Army, 160, 163, 164, 165, 171, 196
  8th Army, 8, 160
  10th Army, 8
  11th Army, 88, 89
  12th Army, 23, 31
  14th Army, 8
  17th Army, 85, 88, 89, 92, 100, 133, 142
    Order of Day after Uman victory, 125–6
    orders for summer 1942, 129
  1st Cavalry Corps, 161
  1st Panzer Corps, 23
  1st SS Panzer Corps, 160
  2nd SS Panzer Corps, 160
  3rd Panzer Corps, 161
  4th SS Panzer Corps, 161
  29th Infantry Corps, 160
  43rd Infantry Corps, 160
  68th Infantry Corps, 161
  72nd Infantry Corps, 160
  Feldherrnhalle Panzer Corps, 160
  1st SS Panzer Division, 161, 167, 183
  2nd SS Panzer Division, 167
  3rd SS Panzer Division, 161, 167
  5th SS Panzer Division, 161
  9th Panzer Division, 103, 106, 108
  11th Panzer Division, 92, 103
  12th SS Panzer Division, 167
  13th Panzer Division, 167
  16th Motorised Division, 103
  16th Panzer Division, 92, 94, 103

25th Motorised Division, 103
44th "Hoch und Deutsch-
meister" Division, 165
97th Light Division, 88, 90,
93–6 *passim*, 105, 106, 115
99th Light Division, xx
125th Infantry Division, 88, 90,
94–8 *passim*, 108, 109,
115, 116
295th Infantry Division, 94, 96,
102
303 SP Brigade, 184, 185
2nd Panzer Grenadier Regiment,
182
18th Mountain Artillery Regiment, 79
95th Mountain Artillery Regiment, 74, 75
477th Regiment, 116, 117, 121
Battle Group Gottwald, 161
Battle Group Groth, 176
Battle Group Raithel, 197
Battle Group Ringel, 154
Battle Group Schweitzer, 161
Battle Group Siegers, 161
Panzer Group 1 (Kleist), 88,
89, 92, 99, 109, 125, 129
Germany,
Alpine Corps of WWI, xix
conscription, 1930s, 3
Gebirgs divisions in 1939, xx
Gebirgsjäger units in WWI,
xviii–xx
increase in Gebirgsjäger units in
WWII, xix–xxi
World War II: invades Poland,
6; victories in West in 1940,
13,14; RN blockade of, 14;
Balkan campaign, 1941,
22–32; battle for Crete,
32–82; forces invading Rus-

sia, 83; defeat in 1945, 153,
154
Gibraltar, 32
"Operation Felix" plan for at-
tack on, 14, 22
Göring, Hermann, 34
Graz, 4, 23, 154, 162, 164, 189
Great Britain,
BEF driven from Continent,
1940, 13; occupies Greek is-
lands, 1941, 22; in action in
Greece, 31; RN destroys sea-
borne invasion of Crete, 42–8
Grechko, Marshal, 142
Greece,
Italian invasion of, 22; German
plan for attack on, 23; Ger-
man invasion of, 27–32; Me-
taxas Line, 27, 31; defeat of,
32
Groth, Major, 168

Halder, Gen., 85
Hannibal,
losses crossing Alps, xvi
Harvey, Major James, 201
Hengl, Gen. Georg Ritter von, 243
Heraklion, Crete, 36–40 *passim*,
43, 74, 80
airfield, 36, 78
Heydrich, Col., 55, 58
Himmler, Heinrich, 215
Hitler, Adolf, xix, 6, 13, 18, 34,
85, 89, 153, 157, 164, 175,
217
reintroduces conscription, 3;
master of Europe, 1940, 14;
plans for 1941, 22; orders attacks on Greece and Yugoslavia, 22–3; plans for summer

offensive, 1942, 128, 129;
death, 189
Hofer, Andreas, 202, 217
Holland,
occupied by Germans, 13
Hötzendorff, Count von, 202

Innsbruck, 4
Italy,
Alpine Corps, 137
World War II: failures in Greek
campaign, 22; anti-German
partisans, 145; German collapse in, 187; British 8th
Army advances, 187; armi-
stice in, 194

Jodl, Gen. Ferdinand, 243

Kiev, 89, 146
encirclement of, 85, 89
King, Adm., 45
Kipling, Rudyard, 97
Kleist, Gen., 23, 88, 89, 92, 99,
109
Kluge, Gen. von, 8
Konrad, Gen. Rudolf, 243
Krakau, Col., 62, 66, 73
combat report from Crete, 63–6
Krause, Gen., 169, 172
Kreysing, Gen. Hans, 244
Kübler, Gen. Ludwig, 8, 93, 107,
109, 110, 119
Kübler, Lt-Gen. Josef, 244
Küchler, Gen., 8
Kursk salient,
Germans fail to take, 145

Lanz, Gen. Hubert, 90, 92, 99,

104, 245
book on 1st Gebirgsjäger Division, 196
Lemberg (Lvov), 8, 26
attacked by 1st Gebirgsjäger Division, 10–11
surrenders, 11
Lemnos, 22
Le Suire, Gen. Karl, 246
List, Gen., 8, 23, 129
Löhr, Col. Gen., 34
Löhr, Field-Marshal, 166, 195, 199
Luftwaffe, 13, 38, 82, 99
radio contact with, 106
World War II: Stuka bombardment in Poland, 10; aerial superiority in Crete, 44, 45;
bombs own troops in Crete,
62, 65; Stuka bombardment in
Russia, 102
Luftwaffe formations (numerically from Fleet down to Regiment),
4th Air Fleet, 35
11th Air Corps, 34, 41
Transport Command, 48
7th Para Division, 34, 35, 41, 43
22nd Air Landing Division, 34
1st Para Regiment, 40
2nd Para Regiment, 40
3rd Para Regiment, 40
Lupo, Italian destroyer, 43, 45, 46

Machine gun,
gives superiority to defence, xvi
Malaparte, Curzio,
Kaputt, 150
Maleme, Crete, 36, 38, 43, 54
airfield, 36, 38, 53, 64
German attack on: air drop, 42;
as German bridgehead, 48; air

lift by Ju 52s, 49–50; German
advance from, 51; build up of
German forces at, 54
Malinovsky, Marshal, 159, 162
Malta, 34
Meindl, Gen., 41
Moscow, 82
Germans fail to take, 85
Mountain warfare,
artillery, 229–34
losses in, throughout history,
xvi, xvii
principles of, xviii
problems of fighting, 139
tactics, 224–8
Munich Crisis of 1938, 6
Mussolini, Benito, 22

Napoleon, 202
losses in St Bernard pass, xvi
Narvik, 13
iron ore port, 15
World War II: RN successes at,
16; fighting round, 16, 18–20;
Norwegians surrender, 20;
Gebirgsjägers leave at end of
war, 201
New Zealand formations,
5th Brigade, 37, 48
10th Infantry Brigade, 57
Kippenberger's Brigade, 57
Petrol Company, 57, 58
New Zealanders,
defence of Crete: dispositions
round Maleme, 49; in action,
52–3; defence of Galatas,
57–62; defence of Canea,
70–1
NKVD, 103
executes Russian troops, 101

Norway, 21
campaign in, 14–20
iron ore for Germany, 15
occupied by Germans, 13
6th Norwegian Division, 18

OKH, 163
OKW, 13, 164, 171, 175, 184, 185
plan for conquest of Norway, 15
plan for conquest of Poland, 8
time-table for destruction of Red
Army, 83
"Operation Barbarossa", xx, 12,
22, 32, 82–5, 88, 128, 164
battles of encirclement, 83, 84,
85
early German successes, 82, 85
false premises behind, 83
"Operation Sealion", 13

Paul, Prince, of Yugoslavia, 23
Paulus, Gen. von, 142
Peter, King, of Yugoslavia, 23
Piraeus, 43
Poland,
Alpine Brigades, 9
German attack on, 7–12
High Tatra mountains, 9
Przemysl group, 9
Rzezov Motorised Brigade, 9
Przemysl, 9

Raeder, Adm.,
plan to conquer Norway, 14
Ramcke, Col., 42, 51, 56
Rauchsteiner, Dr Manfred,
Krieg in Österreich 1945, 158
Red Air Force,
in action in Caucasus, 136

Red Army, 11
desertion from, 182–3
"mountain" troops in Caucasus, 136
rations in Caucasus, 138, 140
size in 1941, 84
size in 1945, 153
system of command, 84
troops executed by NKVD, 101
World War II: early losses, 82, 85; failure of winter offensive, 1941, 127, 128; offensive in Caucasus, 137; offensives in 1945, 153; approaches Austria, 157–8; overruns Austria, 164–200
Red Army formations (numerically from Army down to Regiment),
4th Guards Army, 160
6th Army, 92, 122, 125
6th Guards Tank Army, 160, 162, 187
8th Army, 92
9th Guards Tank Army, 160, 162
12th Army, 125
18th Army, 92
26th Army, 160, 169, 172, 175, 179
27th Army, 160
57th Army, 160
1st Guards Mechanised Corps, 160
1st Guards Motorised Corps, 164
2nd Tank Corps, 122
5th Guards Cavalry Corps, 160, 164, 179
5th Guards Tank Corps, 160, 166
6th Guards Infantry Corps, 160
9th Guards Motorised Corps, 160
16th Tank Corps, 122
17th Infantry Corps, 104
18th Tank Corps, 160
20th Guards Infantry Corps, 160
21st Guards Infantry Corps, 160
30th Infantry Corps, 160, 173
31st Guards Infantry Corps, 160
33rd Infantry Corps, 160, 190
35th Guards Infantry Corps, 160, 176
37th Guards Infantry Corps, 160
37th Infantry Corps, 160
38th Guards Infantry Corps, 160
39th Guards Infantry Corps, 160
64th Infantry Corps, 160
104th Infantry Corps, 160, 176
133rd Infantry Corps, 160
135th Infantry Corps, 160, 172, 176
11th Guards Cavalry Division, 177
20th Mountain Rifle Division, 136
30th Guards Infantry Division, 177
68th Guards Infantry Division, 177
135th Infantry Division, 177
64th Rifle Regiment, 136
174th Rifle Regiment, 136
265th Rifle Regiment, 136
379th Rifle Regiment, 136
Reichenau, Gen., 8, 88, 89
Reichsarbeitsdienst (RAD), 3
Rendulic, Gen., 175, 195, 196
Retimo, Crete, 37, 39, 40, 64, 66, 73

Germans capture, 77, 78
Rhodes, 34
Ringel, Gen. Julius, 19, 27, 28, 30, 31, 35, 42, 49, 57, 71, 89, 169, 245–6
  campaign in Crete: moves to attack from Maleme, 51; sends troops against Galatas and Suda, 55–6; sets up pursuit group, 71; pursues British to Sfakia, 80–1
  on fighting in Crete, 82
Romania, 26
  Ploesti oil fields, 22
  taken over by Red Army, 146
Rovaniemi, Lapland, 148, 151–2
  destruction of, 152
Royal Air Force, 13
  evacuates Crete, 39
Rundstedt, Gen. von, 88
Russia,
  anti-German partisans, 145
  enormous size, 87
  German invasion, 82–5
  inadequate roads and railways, 87
  invades Poland, 1939, 11
  losses in Balkan Wars, 1877, xvii
  losses in Carpathians, WWI, xvii
  political reasons for invasion of Austria, 158
  Stalin Line, 89
  Uman encirclement, 1941, 87–126
  victory in 1945, 153

Sagitario, Italian destroyer, 43
Salzburg, 4
Schlemmer, Gen. Hans, 247
Schlemmer, Lt-Gen. Ernst, 246–7
Schobert, Gen., 88, 89

Schörner, Col. Gen. Ferdinand, 195, 247
Stalin, Josef, 159
Stalingrad, 130, 137
STAVKA, 84, 97, 98, 117, 173, 175, 176
  strategy, 1943–4, 146
Stettner, Lt-Gen. Walter Ritter von, 247–8
Student, Gen., 37, 41, 81
  strategic plans for attacking E. Mediterranean, 34
Stülpnagel, Gen., 88
Styria, 4, 159, 178, 180, 182, 184, 200
  geography of, 161–2
Suda bay, Crete, 37, 39, 51, 62, 70, 71, 74
  abortive Para drop on, 40
  attacked by 85th Gebirgsjäger Regiment, 66
Suez canal, 34
Süssmann, Gen., 41
Suvorov, Gen.,
  losses in St Gotthard, xvi
Sweden,
  iron ore for Germany, 15

Thermopylae, 31, 187
Tito, Marshal, 166–7
Tolbhukin, Marshal, 7, 150, 162, 177, 187

Uman encirclement, 86–126
  Russian attempts to break out, 97, 98, 101–4, 105, 115–22 *passim;* German patrolling round, 111–13; German victory at, 125–6; losses, 126

Utz, Col. (later Lt-Gen.) Willibald, 51, 59, 248

Vienna, 159, 187
"Operation Vienna", 159, 162, 164
Vietinghoff, Col. Gen. von, 187
Vogel, Gen. Emil, 248
Volkssturm, 167, 169, 179
Von Bock, Gen., 129

Weichs, Gen., 23
Weimar Republic, xix
Wittmann, Col. (later Lt-Gen.)
August, 248
combat report, 73–80
Wöhler, Col. Gen., 166, 175

World War I,
mountain warfare in, xviii–xix
World War II,
events of 1939, 7–12
events of 1940, 13–14
events of 1941, 21
events of 1942, 127–8
events of 1943–4, 145–6
events of 1945, 153, 154
finish, 195, 196–200, 201

Yugoslavia,
pact with Germany repudiated, 1941, 23; German invading forces, 23; German invasion, 23–6; collapse of, 31, 32; anti-German partisans, 145; Germans retreat from, 166; Germans captured in, 199